New Junior Cycle English

BE INSPIRED!

Larry Cotter · Kevin McDermott · Della Meade

The Educational Company of Ireland

First published 2016

The Educational Company of Ireland

Ballymount Road

Walkinstown

Dublin 12

www.edco.ie

A member of the Smurfit Kappa Group plc

ISBN: 978-1-84536-663-6

Cover: Red Rattle Design

Cover image: Shutterstock

Design and Layout: Identikit Design Consultants

Editor: Jane Rogers

Proofreader: Jeffrey Gormly

Illustrations: Compuscript, Beehive Illustration (Vince Reid), Bright Children's Illustration (James Davies and Hannah Radenkova)

The paper used in this book comes from Managed Forests in Northern Europe For every tree felled, at least one new tree is planted

While every care has been taken to trace and acknowledge copyright, the publisher tenders its apologies for any accidental infringement where copyright has proved untraceable. The publisher would be pleased to come to a suitable arrangement with the rightful owner in each case.

Web references in this book are intended as a guide for teachers. At the time of going to press, all web addresses were active and contained information relevant to the topics in this book. However, The Educational Company of Ireland and the authors do not accept responsibility for the views or information contained on these websites. Content and addresses may change beyond our control.

Contents

BE INSPIRED!

BE INSPIRED!

Introduction

Dear Student,

We want to inspire you. We want you to love English as much as we do. And that is why *Be Inspired!* is packed with the best stories, poems, personal writing, drama and photos that we could find. And there's a chapter on Media where you'll explore some really clever and imaginative ads and learn about the news.

What's more, there is a brilliant website where you will find loads of interesting videos, interactive games and quizzes.

And we want you to learn by doing all manner of fun and creative activities. You will become a writer, a reporter, a researcher, an actor, a director, a speech-maker and a debater. You will work on your own, with a partner and in small groups, as well as taking part in whole-class activities. You will write poems, stories, letters, diary entries, dialogue and scenes. You will sit in the hot seat and become characters from your favourite stories.

And there's more. There's a *Student Portfolio* where you can keep track of your best work. The portfolio has guidelines to help you to assess and improve your work.

We haven't forgotten your teacher, either. We have a *Teacher's Resource Book*, packed full of ideas.

Be Inspired! is a magic box full of wonders, waiting for you to open it.
Go on – be inspired!

Larry Cotter
Della Meade
Kevin McDermott

Acknowledgements

The authors and publisher would like to thank the following for copyright permission to reproduce the following material:

Texts

'Charles' by Shirley Jackson, from *The Lottery and Other Stories*, used with permission from Linda Allen Literary Agency; 'William's Version' by Jan Mark, from *Nothing to Be Afraid Of*, Puffin Books; Alison Lurie's thoughts on traditional fairy tales, from *Clever Gretchen and Other Forgotten Folktales*, reprinted by permission of United Agents LLP; 'The Practical Princess' by Jay Williams, from *The Practical Princess and Other Liberating Fairy Tales*, published by Parents' Magazine Press/Scholastic Inc. ©1978 by Jay Williams. Used by permission of Scholastic Inc.; 'At the River-Gates' by Philippa Pearce, from *The Shadow Cage and Other Stories*, Penguin Books; 'The Span of Life' by Robert Frost, from *The Poetry of Robert Frost: The Collected Poems, Complete and Unabridged*, Henry Holt and Co.; 'Come to the Edge' by Christopher Logue, from *Selected Poems of Christopher Logue*, reprinted by permission of Faber & Faber; 'Seaview Haiku' by John Foster, from *The Poetry Chest* (Oxford University Press), included by permission of the author © 2007; extract from 'Water Lily' by Ralph Fletcher, reprinted by permission of the author and Marian Reiner Literary Agency; 'Riddle' by Jonathan Swift; extract from 'Three Limericks' from *Michael Rosen's Book of Nonsense* by Michael Rosen, reprinted by permission of Peters Fraser + Dunlop (www.petersfraserdunlop.com) on behalf of Michael Rosen; 'Dreams' by Langston Hughes, from *Winning Words*, ed. William Sieghart, reprinted by permission of David Higham Associates; 'Stars' by Tim Toaster Henderson; 'Epilogue' by Grace Nichols, from *Short and Sweet*, ed. Simon Armitage, Faber & Faber; 'Poem (As the Cat)' by William Carlos Williams, from *The Collected Poems of William Carlos Williams: Volume I, 1990–1939*, ©1938 by New Directions Publishing Corp. Reprinted by permission of Carcanet Press Ltd; 'Fog' by Carl Sandburg, from *The Complete Poems of Carl Sandburg: Revised and Expanded Edition* ©1969, 1970 by Lilian Steichen Sandburg, Trustee. Reprinted by permission of Houghton Mifflin Harcourt Publishing Company. All rights reserved; 'maggie and milly and molly and may' by e.e. cummings, from *Complete Poems: 1904–1962 by e.e. cummings*, ed. George J. Firmage © 1956, 1984, 1991 by the Trustees for the E.E. Cummings Trust, used by permission of Liveright Publishing Corporation; 'The Early Purges' by Seamus Heaney, from *Opened Ground*, reprinted by permission of Faber & Faber; 'Handbag' by Ruth Fainlight, from *New & Collected Poems (2010)*, reprinted by permission of Bloodaxe Books; 'My Papa's Waltz' by Theodore Roethke, from *Collected Poems*, reprinted by permission of Faber & Faber; 'First Love' by Mary Dorcey, from *Bread and Roses: Women's Poetry of the 19th and 20th Centuries*, reprinted by permission of the author; 'What Has Happened to Lulu?' by Charles Causley, from *I Had A Little Cat: Collected Poems for Children*, reprinted by permission of David Higham Associates; 'My First Day at School' from *All I Know Now: Wonderings and Reflections on Growing Up Gracefully* by Carrie Hope Fletcher, Sphere; 'Little Man' by Conor O'Callaghan, from *The Quiet Quarter*, ed. Máire Nic Gearailt, New Island Books; 'The Magic Dress' from *I Know Why the Caged Bird Sings* by Maya Angelou, Little, Brown and Company; 'Captain Hardcastle' from *Boy: Tales of Childhood* by Roald Dahl, reprinted by permission of David Higham Associates; extract from *Zlata's Diary: A Child's Life in Wartime Sarajevo* by Zlata Filipović, Penguin Books; extract from 'Michelle Obama: Twitter Activist' by Christine Sisto in the *National Review*, reproduced with permission from the *National Review*; extract from *Invisible Friends* by Alan Ayckbourn, used by permission of Faber & Faber; extract from *Nobody Here But Us Chickens and The Grey Angel* by Stephanie Miller, Macmillan; extract from *Lovers* by Brian Friel, reprinted by kind permission of the Estate of Brian Friel c/o The Gallery Press, Loughcrew, Oldcastle, County Meath, Ireland; extract from *The Shadow of a Gunman* by Sean O'Casey, reprinted by permission of Faber & Faber; *The Children's Ward* by Ellen Dryden from *Six Primroses Each & Other Plays for Young Actors*, First Writers Collection, published by Samuel French, Micheline Steinberg Literary Agency; 'My Polish Teacher's Tie' from *Ice Cream* by Helen Dunmore, reprinted by permission of AP Watt at United Agents on behalf of Helen Dunmore; 'How Nobody Came to the Graveyard' from *The Graveyard Book* by Neil Gaiman ©2010, reprinted by permission of Bloomsbury Publishing Plc; 'All Summer in a Day' by Ray Bradbury, from *The Stories of Ray Bradbury*, reprinted by permission of Abner Stein; 'The Magic Box' from *Cat among the Pigeons* by Kit Wright (Viking, Kestrel 1987) © Kit Wright, 1984, 1987, Macmillan; 'The Eagle' by Alfred, Lord Tennyson; 'The Vulture' from *The Bad Child's Book of Beasts* by Hilaire Belloc, reprinted by permission of Peters Fraser + Dunlop (www.petersfraserdunlop.com); 'The Listeners' by Walter de la Mare from *The Complete Poems of Walter de la Mare 1975*, is used with permission from the Literary Trustees of Walter de la Mare, represented by the Society of Authors; 'Stopping by Woods on a Snowy Evening' by Robert Frost, from *The Poetry of Robert Frost: Collected Poems*, 2nd revised edition, ed. Edward Connery Latham and Lawrence Thompson, © Henry Holt; 'The Christmas Life' by Wendy Cope from *Two Cures for Love: Selected Poems 1979–2006*, reprinted by permission of Faber & Faber; 'The Trees' by Philip Larkin from *Philip Larkin Poems: Selected by Martin Amis*, reprinted by permission of Faber & Faber; 'The Lake Isle of Innisfree' by William Butler Yeats; 'The Door' by Miroslav Holub, from Poems *Before & After: Collected English Translations*, trans. Ian and Jarmila Milner *et al.* (2006), reprinted with permission of Bloodaxe Books; 'The New Boy' by John Walsh; 'Child on Top of a Greenhouse' by Theodore Roethke, from *The Collected Poems of Theodore Roethke*, Anchor Books, 1974, reprinted by permission of Faber & Faber; 'Climbing' by Amy Lowell; 'Treasure's Pocket Money', from *Treasure: the Trials of a Teenage Terror* by Gina Davidson, Little, Brown and Company; 'Skipping the Queue', from *And When Did You Last See Your Father?* by Blake Morrison, reprinted by permission of Granta Books; 'Mother', from *Are You Somebody?* by Nuala Ó Faoláin, New Island Books; 'St Valentine's Day', from *The Secret World of the Irish Male* by Joseph O'Connor, New Island Books.

Images

Alamy; Corbis; Getty Images; iStock; Shutterstock; TopFoto; Paint it Pink advert, courtesy of the Irish Cancer Society and Chemistry; New Balance advert, courtesy of Athletics Ireland; IKEA advert, used with kind permission of IKEA and DDB; Kit Kat advert, courtesy of J Walter Thompson London and Nestlé; Kleenex Cottonelle advertisement, used with kind permission of Kimberly-Clark Corporation; #MyLastSelfie adverts, courtesy of the World Wide Fund for Nature (WWF) and Uncle Grey, Denmark; Climate Change Hurts advert, courtesy of the World Health Organisation; ISPCC advert, used with kind permission of the ISPCC and photographer Barry McCall; Thomson 'Discover your smile' advert, courtesy of Thomson; Health and Safety Authority (HSA) advert, courtesy of the HSA; *Donegal News* front page, courtesy of the *Donegal News*; *Western People* front page, courtesy of the *Western People*; *Northside People* front page, courtesy of the *Northside People*; *Dublin City Gazette* front page, courtesy of the *Dublin City Gazette*; *Irish Sun* front page © News Syndication; *Irish Times* front page, courtesy of the *Irish Times*; Sleeping students image, courtesy of the Press Association; Refugee crisis image A, courtesy of the Press Association; Refugee crisis image B, courtesy of Getty Images; Refugee crisis image C, © Jason Florio/MOAS_EU, 2015. All rights reserved; Refugee crisis image D, © UNRWA /Alaa Ghosheh; Refugee crisis image E, courtesy of Daniel Etter/*New York Times*/Redux/eyevine; TheJournal.ie image, courtesy of TheJournal.ie; HuffingtonPost.co.uk image, courtesy of PARS International; BuzzFeed.com image, reprinted by permission of BuzzFeed News; RTÉ News Now image © RTÉ; Yes Equality campaign image © Yes Equality; Syrian soldier image, courtesy of the Press Association; Graph of most popular social media platforms among American teenagers in 2015 © Pew Research Center; Graph of photos uploaded and shared per day © Kleiner Perkins; First Pope Francis selfie, courtesy of the Press Association; #NotAMartyr campaign image (left), courtesy of Antoine Amassih; #NotAMartyr campaign image (right), courtesy of Sarah Samaha; Michelle Obama #BringBackOurGirls selfie, courtesy Twitter @Flotus/Associated Press; Dumb show image from *Hamlet*, courtesy of the New American Shakespeare Tavern; Three witches image from *Macbeth*, copyright Utah Shakespeare Festival. Photo by Karl Hugh; *The Shadow of a Gunman* image, courtesy of Sligo Youth Theatre; Image Dublin tenement, 1920s, courtesy of the Royal Society of Antiquaries of Ireland.

Chapter One
STORIES A

Everyone loves a good story. In this chapter you will read about young children, grannies, princesses, ghosts, families and friends. You will laugh and maybe even cry.

Communicating

> You will read a variety of great stories for enjoyment and appreciation.
> You will express your feelings and ideas.
> You will listen actively and take part in class discussions.
> You will work in groups and speak and write with purpose on the stories and each other's work.
> You will plan and write your own stories.
> You will write in a range of forms and styles.

Exploring and Using Language

> You will edit your work and learn from the stories to improve your own writing.
> You will discuss the stories and write about them in thoughtful ways.
> You will learn about different aspects of story writing.
> You will respond to the stories in imaginative ways.
> You will view a range of digital texts.
> You will write and speak in dramatic and interesting ways.
> You will complete online quizzes on the *Be Inspired!* website to practise your knowledge of parts of the sentence.

Understanding Language

> You will write clearly and accurately.
> You will think about the words you choose as you write scripts, compose letters, contribute to class discussions, write a report and plan and write stories.
> You will assess your own writing and that of your fellow students.
> You will experiment with different ways of speaking.
> You will read author biographies on the *Be Inspired!* website and research topics online.

Young Writer's Toolkit

Every writer needs a toolkit – a set of tools to help them write in the best way they can. As you explore the texts in this book, you will learn the art and craft of writing. The Young Writer's Toolkit will help you use words in the best possible ways as you develop your individual style. For Chapter 1, here are some of the tools you will find helpful from the Young Writer's Toolkit (YWT):

> dialogue for stories, p. 192
> the rules of fairy tales, p. 195
> writing poetry, p. 224
> The parts of a short story, p. 190.

Wrapping Up

> To wrap up, you will write your own story.

www.edco.ie/beinspired

*When Laurie goes to school he comes home with tales of Charles,
a boy who is always getting into trouble.*

Charles

SHIRLEY JACKSON

Author Biography
Check out the *Be Inspired!*
website for Shirley Jackson's
author biography.

The day Laurie started kindergarten he renounced corduroy overalls with bibs and began wearing blue jeans with a belt; I watched him go off the first morning with the older girl next door, seeing clearly that an era of my life was ended, my sweet-voiced nursery-school tot replaced by a long-trousered, swaggering character who forgot to stop at the corner and wave goodbye to me.

He came home the same way, the front door slamming open, his cap on the floor, and the voice suddenly become raucous shouting, 'Isn't anybody *here*?'

At lunch he spoke insolently to his father, spilled Jannie's milk and remarked that his teacher said we were not to take the name of the Lord in vain.

'How was school today?' I asked, elaborately casual.

'All right,' he said.

'Did you learn anything?' his father asked.

Laurie regarded his father coldly. 'I didn't learn nothing,' he said.

'Anything,' I said. 'Didn't learn anything.'

'The teacher spanked a boy, though.' Laurie said, addressing his bread and butter. 'For being fresh,' he added with his mouth full.

'What did he do?' I asked. 'Who was it?'

Laurie thought. 'It was Charles,' he said. 'He was fresh. The teacher spanked him and made him stand in a corner. He was awfully fresh.'

'What did he do?' I asked again, but Laurie slid off his chair, took a cookie, and left, while his father was still saying, 'See here, young man.'

The next day Laurie remarked at lunch, as soon as he sat down, 'Well, Charles was bad again today.' He grinned enormously and said, 'Today Charles hit the teacher.'

'Good heavens,' I said, mindful of the Lord's name. 'I suppose he got spanked again?'

'He sure did,' Laurie said. 'Look up,' he said to his father.

'What?' his father said, looking up.

'Look down,' Laurie said. 'Look at my thumb. Gee, you're dumb.'

He began to laugh insanely.

'Why did Charles hit the teacher?' I asked quickly.

'Because she tried to make him colour with red crayons,' Laurie said. 'Charles wanted to colour with green crayons so he hit the teacher and she spanked him and said nobody play with Charles but everybody did.'

The third day – it was Wednesday of the first week – Charles bounced a seesaw onto the head of a little girl and made her bleed and the teacher made him stay inside all during recess. Thursday Charles had to stand in the corner during story time because he kept pounding his feet on the floor. Friday Charles was deprived of blackboard privileges because he threw chalk.

On Saturday I remarked to my husband, 'Do you think kindergarten is too unsettling for Laurie? All this toughness and bad grammar, and this Charles boy sounds like such a bad influence.'

'It'll be all right,' my husband said reassuringly. 'Bound to be people like Charles in the world. Might as well meet them now as later.'

On Monday Laurie came home late, full of news. 'Charles,' he shouted as he came up the hill; I was waiting anxiously on the front steps; 'Charles,' Laurie yelled all the way up the hill, 'Charles was bad again.'

'Come right in,' I said, as soon as he came close enough. 'Lunch is waiting.'

'You know what Charles did?' he demanded, following me through the door. 'Charles yelled so in school they sent a boy in from first grade to tell the teacher she had to make Charles keep quiet, and so Charles had to stay after school. And so all the children stayed to watch him.'

'What did he do?' I asked.

'He just sat there,' Laurie said, climbing into his chair at the table. 'Hi Pop, y'old dust mop.'

'Charles had to stay after school today,' I told my husband.

'Everyone stayed with him.'

'What does this Charles look like?' my husband asked Laurie. 'What's his other name?'

'He's bigger than me,' Laurie said. 'And he doesn't have any boots and he doesn't ever wear a jacket.'

Monday night was the first Parent–Teacher meeting, and only the fact that Jannie had a cold kept me from going; I wanted passionately to meet Charles' mother. On Tuesday Laurie remarked suddenly, 'Our teacher had a friend come see her in school today.'

'Charles' mother?' my husband and I asked simultaneously.

'Naaah,' Laurie said scornfully. 'It was a man who came and made us do exercises. Look.' He climbed down from his chair and squatted down and touched his toes. 'Like this,' he said. He got solemnly back into his chair and said, picking up his fork, 'Charles didn't even *do* exercises.'

'That's fine,' I said heartily. 'Didn't Charles want to do exercises?'

'Naaah,' Laurie said. 'Charles was so fresh to the teacher's friend he wasn't *let* do exercises.'

'Fresh again?' I said.

'He kicked the teacher's friend,' Laurie said. 'The teacher's friend told Charles to touch his toes like I just did and Charles kicked him.'

'What are they going to do about Charles, do you suppose?' Laurie's father asked him.

Laurie shrugged elaborately. 'Throw him out of the school, I guess,' he said.

Wednesday and Thursday were routine; Charles yelled during story hour and hit a boy in the stomach and made him cry. On Friday Charles stayed after school again and so did all the other children.

> ### Explanation –
> ### Spoken English
>
> Did you notice that Laurie used the word 'fresh' instead of 'cheeky', and 'recess' instead of 'break time'? This is because there are differences between the way English is spoken in America and the way it is spoken in Ireland. The way English is spoken changes from place to place and from one era to another.

With the third week of kindergarten Charles was an institution in our family; Jannie was being a Charles when she cried all afternoon; Laurie did a Charles when he filled his wagon full of mud and pulled it through the kitchen; even my husband, when he caught his elbow in the telephone cord and pulled telephone, ash tray, and a bowl of flowers off the table, said, after the first minute, 'Looks like Charles.'

During the third and fourth weeks there seemed to be a reformation in Charles; Laurie reported grimly at lunch on Thursday of the third week, 'Charles was so good today the teacher gave him an apple.'

'What?' I said, and my husband added warily, 'You mean Charles?'

'Charles,' Laurie said. 'He gave the crayons around and he picked up the books afterward and the teacher said he was her helper.'

'What happened?' I asked incredulously.

'He was her helper, that's all,' Laurie said, and shrugged.

'Can this be true, about Charles?' I asked my husband that night. 'Can something like this happen?'

'Wait and see,' my husband said cynically. 'When you've got Charles to deal with, this may mean he's only plotting.'

He seemed to be wrong. For over a week Charles was the teacher's helper; each day he handed things out and he picked things up; no one had to stay after school.

'The PTA meeting's next week again,' I told my husband one evening. 'I'm going to find Charles' mother there.'

'Ask her what happened to Charles,' my husband said, 'I'd like to know.'

On Friday of that week things were back to normal. 'You know what Charles did today?' Laurie demanded at the lunch table, in a voice slightly awed. 'He told a little girl to say a word and she said it and the teacher washed her mouth out with soap and Charles laughed.'

'What word?' his father asked unwisely, and Laurie said, 'I'll have to whisper it to you, it's so bad.' He got down off his chair and went around to his father. His father bent his head down and Laurie whispered joyfully. His father's eye widened.

'Did Charles tell the little girl to say *that*?' he asked respectfully.

> **Explanation –**
> ## Judging characters
>
> People love to talk about other people. One of the best parts of reading a story is thinking about the characters and judging their behaviour. We learn about characters from:
>
> › what the writer tells us
> › what the characters say and do
> › what the characters say about each other.
>
> Not all of these sources are reliable, so readers are like detectives, trying to find evidence for the judgements they make.

'She said it *twice*,' Laurie said. 'Charles told her to say it *twice*.'

'What happened to Charles?' my husband asked.

'Nothing,' Laurie said. 'He was passing out crayons.'

Monday morning Charles abandoned the little girl and said the evil word himself three or four times, getting his mouth washed out with soap each time. He also threw chalk.

My husband came to the door with me that evening as I set out for the PTA meeting. 'Invite her over for a cup of tea after the meeting,' he said. 'I want to get a look at her.'

'If only she's there,' I said prayerfully.

'She'll be there,' my husband said. 'I don't see how they could hold a PTA meeting without Charles' mother.'

At the meeting I sat restlessly, scanning each comfortable matronly face, trying to determine which one hid the secret of Charles. None of them looked to me haggard enough. No one stood up in the meeting and apologised for the way her son had been acting. No one mentioned Charles.

After the meeting I identified and sought out Laurie's kindergarten teacher. She had a plate with a cup of tea and a piece of chocolate cake; I had a plate with a cup of tea and a piece of marshmallow cake. We manoeuvred up to one another cautiously and smiled.

'I've been so anxious to meet you,' I said. 'I'm Laurie's mother.'

'We're all so interested in Laurie,' she said.

'Well he certainly likes kindergarten,' I said. 'He talks about it all the time.'

'We had a little trouble adjusting, the first week or so,' she said primly, 'but now he's a fine little helper. With lapses, of course.'

'Laurie usually adjusts very quickly,' I said. 'I suppose this time it's Charles' influence.'

'Charles?'

'Yes,' I said, laughing, 'you must have your hands full in that kindergarten, with Charles.'

'Charles?' she said. 'We don't have any Charles in the kindergarten!'

Explanation –
Answering questions

Straightforward questions

Some of the questions in this book are straightforward. The answer is usually right there in the text. Here is an example.

Question: What does Laurie say 'Charles' did on the third day of the first week in kindergarten?

Answer: On the third day 'Charles' bounced a seesaw on to a little girl's head.

Thinking out questions

Some questions ask you to think things out. You use the evidence in the text and your own ideas and experience to answer the question. In the following example, your knowledge of parents will help you.

Question: Laurie's mum does not attend the first Parent–Teacher meeting. What might Laurie's teacher think of this?

Answer: At the end of the story we find out that there is no Charles in the kindergarten. We realise that it was Laurie who did all the bad things. I'm sure the teacher must have thought that Laurie's mum was too embarrassed to come to the school because of the way Laurie was behaving.

Personal opinion questions

Some questions ask you for your ideas. The answer will not be found in any one part of the text or story but comes from your thinking about the whole story. You use the evidence in the story to support your ideas.

Question: What, in your view, does the story suggest about the relationship between parents and children? Explain why you think so.

Answer: I think the story suggests that parents can be blind to the behaviour of their children. Laurie comes home every day with stories of the bad things 'Charles' does in school. Even though Laurie's behaviour changes and he is cheeky at home, his parents never think that their son might be the 'bad boy' in school. We are not told how Laurie's mum reacts when she finds out there is no 'Charles'. I'd say she was really embarrassed.

You will find examples of all three types of question as you read this textbook.

1 Describe the changes that came over Laurie during his first week at kindergarten (pre-school).

2 What stories does Laurie tell about Charles in the first week?

3 'Bound to be people like Charles in the world. Might as well meet them now as later.' What kind of people does Laurie's dad have in mind when he says this?

4 Laurie's parents are fascinated by the idea of Charles' mother. How, in your view, do they imagine her?

5 At the end of the story do you feel sympathy for Laurie's mother and father? Explain your thinking.

6 Here are two statements about Charles. Choose the one that most reflects your own view and say why you chose it.

'The reason why Laurie invents Charles is that he wants his parents to love him, even when he is bold.'

Or:

'The reason Laurie invents Charles is that he wants to boast about his own bad behaviour without getting into trouble.'

7 Here are four possible lessons that the story could teach. Which one, do you think, is the most important? Explain your choice of theme.

> The truth comes out in the end.
> Acting up is part of growing up.
> Children embarrass their parents.
> A parent's love is blind.

Groupwork

After the parents' meeting, Laurie's mother phones her sister to tell her what happened. Working in pairs, write in dialogue form the conversation they have. (See the YWT, p. 192, for guidelines on writing dialogue.)

Writing Task

Complete this task in your portfolio, p. 9.

You are Laurie's mother. Write a letter to the principal apologising for Laurie's behaviour in his first weeks in playschool.

Oral Language

Imaginary friends

Prepare a short contribution to a class discussion on imaginary friends and why children invent them. Present your ideas as clearly as you can, choosing your words carefully. Remember, every time you give an opinion, give a reason for thinking as you do. Use the peer assessment guide on oral presentations (in your portfolio, p. 22) to give feedback to each other.

 If you liked 'Charles' you might enjoy the film *New Boy* about a boy's first day at school. Your teacher will find a link to this in the *Be Inspired!* weblinks document.

Language Alert

 Check out the Language Alert quiz on common, proper and abstract nouns on the *Be Inspired!* website.

Common nouns

Nouns are words that name people and things. When children first start to speak they use **common** nouns to identify what they can hear, see, touch or eat. Here are some examples:

| milk | bread | dog | chair | orange | bottle | cat |

When we want to name ordinary, common things, it is easy to find the right word without having to think about it. However, in some situations we have to think about which word to use. Imagine you are on the street with another person and you meet your aunt. She asks if the person with you is your friend. You are not sure what to answer.

Groupwork

Working in small groups, place the following words in order. At the top, place the word that suggests a really close friend; at the bottom, place the word that suggests a distant friend. Everyone in the group must agree on the order of the words.

| acquaintance | companion | best friend | classmate |
| pal | helper | buddy | teammate |

Writing Task

Write a list of ten common nouns a child is likely to use to name the things he or she first sees, hears, touches and tastes. Compare your list with the other lists compiled in the class and see what words you have in common.

Proper nouns

Children quickly learn the names of the important people in their lives. 'Mama' and 'Dada' are among the first words spoken by most babies. The name of a particular person, place or object is called a **proper** noun. It always begins with a capital letter. Some examples are:

> Shirley Jackson   Charles   Laurie   Toyota   Cork   Dublin

Abstract nouns

Words that describe ideas, feelings or states of mind are called **abstract** nouns. Abstract nouns are really important in discussing the theme, tone or mood of the different texts you will read in this book. Here are some examples:

> happiness   sadness   sorrow   jealousy
>
> anger   fear   friendship   loneliness

Collective nouns

A word that describes a group of things is called a **collective** noun. Match the **collective noun** to the phrase.

A _____	of geese	herd
A _____	of mountains	gaggle
An _____	of ants	swarm
A _____	of deer	fleet
A _____	of puppies	pride
A _____	of beads	range
A _____	of lions	army
A _____	of bees	string
A _____	of ships	litter

Check out the Language Alert quiz on collective nouns on the *Be Inspired!* website.

William is a four-year-old boy with attitude. He insists that his granny tell his favourite story his way, and only his way!

William's Version

JAN MARK

William and Granny were left to entertain each other for an hour while William's mother went to the clinic.

'Sing to me,' said William.

'Granny's too old to sing,' said Granny.

'I'll sing to you, then,' said William.

William only knew one song. He had forgotten the words and the tune, but he sang it several times, anyway.

'Shall we do something else now?' said Granny.

'Tell me a story,' said William. 'Tell me about the wolf.'

'Red Riding Hood?'

'No, not *that* wolf, the other wolf.'

'Peter and the wolf?' said Granny.

'Mummy's going to have a baby,' said William.

'I know,' said Granny.

William looked suspicious.

'How do you know?'

'Well ... she told me. And it shows, doesn't it?'

'The lady down the road had a baby. It looks like a pig,' said William. He counted on his fingers. 'Three babies looks like three pigs.'

'Ah,' said Granny. 'Once upon a time there were three little pigs. Their names were – '

'They didn't have names,' said William.

'Yes they did. The first pig was called – '

'Pigs don't have names.'

'Some do. These pigs had names.'

'No they didn't.'

William slid off Granny's lap and went to open the corner cupboard by the fireplace. Old magazines cascaded out as old magazines do when they have been flung into a cupboard and the door slammed shut. He rooted among them until he found a little book covered with brown paper, climbed into the cupboard, opened the book, closed it and climbed out again.

'They didn't have names,' he said.

'I didn't know you could read,' said Granny, properly impressed.

'C-A-T, wheelbarrow,' said William.

'Is that the book Mummy reads to you out of?'

'It's my book,' said William.

'But it's the one Mummy reads?'

'If she says please,' said William.

'Well, that's Mummy's story, then. My pigs have names.'

'They're the wrong pigs.' William was not open to negotiation. 'I don't want them in this story.'

'Can't we have different pigs this time?'

'No. They won't know what to do.'

'Once upon a time,' said Granny, 'there were three little pigs who lived with their mother.'

'Their mother was dead,' said William.

'Oh, I'm sure she wasn't,' said Granny.

'She was dead. You make bacon out of dead pigs. She got eaten for breakfast and they threw the rind out for the birds.'

'So the three little pigs had to find homes for themselves.'

'No.' William consulted his book. 'They had to build little houses.'

'I'm just coming to that.'

'You said they had to *find* homes. They didn't *find* them.'

'The first little pig walked along for a bit until he met a man with a load of hay.'

'It was a lady.'

'A lady with a load of hay?'

'NO! It was a lady-pig. You said *he*.'

'I thought all the pigs were little boy-pigs,' said Granny.

'It says lady-pig here,' said William. 'It says the lady-pig went for a walk and met a man with a load of hay.'

'So the lady-pig,' said Granny, 'said to the man, "May I have some of that hay to build a house?" and the man said, "Yes." Is that right?'

'Yes,' said William. 'You know that baby?'

'What baby?'

'The one Mummy's going to have. Will that baby have shoes on when it comes out?'

'I don't think so,' said Granny.

'It will have cold feet,' said William.

'Oh no,' said Granny. 'Mummy will wrap it up in a soft shawl, all snug.'

'I don't *mind* if it has cold feet,' William explained. 'Go on about the lady-pig.'

'So the little lady-pig took the hay and built a little house. Soon the wolf came along and the wolf said –'

'You didn't tell where the wolf lived.'

'I don't know where the wolf lived.'

'15 Tennyson Avenue, next to the bomb-site,' said William.

'I bet it doesn't say that in the book,' said Granny, with spirit.

'Yes it does.'

'Let me see, then.'

William folded himself up with his back to Granny, and pushed the book up under his pullover.

'I don't think it says that in the book,' said Granny.

'It's in ever so small words,' said William.

'So the wolf said, "Little pig, little pig, let me come in," and the little pig answered, "No." So the wolf said, "Then I'll huff and I'll puff and I'll blow your house down," and he huffed and he puffed and he blew the house down, and the little pig ran away.'

'He ate the little pig,' said William.

'No, no,' said Granny. 'The little pig ran away.'

'He ate the little pig. He ate her in a sandwich.'

'All right, he ate the little pig in a sandwich. So the second little pig –'

'You didn't tell about the tricycle.'

'What about the tricycle?'

'The wolf got on his tricycle and went to the bread shop to buy some bread. To make the sandwich,' William explained, patiently.

'Oh well, the wolf got on his tricycle and went to the bread shop to buy some bread. And he went to the grocer's to buy some butter.' This innovation did not go down well.

'He already had some butter in the cupboard,' said William.

'So then the second little pig went for a walk and met a man with a load of wood, and the little pig said to the man, "May I have some of that wood to build a house?" and the man said, "Yes."'

**Explanation –
Dialogue**

There is very little description in 'William's Version'. The story is mostly made up of dialogue, that is, the words spoken by William and Granny, the two characters in the story. Good dialogue captures the personality of the speakers and seems real. (See the YWT, p. 192, for guidelines on writing dialogue.)

'He didn't say please.'

'"Please may I have some of that wood to build a house?"'

'It was sticks.'

'Sticks *are* wood.'

William took out his book and turned the pages. 'That's right,' he said.

'Why don't you tell the story?' said Granny.

'I can't remember it,' said William.

'You could read it out of your book.'

'I've lost it,' said William, clutching his pullover. 'Look, do you know who this is?' He pulled a green angora scarf from under the sofa.

'No, who is it?' said Granny, glad of the diversion.

'This is Doctor Snake.' He made the scarf wriggle across the carpet.

'Why is he a doctor?'

'Because he is all furry,' said William. He wrapped the doctor round his neck and sat sucking the loose end. 'Go on about the wolf.'

'So the little pig built a house of sticks and along came the wolf – on his tricycle?'

'He came by bus. He didn't have any money for a ticket so he ate up the conductor.'

'That wasn't very nice of him,' said Granny.

'No,' said William. 'It wasn't *very* nice.'

'And the wolf said, "Little pig, little pig, let me come in," and the little pig said, "No," and the wolf said, "Then I'll huff and I'll puff and I'll blow your house down," so he huffed and he puffed and he blew the house down. And then what did he do?' Granny asked, cautiously.

William was silent.

'Did he eat the second little pig?'

'Yes.'

'How did he eat this little pig?' said Granny, prepared for more pig sandwiches or possibly pig on toast.

'With his mouth,' said William.

'Now the third little pig went for a walk and met a man with a load of bricks. And the little pig said, "*Please* may I have some of those bricks to build a house?" and the man said, "Yes." So the little pig took the bricks and built a house.'

'He built it on the bomb-site.'

'Next door to the wolf?' said Granny. 'That was very silly of him.'

'There wasn't anywhere else,' said William. 'All the roads were full up.'

'The wolf didn't have to come by bus or tricycle this time, then, did he?' said Granny, grown cunning.

'Yes.' William took out the book and peered in, secretively. 'He was playing in the cemetery. He had to get another bus.'

'And did he eat the conductor this time?'

'No. A nice man gave him some money, so he bought a ticket.'

'I'm glad to hear it,' said Granny.

'He ate the nice man,' said William.

'So the wolf got off the bus and went up to the little pig's house, and he said, "Little pig, little pig, let me come in," and the little pig said, "No," and then the wolf said, "I'll huff and I'll puff and I'll blow your house down," and he huffed and he puffed and he huffed and he puffed but he couldn't blow the house down because it was made of bricks.'

'He couldn't blow it down,' said William, 'because it was stuck to the ground.'

'Well, anyway, the wolf got very cross then, and he climbed on the roof and shouted down the chimney, "I'm coming to get you!" but the little pig just laughed and put a big saucepan of water on the fire.'

'He put it on the gas stove.'

'He put it on the *fire*,' said Granny, speaking very rapidly, 'and the wolf fell down the chimney and into the pan of water and was boiled and the little pig ate him for supper.'

William threw himself full length on the carpet and screamed.

'He didn't! He didn't! *He didn't*! He didn't eat the wolf.'

Granny picked him up, all stiff and kicking and sat him on her lap.

'Did I get it wrong again, love? Don't cry. Tell me what really happened.'

William wept, and wiped his nose on Doctor Snake.

'The little pig put the saucepan on the gas stove and the wolf got down the chimney and put the little pig in the saucepan and boiled him. He had him for tea, with chips,' said William.

'Oh,' said Granny. 'I've got it all wrong, haven't I? Can I see the book? Then I shall know, next time.'

William took the book from under his pullover. Granny opened it and read, *First Aid for Beginners: a Practical Handbook*.

'I see,' said Granny. 'I don't think I can read this. I left my glasses at home. You tell Gran how it ends.'

William turned to the last page which showed a prostrate man with his leg in a splint; *compound fracture of the femur*.

'Then the wolf washed up and got on his tricycle and went to see his Granny, and his Granny opened the door and said, "Hello, William."'

'I thought it was the wolf.'

'It was. It was the wolf. His name was William Wolf,' said William.

'What a nice story,' said Granny. 'You tell it much better than I do.'

'I can see up your nose,' said William. 'It's all whiskery.'

Thinking about the story

1 Why is Granny minding William?

2 William's mother is expecting a baby. Do you think that William is happy about this? Explain your answer and use the story to support your opinion.

3 a) Go through the story and mark the most obvious changes in William's behaviour.

b) How does Granny react to each of these changes?

4 'William's granny is very patient.' Do you agree? Explain your point of view.

5 Readers have used different words to describe William's behaviour:

> rude
> imaginative
> cheeky

> high-spirited
> bold
> amusing

Which word, do you think, best describes his behaviour? Explain your thinking.

6 Choose your favourite part of the story and say why you liked it.

7 What moral or lesson might a child learn from reading 'William's Version'? Here are some suggestions:

> You should always be kind to your granny.
> If your granny is babysitting, you can get what you want.
> The worse you behave, the more you get your own way.
> Grannies are patient and kind.

Choose one and write a paragraph explaining why you chose it.

Oral Language

Working in groups of three (The Narrator, Granny, William), read the story aloud.

Writing Task

As in 'William's Version', the relationship between members of a family makes for good drama. Write short scripts for the following pairs of characters:

> **A father and his teenage daughter.**
> The daughter wants permission to go to a party in a friend's house. The father intends to refuse permission because he doesn't know the friend.

> **A mother and teenage son.**
> The son wants to persuade his mother to get a dog for his birthday. The mother wants to say no because she dislikes pets. (Short scripts like this are great for making recordings.)

Reminder – Layout of scripts

When you write a script, put the name of the character on the left-hand side and the words he/she speaks on the right, as in this example:

Marcus	Has she gone?
Chris	Valerie? Yes.
Marcus	Good.

Language Alert

 Check out the Language Alert quiz on adjectives on the *Be Inspired!* website.

Adjectives

Adjectives are words that describe or give a fuller picture of a noun. They help to create atmosphere, for example: the **dark** house; the **empty** street; the **still** wind; the **wild** sea. Adjectives can say as much about the person who uses them as the noun they describe.

Groupwork

Working in pairs, read the following three descriptions of William and decide which adjective is the most factual, the most biased and the most sympathetic.

(a) The imaginative boy asked for a story.

(b) The young boy asked for a story.

(c) The bold boy asked for a story.

Most factual *(based on fact)*	(a) ☐ (b) ☐ (c) ☐
Most biased *(based on opinion)* against William	(a) ☐ (b) ☐ (c) ☐
Most sympathetic to William	(a) ☐ (b) ☐ (c) ☐

Noun phrases

When you put adjectives and nouns together you make a noun phrase,
as in the following examples:

The **wild** wind   Replace 'wild' with two different adjectives
to describe the wind.

The **dark, raging** sea   Replace 'dark, raging' with two different adjectives
to describe the sea.

The **rocky** shore   Replace 'rocky' with two different adjectives
to describe the shore.

The **quiet** house   Replace 'quiet' with two different adjectives
to describe the house.

The **dangerous** boy   Replace 'dangerous' with two different adjectives
to describe the boy.

Noun phrases are central to writing good descriptions.

Writing Task

Write a list poem, consisting of five colourful noun phrases, to describe the moon
or the sun.

Before you read ...

Before you begin 'The Practical Princess', read Alison Lurie's thoughts on traditional fairy tales and what they say about the roles of boys and girls.

In the fairy tales that we know best today, the heroes seem to have all the interesting adventures. They get to kill dragons and outwit giants and rescue princesses and find the magic treasure. As for the heroines, things just happen to them: they are persecuted by wicked stepmothers, eaten by wolves, or fall asleep for a hundred years. All most of them ever seem to do is wait patiently for the right prince to come, or for someone else to rescue them from danger and enchantments. This has made people say that modern children ought not to read fairy tales because they will get the idea that girls are supposed to be beautiful and good and helpless and dull.

But there are thousands of folktales in the world that are not at all like this. They have heroines who can fight and hunt as well as any man, heroines who defeat giants, answer riddles, outwit the Devil, and rescue their friends and relatives from all sorts of dangers and evil spells. They are not only beautiful and good, but also strong, brave, clever, and resourceful.

Why don't we know these stories as well as the others? It is because the first collections of fairy tales for children were put together over a hundred years ago, when women were supposed to be weak and helpless; and the editors who picked the stories out of the many that were available chose ones like 'Snow White', 'Cinderella', 'Sleeping Beauty' and 'Little Red Riding-Hood'. These tales were printed over and over again, while the rest were forgotten.

Most of the editors who chose these stories were men. The original tellers of folktales, on the other hand, were mainly women. And they were… working women: farmers' wives, shopkeepers, craftswomen, household servants, children's nurses, and midwives. They lived active, interesting lives, and the stories they told show it.

 Not all princesses are 'beautiful and good and helpless and dull' – your teacher can find some movie trailers in the *Be Inspired!* weblinks document on edcodigital that challenge this description!

The Practical Princess

JAY WILLIAMS

Princess Bedelia was as lovely as the moon shining upon a lake full of waterlilies. She was as graceful as a cat leaping. And she was also extremely practical.

When she was born, three fairies had come to her cradle to give her gifts as was usual in that country. The first fairy had given her beauty. The second had given her grace. But the third, who was a wise old creature, had said, 'I give her common sense.'

'I don't think much of that gift,' said King Ludwig, raising his eyebrows. 'What good is common sense to a princess? All she needs is charm.'

Nevertheless, when Bedelia was eighteen years old, something happened which made the king change his mind.

A dragon moved into the neighbourhood. He settled in a dark cave on top of a mountain, and the first thing he did was to send a message to the king. 'I must have a princess to devour,' the message said. 'Or I shall breathe out my fiery breath and destroy the kingdom.'

Sadly, King Ludwig called together his councillors and read them the message. 'Perhaps,' said the Prime Minister, 'we had better advertise for a knight to slay the dragon? That is what is generally done in these cases.'

'I'm afraid we haven't time,' answered the king. 'The dragon has only given us until tomorrow morning. There is no help for it. We shall have to send him the princess.' Princess Bedelia had come to the meeting because, as she said, she liked to mind her own business and this was certainly her business.

'Rubbish!' she said. 'Dragons can't tell the difference between princesses and anyone else. Use your common sense. He's just asking for me because he's a snob.'

'That may be so,' said her father, 'but if we don't send you along, he'll destroy the kingdom.'

'Right!' said Bedelia. 'I see I'll have to deal with this myself.' She left the council chamber. She got the largest and gaudiest of her state robes and stuffed it with straw, and tied it together with string. Into the centre of the bundle she packed about fifty kilos of gunpowder. She got two strong young men to carry it up the mountain for her. She stood in front of the dragon's cave, and called, 'Come out! Here's the princess!'

The dragon came blinking and peering out of the darkness. Seeing the bright robe covered with gold and silver embroidery, and hearing Bedelia's voice, he opened his mouth wide.

At Bedelia's signal, the two young men swung the robe and gave it a good heave, right down the dragon's throat. Bedelia threw herself flat on the ground, and the two young men ran.

As the gunpowder met the flames inside the dragon, there was a tremendous explosion.

Bedelia got up, dusting herself off. 'Dragons,' she said, 'are not very bright.'

She left the two young men sweeping up the pieces, and she went back to the castle to have her geography lesson.

The lesson that morning was local geography. 'Our kingdom, Arapathia, is bounded on the north by Istven,' said the teacher. 'Lord Garp, the ruler of Istven, is old, crafty, rich and greedy.' At that very moment, Lord Garp of Istven was arriving at the castle. Word of Bedelia's destruction of the dragon had reached him. 'That girl,' said he, 'is just the wife for me.' And he had come with a hundred finely-dressed courtiers and many presents to ask King Ludwig for her hand.

The king sent for Bedelia. 'My dear,' he said, clearing his throat nervously, 'just see who is here.'

'I see. It's Lord Garp,' said Bedelia. She turned to go.

'He wants to marry you,' said the king.

Bedelia looked at Lord Garp. His face was like an old napkin, crumpled and wrinkled. It was covered with warts, as if someone had left crumbs on the napkin. He had only two teeth. Six long hairs grew from his chin, and none on his head. She felt like screaming.

However, she said, 'I'm very flattered. Thank you, Lord Garp. Just let me talk to my father in private for a minute.' When they had retired to a small room behind the throne, Bedelia said to the king, 'What will Lord Garp do if I refuse to marry him?'

'He is rich, greedy, and crafty,' said the king unhappily. 'He is also used to having his own way in everything. He will be insulted. He will probably declare war on us, and then there will be trouble.'

'Very well,' said Bedelia. 'We must be practical.'

She returned to the throne room. Smiling sweetly at Lord Garp, she said, 'My Lord, as you know, it is customary for a princess to set tasks for anyone who wishes to marry her. Surely you wouldn't like me to break the custom. And you are bold and powerful enough, I know, to perform any task.'

'That is true,' said Lord Garp smugly, stroking the six hairs on his chin. 'Name your task.'

'Bring me,' said Bedelia, 'a branch from the Jewel Tree of Paxis.'

Lord Garp bowed and off he went. 'I think,' said Bedelia to her father, 'that we have seen the last of him. For Paxis is fifteen hundred kilometres away, and the Jewel Tree is guarded by lions, serpents and wolves.'

But in two weeks Lord Garp was back. With him he bore a chest, and from the chest he took a wonderful twig. Its bark was of rough gold. The leaves that grew from it were of fine silver. The twig was covered with blossoms and each blossom had petals of mother-of-pearl and centres of sapphires, the colour of the evening sky.

Bedelia's heart sank as she took the twig. But then she said to herself, 'Use your common sense, my girl! Lord Garp never travelled three thousand kilometres in two weeks, nor is he the man to fight his way through lions, serpents and wolves.'

She looked carefully at the branch. Then she said, 'My lord, you know that the Jewel Tree of Paxis is a living tree, although it is all made of jewels.'

'Why, of course,' said Lord Garp. 'Everyone knows that.'

'Well,' said Bedelia, 'then why is it that these blossoms have no scent?'

Lord Garp turned red.

'I think,' Bedelia went on, 'that this branch was made by the jewellers of Istven, who are the best in the world. Not very nice of you, my lord. Some people might even call it cheating.'

Lord Garp shrugged. He was too old and rich to feel ashamed. But like many men used to having their own way, the more Bedelia refused him, the more he was determined to have her.

'Never mind all that,' he said. 'Set me another task. This time, I swear I will perform it.'

Bedelia sighed. 'Very well. Then bring me a cloak made from the skirts of the salamanders who live in the Volcano of Scoria.'

Lord Garp bowed, and off he went. 'The Volcano of Scoria,' said Bedelia to her father, 'is covered with red-hot lava. It burns steadily with great flames, and pours out poisonous smoke so that no one can come within a metre of it.'

'You have certainly profited by your geography lessons,' said the king, with admiration.

Nevertheless, in a week, Lord Garp was back. This time he carried a cloak that shone and rippled like all the colours of fire. It was made of scaly skins, stitched together with golden wire as fine as a hair; and each scale was red and orange and blue, like a tiny flame.

Bedelia took the splendid cloak. She said to herself, 'Use your head, miss! Lord Garp never climbed the red-hot slopes of the Volcano of Scoria.'

A fire was burning in the fireplace of the throne room. Bedelia hurled the cloak into it. The skins blazed up in a flash, blackened, and fell to ashes.

Lord Garp's mouth fell open. Before he could speak, Bedelia said, 'That cloak was a fake, my lord. The skins of salamanders who can live in the Volcano of Scoria wouldn't burn in a little fire like that one.'

Lord Garp turned pale with anger. He hopped up and down, unable at first to do anything but splutter.

'Ub-ub-ub!' he cried. Then, controlling himself, he said, 'So be it. If I can't have you, no one shall!'

He pointed a long, skinny finger at her. On the finger was a magic ring. At once a great wind arose. It blew through the throne room. It sent King Ludwig flying one way and his guards the other. It picked up Bedelia and whisked her off through the air. When she could catch her breath and look around her, she found herself in a room at the top of a tower.

Bedelia peered out of the window. About the tower stretched an empty, barren plain. As she watched, a speck appeared in the distance. A plume of dust rose behind it. It drew nearer and became Lord Garp on horseback.

He rode up to the tower and looked up at Bedelia. 'Aha!' he croaked. 'So you are safe and snug, are you? And will you marry me now?'

'Never,' said Bedelia, firmly.

'Then stay there until never comes,' snarled Lord Garp.

Away he rode.

For the next two days, Bedelia felt very sorry for herself. She sat wistfully by the window, looking out at the empty plain. When she was hungry, food appeared on the table. When she was tired, she lay down on the narrow cot and slept. Each day, Lord Garp rode by and asked her if she had changed her mind, and each day she refused him. Her only hope was that, as so often happens in old tales, a prince might come riding by who would rescue her.

But on the third day, she gave herself a shake.

'Now then, pull yourself together,' she said sternly. 'If you sit waiting for a prince to rescue you, you may sit here forever. Be practical! If there's any rescuing to be done, you're going to have to do it yourself.'

She jumped up. There was something she had not yet done, and now she did it. She tried the door.

It opened.

Outside were three other doors. But there was no sign of a staircase, or any way down from the top of the tower.

She opened two of the doors and found that they led into cells just like hers, but empty.

Behind the fourth door, however, lay what appeared to be a haystack.

From beneath it came the sound of snores. And between snores, a voice said, 'Sixteen million and twelve … *snore* … sixteen million and thirteen … *snore* … sixteen million and fourteen …'

Cautiously, she went closer. Then she saw that what she had taken for a haystack was in fact an immense pile of blond hair. Parting it, she found a young man, sound asleep.

As she stared, he opened his eyes. He blinked at her. 'Who –?' he said. Then he said, 'Sixteen million and fifteen,' closed his eyes and fell asleep again.

Bedelia took him by the shoulder and shook him hard. He awoke, yawning, and tried to sit up. But the mass of hair made this difficult.

'What on earth is the matter with you?' Bedelia asked. 'Who are you?'

'I am Prince Perian,' he replied, 'the rightful ruler of – oh, dear! here I go again. Sixteen million and ...' His eyes began to close.

Bedelia shook him again. He made a violent effort and managed to wake up enough to continue, '– of Istven. But Lord Garp has put me under a spell. I have to count sheep jumping over a fence, and this puts me to slee-ee-ee-'

He began to snore lightly.

'Dear me,' said Bedelia. 'I must do something.'

She thought hard. Then she pinched Perian's ear, and this woke him with a start. 'Listen,' she said. 'It's quite simple. It's all in your mind, you see. You are imagining the sheep jumping over the fence – no! don't go to sleep again!

'This is what you must do. Imagine them jumping backwards. As you do, *count* them backwards and when you get to *one*, you'll be wide awake.'

The prince's eyes snapped open. 'Marvellous!' he said. 'Will it work?'

'It's bound to,' said Bedelia. 'For if the sheep going one way will put you to sleep, their going back again will wake you up.'

Hastily, the prince began to count, 'Six million and fourteen, six million and thirteen, six million and twelve ...'

'Oh, my goodness,' cried Bedelia, 'count by hundreds or you'll never get there.'

He began to gabble as fast as he could, and with each moment that passed, his eyes sparkled more brightly, his face grew livelier, and he seemed a little stronger, until at last he shouted, 'Five, four, three, two, ONE!' and awoke completely.

He struggled to his feet, with a little help from Bedelia.

'Heavens!' he said. 'Look how my hair and beard have grown. I've been here for years. Thank you, my dear. Who are you, and what are you doing here?'

Bedelia quickly explained.

Perian shook his head. 'One more crime of Lord Garp's,' he said. 'We must escape and see that he is punished.'

'Easier said than done,' Bedelia replied. 'There are no stairs in this tower, as far as I can tell, and the outside wall is much too smooth to climb.'

Perian frowned. 'This will take some thought,' he said. 'What we need is a long rope.'

'Use your common sense,' said Bedelia. 'We haven't any rope.'

Then her face brightened, and she clapped her hands. 'But we have your beard,' she laughed.

Perian understood at once, and chuckled, 'I'm sure it will reach almost to the ground,' he said. 'But we haven't any scissors to cut it off with.'

'That is so,' said Bedelia. 'Hang it out of the window and let me climb down. I'll search the tower and perhaps I can find a ladder, or a hidden stair. If all else fails, I can go for help.'

She and the prince gathered up great armfuls of the beard and staggered into Bedelia's room, which had the largest window. The prince's long hair trailed behind and nearly tripped him.

He threw the beard out of the window, and sure enough the end of it came to within a metre of the ground.

Perian braced himself, holding the beard with both hands to ease the pull on his chin. Bedelia climbed out of the window and slid down the beard. She dropped to the ground and sat for a moment, breathless.

And as she sat there, out of the wilderness came the drumming of hoofs, a cloud of dust, and then Lord Garp on his swift horse.

With one glance he saw what was happening. He shook his fist up at Prince Perian.

'Meddlesome fool!' he shouted. 'I'll teach you to interfere.'

He leapt from his horse and grabbed the beard. He gave it a tremendous yank. Head-first came Perian, out of the window. Down he fell, and with a thump, he landed right on top of old Lord Garp.

This saved Perian, who was not hurt at all. But it was the end of Lord Garp.

Perian and Bedelia rode back to Istven on Lord Garp's horse.

In the great city, the prince was greeted with cheers of joy – once everyone had recognised him after so many years and under so much hair.

And of course, since Bedelia had rescued him from captivity, she married him. First, however, she made him get a haircut and a shave so that she could see what he really looked like.

For she was always practical.

Thinking about the story

1 What were the three gifts presented to Bedelia when she was born?

2 In what way was the gift of the third fairy different from the usual gifts presented to princesses on their birth? Explain your thinking.

3 What is your favourite example of Bedelia's common sense in the story?

4 Which of these three phrases best describes Lord Garp?

> greedy and dishonest   > powerful and determined   > imaginative and clever

Explain your thinking.

5 Which of these three phrases best describes Bedelia?

> beautiful and dull   > patient and helpless   > clever and brave

Explain your thinking.

6 a) Can you think of any recent fairy-tale film in which the princess is the action hero?

b) Why, in your view, are filmmakers beginning to move away from the image of the princess as helpless and dependent on a prince to save her?

7 Watch the video 'Like a Girl' on the *Be Inspired!* website. What, in your view, is the message that both the video and 'The Practical Princess' share?

 Video

Writing Task

In your portfolio, p. 10, write a tale which involves one of the following:

> a dangerous journey   > the lifting of an evil spell   > the release of a prisoner

Consider making your heroine a resourceful and spirited young woman.

Oral Language

Working in groups of three, take a section of the story (the defeat of the dragon; or the outwitting of Lord Garp; or the escape from the tower) and prepare a reading of it for the rest of the class.

 You might like to watch a retelling of a traditional tale for ideas on making a story come alive. Your teacher can check out *Granny O'Grimm's Sleeping Beauty* through the *Be Inspired!* weblinks document on edcodigital.

 If you enjoyed 'The Practical Princess' you will enjoy Dave Rudden's poem 'Princes Come to Those who Wait' on the *Be Inspired!* website.

Verbs

Verbs are sometimes called action words. This is a useful idea if we include speech, feelings and thoughts as actions. A simple way to recognise a verb is to think of words that follow 'I':

I think	I love	I forget	I write	I run
I dream	I imagine	I suggest	I laugh	I talk

Forming the past tense

> Check out the Against the Clock quiz on forming the past tense on the *Be Inspired!* website.

For many regular verbs, changing the ending of a verb changes the meaning. Take the verb 'play': add 's' to the end and you get the present tense; add 'ed' and you get the past.

Verb	Present	Past	Impersonal past
play	he plays	she played	the match was played

For irregular verbs, it's not as simple. Think of 'he runs' and 'he ran'.

Working in a small group, fill in this chart of verbs. Consult a dictionary if you're not sure.

Verb	Present	Past	Impersonal past
run	he ...	she ...	the race was ...
send	she ...	he ...	the letter was ...
keep	he ...	she ...	the money was ...
teach	she ...	he ...	the lesson was ...
take	he ...	she ...	the photo was ...
see	she ...	he ...	the fox was ...
catch	he ...	she ...	the chicken was ...
come	she ...	he ...	the time had ...
burn	he ...	she ...	the toast had ...
begin	she ...	he ...	the storm had ...

In this ghost story, a ghost comes to help his family.
This is a great story to hear read aloud by your teacher.

> **Author Biography**
> Check out the *Be Inspired!* website for Philippa Pearce's author biography.

At the River-Gates

PHILIPPA PEARCE

Lots of sisters I had (said the old man), good girls too; and one elder brother. Just the one. We were at either end of the family: the eldest, my brother John – we always called him Beany, for some reason; then the girls, four of them, then me. I was Tiddler, and the reason for that was plain.

Our father was a flour miller, and we lived just beside the mill. It was a watermill, built right over the river, with the mill-wheel underneath. To understand what happened that wild night, all those years ago, you have to understand a bit about the working of the mill-stream. About a hundred yards before the river reached the mill, it divided: the upper river flowed on to power the mill, as I've said; the lower river, leaving the upper river through sluice-gates, flowed to one side of the mill and past it; and then the upper and lower rivers joined up again well below the mill. The sluice-gates could be opened or shut by the miller to let more or less water through from the upper to the lower river. You can see the use of that: the miller controlled the flow of water to power his mill; he could also draw off any floodwaters that came down.

Being a miller's son, I can never remember not understanding that. I was a little tiddler, still at school, when my brother, Beany, began helping my father in the mill. He was as good as a man, my father said. He was strong, and he learnt the feel of the grain, and he was clever with the mill machinery, and he got on with the other men in the mill – there were only ten of them, counting two carters. He understood the gates, of course, and how to get just the right head of water for the mill. And he liked it all: he liked the work he did, and the life; he liked the mill, and the river, and the long river-bank. One day he'd be the miller after my father, everyone said.

I was too young to feel jealousy about that; but I would never have felt jealous of Beany, because Beany was the best brother you could have had. I loved and admired him more than anyone I knew or could imagine knowing. He was very good to me. He used to take me with him when you might have thought a little boy would have been in the way. He took me with him when he went fishing, and he taught me to fish. I learnt patience, then, from Beany. There were plenty of roach and dace in the river; and sometimes we caught trout or pike; and once we caught an eel, and I was first of all terrified and then screaming with excitement at the way it whipped about on the bank, but Beany held it and killed it, and my mother made it into eel-pie. He knew about the fish in the river, and the little creatures, too. He showed me fresh-water shrimps, and leeches – 'Look, Tiddler, they make themselves into croquet-hoops when they want to go anywhere!' and he showed me the little underwater cottages of caddis-worms. He knew where to get good watercress for Sunday tea – you could eat watercress from our river, in those days.

We had an old boat on the river, and Beany would take it upstream to inspect the banks for my father. The banks had to be kept sound: if there was a breach, it would let the water escape and reduce the water-power for the mill. Beany took Jess, our dog, with him in the boat, and he often took me. Beany was the only person I've ever known who could point out a kingfisher's nest in the river-bank. He knew about birds. He once showed me a flycatcher's nest in the brickwork below the sluice gates, just above where the water dashed and roared at its highest. Once, when we were in the boat, he pointed ahead to an otter in the water. I held on to Jess's collar then.

It was Beany who taught me to swim. One summer it was hotter than anyone remembered, and Beany was going from the mill up to the gates to shut in more water. Jess was following him, and as he went he gave me a wink, so I followed too, although I didn't know why. As usual, he opened the gates with the great iron spanner, almost as long in the handle as he was tall. Then he went down to the pool in the lower river, as if to see the water-level there. But as he went he was unbuttoning his flour-whitened waistcoat; by the time he reached the pool he was naked, and he dived straight in. He came up with his hair plastered over his eyes, and he called to me: 'Come on, Tiddler! Just time for a swimming lesson!' Jess sat on the bank and watched us.

Jess was really my father's dog, but she attached herself to Beany. She loved Beany. Everyone loved Beany, and he was good to everyone. Especially, as I've said, to me. Just sometimes he'd say, 'I'm off on my own now, Tiddler,' and then I knew better than to ask

BE INSPIRED!

to go with him. He'd go sauntering up the river-bank by himself, except for Jess at his heels. I don't think he did anything very particular when he went off on his own. Just the river and the river-bank were happiness enough for him.

He was still not old enough to have got himself a girl, which might have changed things a bit; but he wasn't too young to go to the War. The War broke out in 1914, when I was still a boy, and Beany went.

It was sad without Beany; but it was worse than that. I was too young to understand then; but, looking back, I realise what was wrong. There was fear in the house. My parents became gloomy and somehow secret. So many young men were being killed at the Front. Other families in the village had had word of a son's death.

The news came in a telegram. I overheard my parents talking of those deaths, those telegrams, although not in front of the girls or me. I saw my mother once, in the middle of the morning, kneeling by Beany's bed, praying.

So every time Beany came home on leave, alive, we were lucky.

But when Beany came, he was different. He loved us so much, but he was different. He didn't play with me as he used to do; he would sometimes stare at me as though he didn't see me. When I shouted 'Beany!' and rushed at him, he would start as if he'd woken up. Then he'd smile, and be good to me, almost as he used to be. But, more often than he used to, he'd be off all by himself up the river-bank, with Jess at his heels. My mother, who longed to have him within her sight for every minute of his leave, used to watch him go, and sigh. Once I heard her say to my father that the river-bank did Beany good, as if he were sickening for some strange disease. Once one of the girls was asking Beany about the Front and the trenches, and he was telling her this and that, and we were all interested, and suddenly he stopped and said, 'No. It's hell.' And walked away alone, up the green, quiet river-bank. I suppose if one place was hell, then the other was heaven to him.

After Beany's leaves were over, the mill-house was gloomy again; and my father had to work harder, without Beany's help in the mill. Nowadays he had to work the gates all by himself, a thing that Beany had been taking over from him. If the gates needed working at night, my father and Beany had always gone there together. My mother hated it nowadays when my father had to go to the gates alone at night: she was afraid he'd slip and fall in the water, and, although he could swim, accidents could happen to a man alone in the dark. But, of course, my father wouldn't let her come with him, or any of my sisters, and I was still considered much too young. That irked me.

Well, one season had been very dry and the river level had dropped. The gates were kept shut to get a head of water for the mill. Then clouds began to build up heavy on the horizon, and my father said he was sure it was going to rain; but it didn't. All day storms rumbled in the distance. In the evening the rain began. It rained steadily: my father had already been once to the gates to open the flashes. He was back at home, drying off in front of the fire. The rain still drove against the windows. My mother said, 'It can't come down worse than this.' She and my sisters were still up with my father. Even I wasn't in bed, although I was supposed to have been. No one could have slept for the noise of the rain. Suddenly the storm grew worse – much worse. It seemed to explode over our heads. We heard a pane of glass in the skylight over the stairs shatter with the force of it, and my sisters ran with buckets to catch the water pouring through. Oddly, my mother didn't go to see the damage: she stayed with my father, watching him like a lynx. He was fidgeting up and down, paying no attention to the skylight either, and suddenly he said he'd have to go up to the gates again and open everything to carry all possible floodwater into the lower river. This was what my mother had been dreading. She made a great outcry, but she knew it was no use. My father put on his tarpaulin jacket again and took his oil lamp and a thick stick – I don't know why, nor did he, I think. Jess always hated being out in the rain, but she followed him. My mother watched him from the back door, lamenting, and urging him to be careful. A few steps from the doorway and you couldn't see him any longer for the driving rain.

My mother's lingering at the back door gave me my chance. I got my boots on and an oilskin cape I had (I wasn't a fool, even if I was little) and I whipped out of the front door and worked my way round in the shelter of the house to the back and then took the path my father had taken to the river, and made a dash for it, and caught up with my father and Jess, just as they were turning up the way towards the gates. I held on to Jess's tail for quite a bit before my father noticed me. He was terribly angry, of course, but he didn't like to send me back alone, and perhaps in his heart of hearts he was glad of a little human company on such a night. So we all three struggled up to the gates together. Just by the gates my father found me some shelter between a tree trunk and a stack of drift-wood. There I crouched, with Jess to keep me company.

I was too small to help my father with the gates, but there was one thing I could do. He told me to hold his lamp so that the light shone on the gates and what he was doing. The illumination was very poor, partly because of the driving rain, but at least it was better than nothing, and anyway my father knew those gates by heart. Perhaps he gave me the job of holding the light so that I had something to occupy my mind and keep me from being afraid.

There was plenty to be afraid of on that night of the storm.

Directing what light I could on to my father also directed and concentrated my attention on him. I could see his laborious motions as he heaved the great spanner into place. Then he began to try to rack up with it, but the wind and the rain were so strong that I could see he was having the greatest difficulty. Once I saw him stagger sideways nearly into the blackness of the river. Then I wanted to run out from

my shelter and try to help him, but he had strictly forbidden me to do any such thing, and I knew he was right.

Young as I was, I knew – it came to me as I watched him – that he couldn't manage the gates alone in that storm. I suppose he was a man already just past the prime of his strength: the wind and the rain were beating him; the river would beat him.

I shone the light as steadily as I could, and gripped Jess by the collar, and I think I prayed.

I was so frightened then that, afterwards, when I wasn't frightened, I could never be sure of what I had seen, or what I thought I had seen, or what I imagined I had seen. Through the confusion of the storm I saw my father struggling and staggering, and, as I peered and peered, my vision seemed to blur and to double, so that I began sometimes to see one man, sometimes two. My father seemed to have a shadow-self besides himself, who steadied him, heaved with him, worked with him, and at last together they had opened the sluice-gates and let the flood through.

When it was done, my father came back to where Jess and I were, and leant against the tree. He was gasping for breath and exhausted, and had a look on his face that I cannot describe. From his expression I knew that he had *felt* the shadow with him, just as I had seen it. And Jess was agitated too, straining against my hold, whining.

I looked past my father, and I could still see something by the sluice-gates: a shadow that had separated itself from my father, and lingered there. I don't know how I could have seen it in the darkness. I don't know. My father slowly turned and looked in the direction that he saw me looking. The shadow began to move away from the gates, away from us; it began to go up the long river-bank beyond the gates, into the darkness there. It seemed to me that the rain and the wind stilled a little as it went.

Jess wriggled from my grasp and was across the gates and up the river-bank, following the vanished shadow. I had made no move, uttered no word, but my father said to me, 'Let them go!' I looked up at him, and his face was streaming with tears as well as with rain.

He took my hand and we fought our way back to the house. The whole house was lit up, to light us home, and my mother stood at the back door, waiting. She gave a cry of horror when she saw me with my father; and then she saw his face, and her own went quite white. He stumbled into her arms, and he sobbed and sobbed. I didn't know until that night that grown men could cry. My mother led my father indoors, and I don't know what talk they had together. My sisters looked after me, dried me, scolded me, put me to bed.

The next day the telegram came to say that Beany had been killed in action in Flanders.

It was some time after that that Jess came home. She was wet through, and my mother thought she was ill, for she sat shivering by the fire, and for two days would neither eat nor drink. My father said: 'Let her be.'

I'm an old man: it all happened so many years ago, but I've never forgotten my brother Beany. He was so good to us all.

Thinking about the story

1 The story is told by an old man. In five or six sentences, summarise the story he tells.

2 The old man 'loved and admired' his brother, Beany. In what ways was Beany good to him? Give three examples and explain why you chose them.

3 'It was sad without Beany; but it was worse than that.' Describe the changes in the household brought about by the war. Suggest one or two other changes that you imagine the war caused, but which are not mentioned in the story.

4 Read the end of the story from the paragraph beginning 'I was so frightened then ...' Do you think it is a good ending? Explain your thinking.

5 The story is told by an old man. Does this make the story more or less believable? Explain your answer as clearly as you can.

Groupwork

All short stories have some, if not all, of the following ingredients:

> The **main character**: the person who is at the centre of the story
> The **situation**: the family or personal situation of the main character
> The **setting**: the place where the story takes place, but also the atmosphere of that place
> The **problem/crisis/conflict**: the problem or conflict that the main character has to face
> The **decisive moment**: the most important moment in the story, after which things can never be the same again
> The **ending/aftermath**: most endings let us know how things work out for the character, though sometimes the ending is not clear.

Each story also has its own events or action. (See the YWT, p. 190, for more on short stories.) Working in pairs, complete the following sentences for 'At the River-Gates'.

> 'The main character in the story is ...'
> 'The crisis happens when ...'
> 'The decisive moment is when ...'
> 'This is how the story ends ...'

'"Let them go!" I looked up at him, and his face was streaming with tears as well as with rain.'

Using some of the ideas in the YWT on writing poetry (p. 224), write a short poem which captures the father's thoughts and feelings at this moment in the story. Speak or perform your poem aloud to the class.

Writing Task

Plan the outline for a short story in which a young boy or girl alerts his/her family and neighbours that a river has burst its banks and is threatening to flood the area. Use the information on the parts of a story in the YWT, p. 193, to help you to organise your ideas.

Research

Ask your grandparents or older relatives about ghostly experiences they may have had or heard about. Share their stories with the class.

Or:

Working in pairs, look for letters or diary entries written by troops from the front in the First World War. Your teacher will find some useful links in the *Be Inspired!* weblinks document on edcodigital to help you start your research.

More about verbs

When you place any of the following words before a **verb,** you are suggesting the likelihood of something happening:

will	**would**	**should**	**may**
can	**could**	**must**	**might**

These small words really change the meaning of what is being said.

Groupwork

Working in small groups, look at each of the following statements and say how the meaning changes depending on which word is placed before the verb. You must all agree on the meaning of each sentence before moving on to the next one. You may add to each statement to make the meaning clear, for example 'Beany **must** open the sluice-gates to save the mill.' It will help if you imagine someone speaking and think of that person's relationship with Beany.

> Beany *will* open the sluice-gates ...
> Beany *would* open the sluice-gates ...
> Beany *should* open the sluice-gates ...
> Beany *may* open the sluice-gates ...
> Beany *might* open the sluice-gates ...
> Beany *can* open the sluice-gates ...
> Beany *could* open the sluice-gates ...
> Beany *must* open the sluice-gates ...

Revealing verbs

Choosing the right verb is an important part of becoming a good writer or speaker. A verb can describe an action in a factual way. But it can also do more than that. It can, for example, reveal something about the person doing the action or the person describing the action.

Oral Language

Working with a partner, match the three sentences to the three descriptions and explain your choices.

Sentence	Description
Little Red Riding Hood ran home.	Suggests that the writer is not sympathetic
Little Red Riding Hood scurried home.	Suggests that Little Red Riding Hood is excited
Little Red Riding Hood raced home.	Factual description

Adverbs

Adverbs are words that give more information about verbs. Some are easy to recognise because they end in '-ly'.

I walked quietly.   **He drove slowly.**

We ate quickly.   **They laughed loudly.**

Prepositions and adverbial phrases

Check out the Language Alert quizzes on prepositions and adverbial phrases on the *Be Inspired!* website.

Many sentences say where or when an action took place and use words like:

above	between	behind	after	from
at	below	through	of	beside
around	in	under	with	across
like	before	to	over	up

These small words are called *prepositions*. Using a preposition and a noun or a noun phrase, we form what is called an *adverbial phrase*. This tells us where, when or how an action takes place.

Groupwork

Working in pairs, match the sentence starter with a suitable adverbial phrase.

The children played	across the hills
The bird flew	over the moon
The plane soared	on the rocky shore
The cow jumped	through the night
The boat sailed	all summer long
I stood	in the quiet house
The boy raced	above the clouds
The wolves howled	on the dark, raging sea
The music played	like the wind

Wrapping up

Now that you have finished this chapter, let's recap on what you have learned. You have:

> read and written about stories
> given your interpretation and personal responses
> made arguments for your opinions and point of view
> discussed with others the themes of the stories and ideas which come from them
> responded in imaginative ways to what you've read and heard
> been reminded of some important features of writing.

Here is the final task to wrap up this chapter.

Earlier you were asked to write an idea for a short story in which a young boy or girl alerts his/her family and neighbours about a threatened flood. Now, in your portfolio, p. 12, write your story.

Chapter Two
POETRY A

Poems can be riddles, stories or jokes. In this chapter, poems will make you ask questions, laugh out loud or imagine something new.

Communicating

> You will enjoy reading and listening to a wide variety of poems.

> You will discuss your own response to poems and listen to the views of others.

> You will express your ideas by speaking and writing about the poems you read.

> You will work on your own, in pairs and in small groups, to explore, create and perform in a variety of ways.

Exploring and Using Language

> You will respond to and talk about poems using appropriate language.

> You will examine the poet's choice of language and the effects of various words in the poems.

> You will find out about the key elements of a poem and the various styles of poetry.

> You will respond to several poems in creative and imaginative ways.

Understanding Language

> You will read poems and learn from them how to improve your own writing.

> You will learn to plan, draft and edit your own work and offer helpful feedback to others.

> You will enjoy the pleasure of writing clearly in your own personal voice.

> You will write for different audiences using suitable language in a number of different styles.

Wrapping Up

> To wrap up, you will write a poem of your own.

www.edco.ie/beinspired

Theme: Growing

Poetry Sampler

Before you read ...

1 What do you think of when you hear the word 'poem'?
2 What poems do you remember from primary school?
3 How is poetry different from other types of writing, like stories or newspaper articles?

The poems below are all quite short. Think of the eleven poems on these pages as a sample of what goes on in poetry. Read the poems and do the exercises that follow. Sometimes you will be asked to write an answer, sometimes to talk to a partner in class, sometimes to work with a small group to deal with a question.

Seaview Haiku

JOHN FOSTER

Bright as butterflies
With folded wings, the windsurfs
Skim across the bay.

FROM ...
Water Lily

RALPH FLETCHER

My petals enfold stamens[1] of gold.
I float, serene,[2] while down below

these roots of mine are deeply stuck
in the coolest most delicious muck.

---

[1] the part of a flower that produces pollen
[2] calm, tranquil

The Span of Life

ROBERT FROST

The old dog barks backward without getting up.
I can remember when he was a pup.

 Come to the Edge

CHRISTOPHER LOGUE

Come to the edge.
We might fall.
Come to the edge.
It's too high!
COME TO THE EDGE!
And they came,
And he pushed,
And they flew.

Riddle

JONATHAN SWIFT

We are little airy Creatures,
All of diff'rent Voice and Features,
One of us in Glass is set,
One of us you'll find in Jet,
T'other you may see in Tin,
And the fourth a Box within,
If the fifth you should pursue,
It can never fly from you.

What are we?

FROM …
Three Limericks
MICHAEL ROSEN

There was a young man with a pimple
who said everything in life is simple.
For weeks and weeks
he sucked in his cheeks
and now his pimple's a dimple.

Epilogue[3]
GRACE NICHOLS

I have crossed an ocean
I have lost my tongue
from the root of the old one
a new one has sprung

---

[3] epilogue – the end of a story, giving a
summary of what happened

Dreams
LANGSTON HUGHES

Hold fast to dreams
For if dreams die
Life is a broken-winged bird
That cannot fly.
Hold fast to dreams
For when dreams go
Life is a barren field
Frozen with snow.

Poem (As the Cat)
WILLIAM CARLOS WILLIAMS

As the cat
climbed over
the top of

the jamcloset
first the right
forefoot

carefully
then the hind
stepped down

into the pit of
the empty
flowerpot

Fog
CARL SANDBURG

The fog comes
on little cat feet.

It sits looking
over harbor and city
on silent haunches[4]
and then moves on.

---

[4] hindquarters

Stars
TIM TOASTER HENDERSON

Black outs
Were the only time
I saw the stars in the city.

Clouds were easy to find,
Just enough sky
To know what you're missing,

What you have,
What it means.

Thinking about the poems

1 Choose a poem you liked and think about what makes it enjoyable to read.

2 How does it make you feel?

3 What do you think of when you read the poem?

4 Find a pattern in the words or sounds of a poem.

5 Did you find any surprises when you read the poems?

Oral Language

1 Choose a poem and think about how it might sound read out loud.

2 What kind of voice do you imagine speaking in the poem?

3 Working with a partner, listen to each other reading a number of poems you like.

4 What feelings do you hear being expressed?

5 Describe the pictures the poem creates in your mind.

> ### Explanation –
> ### Image
> An image is a group of words that paints a picture in your mind, e.g. 'windsurfs skim across the bay'.

Groupwork

In small groups, share your ideas about the poems you enjoyed from the poetry sampler.

Listen to others reading the poems out loud.

1 Which poem puts pictures in your mind? Describe the images.

2 Which poem do you have most questions about?

3 Are there any poems here you dislike? Why?

As a group, come up with your own explanation of what poetry is.

Design a poster for your classroom illustrating some of your ideas about poetry.

Research

Choose one or two poets from the sampler pages and see what you can find out about them. Your teacher can find some helpful sites on the *Be Inspired!* weblinks document on edcodigital. When you have collected some interesting information, write out some notes and give a short talk to your class about what you have learned.

In this poem a group of people travel to the coast together.

Maggie and Milly and Molly and May

E.E. CUMMINGS

maggie and milly and molly and may
went down to the beach (to play one day)

and maggie discovered a shell that sang
so sweetly she couldn't remember her troubles, and

milly befriended a stranded star
whose rays five languid fingers were;

and molly was chased by a horrible thing
which raced sideways while blowing bubbles: and

may came home with a smooth round stone
as small as a world and as large as alone.

For whatever we lose (like a you or a me)
it's always ourselves we find in the sea

> **Explanation – Rhyme**
>
> Rhyme is when two or more words have the same sound, e.g. m*ay*/d*ay* and m*e*/s*ea*.

Thinking about the poem

1 There are four people named in the poem. How old do you think they are?
2 Each person discovered something different on their visit to the beach. Which one do you find most interesting?

Oral Language

1 Do you agree that the poem is like a nursery rhyme? Explain your views.
2 What lesson can we learn from this poem? Choose one of the following or suggest a moral of your own.

> At the sea we all discover something.   > Everyone is unique.

Writing Task

Write a paragraph describing a visit to the seaside. Give lots of details of what you saw, heard, tasted, smelled and felt on your skin.

A 'purge' is when you get rid of something unwanted. In the poem below, Seamus Heaney remembers a dramatic event from his childhood and learns a harsh lesson.

The Early Purges

SEAMUS HEANEY

I was six when I first saw kittens drown.
Dan Taggart pitched them, 'the scraggy wee shits',
Into a bucket; a frail metal sound,

Soft paws scraping like mad. But their tiny din
Was soon soused. They were slung on the snout
Of the pump and the water pumped in.

'Sure, isn't it better for them now?' Dan said.
Like wet gloves they bobbed and shone till he sluiced
Them out on the dunghill, glossy and dead.

Suddenly frightened, for days I sadly hung
Round the yard, watching the three sogged remains
Turn mealy and crisp as old summer dung

Until I forgot them. But the fear came back
When Dan trapped big rats, snared rabbits, shot crows
Or, with a sickening tug, pulled old hens' necks.

Still, living displaces false sentiments
And now, when shrill pups are prodded to drown
I just shrug, 'Bloody pups'. It makes sense:

'Prevention of cruelty' talk cuts ice in town
Where they consider death unnatural
But on well-run farms pests have to be kept down.

> **Explanation – Simile**
>
> A simile is when one thing is compared to another using the words 'like' or 'as', e.g. 'Like wet gloves …'

BE INSPIRED!

Thinking about the poem

1 How did the kittens die?

2 What was the reaction of the small boy to their deaths?

3 Is Dan Taggart the villain of this poem? Give reasons for your answer.

4 Search through 'The Early Purges' to find something you could:

see	hear	smell	touch	taste

Oral Language

1 At one point in the poem Dan asks: 'Sure, isn't it better for them now?' What, do you imagine, was he thinking at the time? Discuss your ideas with a partner.

2 Dan uses colloquial and vulgar language. Is this necessary in the poem? Outline your thoughts about the language used. Have a discussion in class about what makes language suitable or inappropriate.

Groupwork

The poem ends with the line: 'on well-run farms pests have to be kept down'.

Have a class debate in which two teams argue *for* and *against* the motion. You will need to plan your speech before you write it.

Ask yourself:

1 Do I agree with 'putting down' pests?

2 What are my reasons for agreeing or disagreeing?

3 What examples can I give to support my point of view?

4 Can I find strong words or phrases to exaggerate the effects of putting down pests?

When your speeches are ready, speak them aloud in class. Try to convince your classmates to accept your position on the subject.

Imagine you could save only one prized possession from your home. What would you choose?

Talk to a classmate about why it is so valuable to you and listen as your classmate explains his/her own choice.

Handbag

RUTH FAINLIGHT

My mother's old leather handbag,
crowded with letters she carried
all through the war. The smell
of my mother's handbag: mints
and lipstick and Coty powder.
The look of those letters, softened
and worn at the edges, opened,
read, and refolded so often.
Letters from my father. Odour
of leather and powder, which ever
since then has meant womanliness,
and love, and anguish, and war.

Explanation – Symbol

A symbol is something that is used to 'stand for' or represent something else. For example, the 'odour' of the handbag stands for 'womanliness, and love, and anguish, and war'. Symbols can bring out strong emotions in people.

Thinking about the poem

1 A person's belongings can give us clues about his/her personality. Think about the handbag and its contents. What does it tell you about the poet's mother?

2 What made the 'letters from my father' so special, do you think?

3 How does the poem appeal to your senses?

Oral Language

1 Choose two of the following and say in each case why you think the handbag came to 'stand for' that thing.

> womanliness > anguish
> love > war

2 a) Bring in an object you think of as precious and show it to the class. Explain why it is special for you.

b) Your teacher will find a link to the video 'Dad' in the *Be Inspired!* weblinks document. In your opinion, what object would the young girl in the video bring in to show her class? Explain your answer.

Writing Task

Complete this task in your portfolio, p. 16.

We never find out what was written in the precious letters home. Imagine you are a soldier in wartime who has been away from home for a long time. Write a personal letter or email to your partner or your child.

Writing Task

Think about the bedtime routine at home when you were a small child. Write a paragraph describing a typical night. Use some of the following to help prompt your writing.

1 Who put you to bed?
2 What was your bedtime?
3 Did your siblings go to bed before or after you or at the same time?
4 Were there songs or stories told before you fell asleep?
5 Did you have a favourite cuddly toy?

Now read Theodore Roethke's poem about a night at home with his parents.

My Papa's Waltz

THEODORE ROETHKE

The whiskey on your breath
Could make a small boy dizzy;
But I hung on like death:
Such waltzing was not easy.

We romped until the pans
Slid from the kitchen shelf;
My mother's countenance
Could not unfrown itself.

The hand that held my wrist
Was battered on one knuckle;
At every step you missed
My right ear scraped a buckle.

You beat time on my head
With a palm caked hard by dirt,
Then waltzed me off to bed
Still clinging to your shirt.

> **Explanation –**
> **Stanza**
>
> A stanza is a group of lines in a poem. 'My Papa's Waltz' is made up of four stanzas, with four lines in each stanza.

Thinking about the poem

1 In this poem there are three characters. Say who each character is and what you discovered about them. Give as much detail as possible in your answer.

2 Which of the three characters did you like most?

3 Choose your favourite word or phrase in the poem and say why you like it.

Oral Language

1 'I hung on like death' in the first stanza is an unusual simile. What does it tell us?

2 Why, do you think, has this moment stood out in the poet's memory? Explain your answer using words from the poem to help you.

3 How would you describe the mood of this poem? Is the mood:

> cheerful   > fearful
> carefree   > excited
> nervous   > regretful?

Explain your choice using some words from the poem to support your ideas.

Explanation –
Mood

The feeling or atmosphere of a particular time and place in a poem is called the *mood*, e.g. a sad mood, a mysterious mood.

Writing Task

Think about the various sounds mentioned in 'My Papa's Waltz'. Now write a paragraph beginning with these words:

'When I listen to this poem I hear the sound of ...'

Before you read ...

Think about the title of the poem 'First Love'.

Write a few words about what you expect to happen in the poem.
You can use the following as prompts for your own ideas:

> characters   > events   > setting   > mood

First Love

MARY DORCEY

You were tall and beautiful.
You wore your long brown hair
wound about your head,
your neck stood clear and full
as the stem of a vase.
You held my hand in yours
and we walked slowly, talking
of small familiar happenings
and of the lost secrets of
your childhood. It seems it was

Always autumn then.
The amber trees shook. We laughed
in a wind that cracked the leaves
from black boughs and set them scuffling
about our feet, for me to trample still
and kick in orange clouds
about your face. We would climb dizzy
to the cliff's edge and stare down
at a green and purple sea, the

Wind howling in our ears, as it
tore the breath from white cheeked waves.
You steadied me against
the wheeling screech of gulls, and i
loved to think that but for your strength
i would tumble to the rocks below
to the fated death, your stories made me
dream of. I don't remember
that i looked in your eyes or that we
ever asked an open question. Our thoughts

Explanation –
Metaphor

Comparing one thing to
something else is called
a metaphor. For example,
'wind howling' compares the
weather to a creature.

Passed through our blood, it seemed,
and the slightest pressure of our hands
decided all issues wordlessly.
We watched in silence by the shore
the cold spray against our skin,
in mutual need of the water's fierce,
inhuman company, that gave promise
of some future, timeless refuge from
all the fixed anxieties of our world.
As we made for home

We faced into the wind, my thighs
were grazed by its icy teeth, you
gathered your coat about me and i
hurried our steps towards home, fire
and the comfort of your sweet, strong tea.
We moved bound in step.
You sang me songs of Ireland's sorrows
and of proud women, loved and lost.
I knew then, they set for me
a brilliant stage of characters, who

Even now, can seem more real
than my most intimate friends.
We walked together, hand in hand.
You were tall and beautiful,
you wore your long brown hair wound
about your head, your neck stood
clear and full as the stem of a vase.
I was young — you were my mother
and it seems, it was always
autumn then.

Thinking about the poem

1 There are two characters in the poem
'First Love'. Who are these characters?

2 How does the poet let us know that
the cliff walk was dangerous?

3 Why does she wait until the end of
the poem to mention her mother?

1 'We watched in silence by the shore'. Why did they not speak much?

2 'You were tall and beautiful,
you wore your long brown hair wound
about your head …'

These lines are repeated towards the end of the poem. Can you think of a good reason why the poet did this?

Writing Task

There are many striking images in 'First Love'. Choose one you like and write a short paragraph explaining the reasons why you like it.

Groupwork – Storyboard

Working in small groups, use the grid below to draw a series of cartoons or pictures telling the story of the poem.

1 Think about the name Lulu. Is it a formal name or is it a casual name?

2 Could Lulu be a nickname or a pet name?

3 What names could be shortened to Lulu?

What Has Happened To Lulu?*

CHARLES CAUSLEY

What has happened to Lulu, mother?
    What has happened to Lu?
There's nothing in her bed but an old rag doll
    And by its side a shoe.

Why is her window wide, mother,
    The curtain flapping free,
And only a circle on the dusty shelf
    Where her money-box used to be?

Why do you turn your head, mother,
    And why do tear-drops fall?
And why do you crumple that note on the fire
    And say it is nothing at all?

I woke to voices late last night,
    I heard an engine roar.
Why do you tell me the things I heard
    Were a dream and nothing more?

I heard somebody cry, mother,
    In anger or in pain,
But now I ask you why, mother,
    You say it was a gust of rain.

Why do you wander about as though
    You don't know what to do?
What has happened to Lulu, mother?
    What has happened to Lu?

> **Explanation –**
> **Ballad**
>
> This poem is a ballad. A ballad always tells a story, has regular rhyme and a refrain or chorus that is repeated, e.g. 'What has happened to Lulu, mother?'

---

* For an alternative ballad see the Poetry Appendix in the *Teacher's Resource Book*.

Thinking about the poem

1 What can you tell about the person speaking in the poem?
2 Why is the 'circle on the dusty shelf' a useful clue about the missing girl?
3 Why are there so many questions in this poem?
4 Describe the relationship between the speaker and the mother in the poem.

Oral Language

1 Work with a partner and practise speaking the lines of the poem out loud.
2 Think about what tone of voice to use, where you could pause for dramatic effect and which words you think you should highlight.
3 Learn the poem for homework.
4 Perform your reading for the class.

Writing Task

Complete this task in your portfolio, p. 17.

Imagine you are the mother in the poem whose daughter has just run away from home. The police have asked you to broadcast a video message to your child to help them find her. Write out the text of a short message from the anxious parent to her child.

Wrapping up

Now that you have finished this chapter, let's recap on what you have learned so far. You have:

> read a wide variety of poems using different language in different ways
> discussed your thoughts and feelings about the poems you read
> come up with your own explanation of what poetry is
> listened carefully for the sounds of words and the patterns they make
> spoken poems out loud, on your own, in pairs, and together with the full class
> written sentences explaining your thoughts and paragraphs discussing your opinions
> composed work of your own, expressing ideas and feelings
> illustrated your ideas in posters and comic strips.

Complete this task in your portfolio.

Now that you have explored a variety of poems, try writing some poems of your own. You will find helpful guidelines for writing acrostic, autobiographical, haiku and riddle poems in your portfolio (pp. 18–21).

Chapter Three
PERSONAL WRITING A

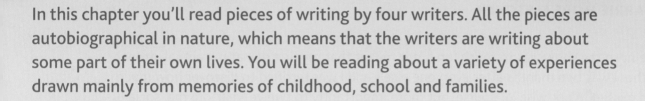

In this chapter you'll read pieces of writing by four writers. All the pieces are autobiographical in nature, which means that the writers are writing about some part of their own lives. You will be reading about a variety of experiences drawn mainly from memories of childhood, school and families.

Communicating

> You will have the opportunity to work with others in pairs and small groups:
>> To listen actively
>> To explain your thoughts, feelings and opinions
>> To imagine, speculate and make judgements
> You will read these texts in order to:
>> Understand, enjoy and respond to them
>> Question and analyse them
>> Respond both orally and in writing in a variety of forms

Exploring and Using Language

> You will read these texts both for pleasure and to understand and appreciate all their aspects including character, language, images.
> You will understand and comment, orally and in writing, on how these texts are enhanced by their authors' use of language and imagery.
> You will complete quizzes on the *Be Inspired!* website that focus on paragraphs and sentences.

Understanding Language

> You will also use sources such as a dictionary, websites and a thesaurus to help you with vocabulary.
> You will apply what you learn from these texts to improve your own writing.
> You will also make judgements about your own and others' work and think about how to improve your skills.
> You will learn to choose appropriate language as you work alone and with others to create a simile, an email, a dialogue, a blog, a story, a book cover, and write using a photograph as stimulus.
> You will read author biographies on the *Be Inspired!* website and research topics online.

Wrapping Up

> To wrap up, you will be asked to think and record some details in your portfolio, p. 26, to help you to create your own life story and to write a letter to your older self.

www.edco.ie/beinspired

Before you read ...

Can you remember your first day at school? How did you feel – happy, sad, excited ...?
Swap stories with your neighbour.

Carrie is an actress, musician and vlogger from London, who has a huge fan base for her YouTube channel, 'It'sWayPastMyBedtime'. She did not begin secondary school on the same day as all the other pupils in her class as she was appearing as an actress in Mary Poppins *in the theatre.*

My First Day at School

CARRIE HOPE FLETCHER

Being in the show was so much fun but it meant that my first day at my actual, proper school was two months after everyone else's and I was terrified to discover how much I'd missed. Work-wise, of course, but more importantly to twelve-year-old me, socially. The school was rather a large one with around eight hundred girls from the ages of three to eighteen – I felt like a little tadpole in an ocean. I walked into a classroom full of kids who had already decided who was cool and who wasn't, what the cliques were and who was in them and who sat where at lunchtime in the cafeteria. Everyone already knew that they could get away with not wearing their blazers, that they could roll their skirts up so they hung just *above* the knee and that the rule about having *only black* school bags was more like a guideline and not something that would land you in detention. All of this had been learnt while I was away. So, in I walked, through the blue school gates in my blue blazer that was a little on the large side with a five pound note from my dad in the inside pocket, an exceedingly long skirt, swaying way past my knees, and my hefty black rucksack that made me look like a gothic turtle, not knowing what clique I'd fit into, or even if I was going to fit into any.

I'm not going to lie or sugar-coat it ... it was terrifying. It always is when you walk into a room full of peers you don't know, all of them ogling you like you're a bridge troll that's just swaggered in trailing a length of moss and slime with cat skulls tangled in its weeds. For me, it was particularly scary because, as I'd gathered from the girl who had been sent to meet me

54

from the school office, all the girls had long ago been told I had been in a show and that I was 'Tom from McFly's sister'. Snap judgements of me had been made instantly and I didn't realise until I walked into my form just how hard it would be to change their minds after they'd lived with that image of me in their heads for so long. Making friends comes naturally to some but I always used to be a little uncertain of how to approach people [...] but, believe me, it's even harder to make friends when they've all decided what kind of person you are before you've even said hello.

I bet she's really stagey. A proper theatre snob!

I bet she thinks she's better than everyone because her brother's in a famous band.

I bet she's on the verge of a nervous breakdown because she's got pushy parents!

How do you even begin to break down those judgements and prove to your peers that you're just a normal, nervous girl in year seven, trying to make friends? It's extremely hard, I'll tell you that for free!

In the midst of this generally petrifying day, the few friendly faces I saw shone out like beacons. When I sat down in one of my first classes, the girl in front of me, who had golden skin, dark brown hair and the sort of cheeks you just want to pinch between your fingers, turned around and said, 'Harriet, can I borrow a pencil?'

'Harriet?' she said a little louder, and when I didn't answer ... 'HARRIET'!

I finally looked up but, as I did, the girl sitting at the desk next to me gently told the girl in front, 'Erm, her name's Carrie.'

Instead of looking mortified, like I expected, she burst into a fit of giggles and introduced herself as Saffron. I can't tell you how relieved I was. But truth be told, the friendly faces were in the minority. I had to do that awful clichéd introduction that schools usually make you do when you're 'the new girl'. They made me stand in front of the class and state my name and 'a little bit about myself'. When I sat back down, a little flushed and flustered, the girl to my right sidled up to me and said, 'So, can you get me free McFly tickets?' This was a situation I'd been in all too frequently at my

primary school so I knew my correct response was to shake my head and to ignore 'those sorts of people'. I felt like Harry Potter when Draco Malfoy tells him he doesn't want to be making friends with 'the wrong sort'. Thankfully, like Harry, I could tell the wrong sort for myself! Later on, after lunchtime when the bell had rung, signalling that we all had to make our way to our next class, and I had my books ready for the last four lessons of the day, I walked through my form room doorway only to trip over a well-placed foot in the hall.

'Whoops! Was that me?' The same girl grinned as she strutted off, leaving me and my books strewn across the hallway in front of the upper school girls who were lined up waiting to go into the opposite classroom for Spanish. Instead of laughing at me, they helped me up and collected my books for me and explained that that girl had always been a troublemaker. I'd already made an enemy? Presumably because I couldn't (and wouldn't if I could) get her tickets to see my brother's band? Wonderful. [...]

My first day at school was a bit unusual because it really was only a first for me. And as you can see it didn't go all that well. The girl who tripped me up went on to cause all sorts of trouble for me over my first three years at high school. [...] But even knowing everything she had in store for me, I can still look back and take some positives from that day.

> **Reminder –**
> **Similes**
>
> Similes are phrases that use 'like' or 'as' to make comparisons between one thing and another. One example from this text is 'I felt like a little tadpole in an ocean' in the first paragraph. Look out for others as you read.

Thinking about the text

1 Starting school later than the rest of her peers, what was Carrie most worried about?

2 What kind of things had the others picked up about life in school that Carrie hadn't yet learned? What evidence can you find to show that she didn't know these things?

3 What did the rest of her classmates know about her before she arrived?

4 Do you agree that it is frightening to walk into a room full of people you don't know? Explain your opinion.

5 Some of the girls wanted tickets for her brother's band's performance. If you had a choice, what current group would you really like tickets for? Explain.

6 The writer uses a number of similes (see Reminder above).

a) Find two other similes in this extract and say whether they help you understand a little more about how Carrie feels.

b) Think about your own first day in your new secondary school and create your own simile to express how you felt.

Oral Language

'I walked into a classroom full of kids who had already decided who was cool and who wasn't, what the cliques were and who was in them and who sat where at lunchtime in the cafeteria.' (Paragraph 1)

From your own experience of school:

> Do pupils form into cliques or groups?
> Do all students make judgements about who is 'cool' or not?
> Does it matter where people sit in the canteen?

Share your opinion with at least one other student or a small group. Be prepared to explain your opinion in a full class discussion on the topic.

Writing Task

Imagine that you are one of the students in Carrie's class that first day. Email her a short note (about two paragraphs) offering her some advice for her second day.

Groupwork

Work in small groups of three or four to talk about and create a dialogue between some of her classmates on the day before they meet Carrie (see paragraph 2). Join with another group to role-play your scripts for each other.

Comment on each other's performances as follows:

> One thing we enjoyed about your performance was …
> One way to make it better would be …

Research

As you read in the introduction, this writer has a YouTube channel called 'It'sWayPastMyBedtime'. Write a short report on (a) this channel *or* (b) your own favourite channel to share with your class. (See your portfolio, p. 68, for help with writing a report.)

Sentences: subjects and verbs

 Check out the Language Alert quiz on sentences on the *Be Inspired!* website.

A **sentence** is a statement (spoken or written) that makes complete sense. A sentence always begins with a capital letter and usually ends with a full stop. A sentence can also end with a question mark or exclamation mark. A sentence must have at least two parts: the **subject** and the **verb**.

The **subject** does the action.

The **verb** describes the action.

Sentence: The rain fell.

Subject: the rain   **Verb:** fell

Sentence: I ran.

Subject: I   **Verb:** ran

Sentences: objects and adverbials

All sentences must have a subject and a verb. Many also have one or more of these elements:

The **object** describes who or what has been affected by the action of the verb.
The **adverbial** describes when, where or how the action took place.

Sentence: The student threw my bag on the ground.

Subject: the student   **Verb:** threw   **Object:** my bag   **Adverbial:** on the ground

Groupwork

Working in pairs, divide the following sentences into Subject–Verb–Object–Adverbial:

> The red car hit the lamppost yesterday evening.
> The red fox stole the chicken from the hen house.
> The clumsy man smashed the expensive vase on the floor.
> The new boy lost his bag in the river.

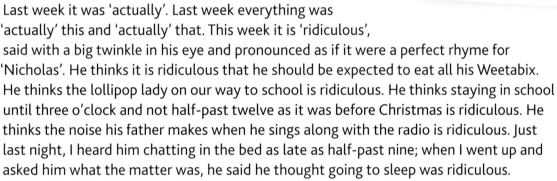

In this piece the author writes about his four-year-old son who, as his vocabulary expands, develops a fondness for particular words, which he applies to every possible subject.

Little Man

CONOR O'CALLAGHAN

Last week it was 'actually'. Last week everything was 'actually' this and 'actually' that. This week it is 'ridiculous', said with a big twinkle in his eye and pronounced as if it were a perfect rhyme for 'Nicholas'. He thinks it is ridiculous that he should be expected to eat all his Weetabix. He thinks the lollipop lady on our way to school is ridiculous. He thinks staying in school until three o'clock and not half-past twelve as it was before Christmas is ridiculous. He thinks the noise his father makes when he sings along with the radio is ridiculous. Just last night, I heard him chatting in the bed as late as half-past nine; when I went up and asked him what the matter was, he said he thought going to sleep was ridiculous.

Our son is four. He seems to have it in his head that four is when you come of age. He has already taken to beginning sentences with phrases like – 'When I was a small boy' or 'Now that I'm big'. He thinks he should be allowed to come out playing snooker with me and his uncle on Tuesday nights. He really believes that he could manage the car – if only his parents would let him. The odd evening when he and his sister are feeling giddy, he stands in the hall in his pyjamas and my jacket and boots and calls back to us in the kitchen, 'I'm away out for a pint of Guinness.'

Since turning four, he has become philosophical. He has begun to ask awkward questions, although about nothing so trivial as the birds and the bees. Umpteen times now, we have found ourselves sitting there nodding at each other, as if to say, 'It's your turn to answer the unanswerable.' He wants to know what it means to be old, he wants to know why dolls don't die, he wonders why the sky

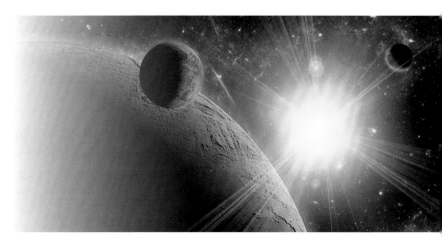

is blue. His mother goes for the truth. Once, I stepped into the kitchen to find she had arranged soggy pears and kiwis into a DIY solar system. He was sitting on the sideline with binoculars and a stethoscope, looking as if he regretted asking where the sun goes at night. Later, I told him that two men go up every night and carry the sun down in a net hung between their separate helicopters. I told him that they keep the sun in a big shed, in a small coastal village three miles from where we live, and that they clean it once a week. He prefers my stories, but I think he believes his mother.

Since starting school, he has become conscious of his appearance in a way that he never was before. It used to be that the morning after we gave them a bath, he would wake up with his hair standing on end, looking as if he had been struck by lightning in his dreams – and it didn't bother him in the slightest. Then, one of the other boys at school said something about his hair to his best friend Desmond, and then Desmond said it back to him. Now, he insists on wearing a baseball cap while eating his breakfast. Time and again, I am struck by how strange the day-to-day life of a four-year-old is. When he was teething – a couple of years ago – he used to soothe his aching gums by chewing a Volkswagen Beetle. Nowadays, he takes a Wagon Wheel for his break and he alternates between an alien (with alien babies) and a penguin for company. He keeps the shaft of a plastic golf club beside his bed and calls it a 'gun'. He drifts off every night to the sound of my grandmother's music box, unwinding through 'The Isle of Capri'. And he thinks you don't die, until you're ninety-nine.

In his teens, years from now, he will spend his summers sleeping in until two in the afternoon and shaving twice a day. He will beg for money from us and accuse us of never loving him – all in the same breath. So, for the time being, I'm inclined just to enjoy him being my little man. And I have begun to realise – that four is probably as good as it gets.

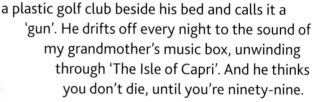

Explanations –

Point of view

This refers to the stance from which the story is told in a piece of writing. For example, in this piece the dad is writing from his own point of view.

Repetition of words and phrases

Many writers use this technique to good effect – it can pull together a piece of writing and create a feeling that everything fits well together. However, repeating the same words or phrases can also sound boring and dreary. Think about this as you read this story and ask yourself whether you think it works well for this writer.

Thinking about the text

1 Make a list of all the things the little boy regards as 'ridiculous'.

2 What kinds of questions does he ask? Can you find at least three?

3 Why does he keep a plastic golf club beside his bed?

4 What evidence does the writer offer as proof that the child has become anxious about his appearance since he started school?

5 a) This little boy obviously regards himself as much older than four years of age. Can you find at least two pieces of evidence that would support this statement?

   b) Your teacher will find a link to the video 'Let Me Get What I Want' in the *Be Inspired!* weblinks document. Watch the video and write two paragraphs comparing the two little boys under the heading 'Two Boys in a Hurry'.

6 Overall, did you or did you not find the entire piece amusing and entertaining? Explain your opinion.

7 'Since becoming four, he has turned philosophical.' Look up the word 'philosophical' in a dictionary and say what you think the writer means by this statement. Write down your own view before sharing your answer with a partner.

Oral Language

Re-read the final paragraph and say whether you agree with the writer's view of teenagers. Make some notes about your own ideas before swapping ideas with your partner. Then join another pair of students and exchange thoughts on the issue.

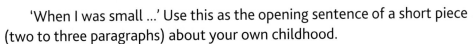

Writing Task

Complete this task in your portfolio, p. 23.

'When I was small ...' Use this as the opening sentence of a short piece (two to three paragraphs) about your own childhood.

Research

Carry out some research to find a poem, story, book or film that appeals to you and that features a young child. Give a short oral presentation to your group or class saying why you would recommend it to other students. Create a colourful poster to accompany your talk. You may find www.glogster.com useful for this task.

Groupwork

Divide into groups of four. Each member of each group will be given a role as follows:

1 **Recorder:** notes the main points you all agree on

2 **Turn-taker:** makes sure that everyone gets a chance to contribute

3 **Time-keeper:** keeps an eye on time and ensures that each person gets an equal amount of time

4 **Reporter:** reports the results of your discussion back to the rest of the class.

Each of you should have written some notes on what you learned about the writer's use of repetition in this piece. Did you think it pulled the story together and gave it a sense of unity, a sense that he really thought about what he was doing? As stated in the Explanations above, if repetition is over-used or used unthinkingly, it can take away from the writing and make it dull and boring.

You should be able to tell each other whether you liked it or not, and if you thought it worked well with this topic. Be prepared to give reasons for your opinions.

Language Alert

Extending sentences

'The boy put on his dad's jacket' is a simple sentence. Another simple sentence is 'The boy wore his new baseball hat.'

Conjunctions

We can make two simple sentences into one sentence using a link word or a conjunction: 'The boy put on his dad's jacket and wore his new baseball hat.' The most common conjunctions are:

> **and**   **but**   **or**

Relative pronouns

Another way to extend a sentence is to use a relative pronoun to link information back to the subject or the object. The relative pronouns are:

> **who**   **whom**   **whose**   **which**   **that**

Look at the following example and see how the relative pronoun is used:
'The boy, *who was starting school,* put on his dad's jacket.'

Three ways to extend a sentence

1 Use **adjectives** to describe the subject and the object of the sentence:

   Subject The boy ➜ The small scared boy
   Object his dad's jacket ➜ his dad's old jacket

2 Use **relative pronouns** to link information back to the subject and the object:
   'The small scared boy, who was crying for his mother, put on his dad's jacket, which was too big for him.'

3 Use **conjunctions** ('and', 'but', 'or') to add information at any point in the sentence.

Complete sentences

When you are invited to give your opinion on a text, it is best to write complete sentences that express your full thoughts. For example, if you are asked to give a reason why you like a character, it is not a good idea to start, 'Because …'. When you start with 'because' you leave out the most important part of an opinion sentence, the *subject* 'I' and the verb. When you are discussing texts in class, many of the complete sentences you use will have this basic structure:

➤ I think that … because …
➤ I know this … because …
➤ I feel this … because …
➤ I wonder about this … because …

Try to develop the habit of writing complete sentences when you are asked for your opinions and feelings.

Groupwork

This is a class activity. Using 'The boy put on his dad's jacket' as your starting point, see how far you can expand the sentence, using adjectives, relative pronouns and conjunctions. The first person begins by saying 'The boy' and then passes it on to the next person. The next person tries to expand the phrase before passing it on. Each person has to repeat what the last person said before adding to it. If a person cannot think of anything to add, he/she says the next word in the sentence. Try to extend the sentence so that everyone in the class gets to add to it. This is a fun exercise but it can help us to remember that there are different ways of making our sentences flow.

Young Writer's Toolkit

Paragraphs

A paragraph is a group of sentences on a single point or idea. We often write paragraphs to explain, make an argument or put forward an idea. Each paragraph should make one point and this should be clear to the reader. A good routine that works when you have to explain or make an argument is to present your idea in the first sentence. Once you have stated the idea, use the other sentences to support it. The other sentences can:

Check out the Language Alert quiz on paragraphs on the *Be Inspired!* website.

> explain or discuss what you mean
> use examples or evidence to support your idea
> draw conclusions from the evidence
> wrap up the idea and/or prepare for the next idea in the next paragraph.

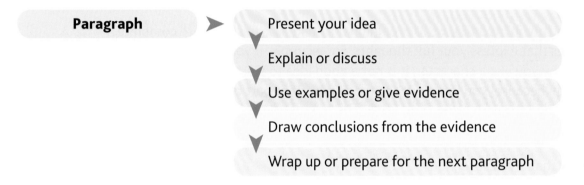

Paragraph ➤ Present your idea
Explain or discuss
Use examples or give evidence
Draw conclusions from the evidence
Wrap up or prepare for the next paragraph

In the following paragraph, the writer uses an imaginary example to make his point: 'Imagine learning a word in a foreign language …' He also introduces his idea by asking a question.

This allows him to begin his paragraph by answering his own question!

Baby Talk

How do we know that a baby has no idea what it's saying? Because we hear the same 'ma-ma-ma' sound being used in all sorts of situations, whether the mother is there or not. Imagine learning a word in a foreign language, such as French – the word 'porte', for instance. It means 'door'. But if we were heard saying 'porte' when we saw a cat, or an apple, or a bed, people would quickly conclude that we had no idea what 'porte' meant. They'd change their minds only when they heard us saying it every time we saw a door. It's the same with babies. There will come a time when they will learn that, in English, 'mama' is the sound they need to use when they want to talk about 'mother' or call for her. At six months of age, they haven't reached that stage.

The first sentence, written as a question, introduces the main idea of the paragraph.

The second sentence answers the question.

Much of the paragraph is taken up with an imagined example.

The writer finally draws a conclusion based on the example. Note how, in 'Baby Talk', the last sentence wraps up the idea and also sets the scene for the following paragraph.

Groupwork

Working in pairs, answer the following questions.

Baby Talk ➤

What argument is the writer making?

How does the writer introduce the idea?

What example does the writer give?

How does the writer prepare for the next paragraph?

Paragraphs: a Brief Summary

The key to writing a good paragraph is to think through your ideas before you write them down; the clearer your thinking, the clearer the paragraph. Here are a few final tips on writing a good paragraph.

> Brainstorming can help you to develop the idea for your paragraph.

> Begin with a sentence that introduces your idea or your point.

> Make sure that each sentence that follows is linked to the subject of the paragraph. Check that the order of the sentences makes sense.

> Think of a good sentence to end your paragraph.

> Review what you've written. Does it seem complete? Could you add anything more?

> If you are writing more than one paragraph, leave a space between them so that it is clear where one ends and the next begins.

In this extract from I Know Why the Caged Bird Sings, *Maya Angelou recounts an episode from her childhood when her grandmother made her a dress for an Easter ceremony with the Colored Methodist Episcopal Church. This piece is from the opening chapter and comes directly after the moment she forgets her lines when it comes to her turn to say something.*

Author Biography

Check out the *Be Inspired!* website for Maya Angelou's author biography.

The Magic Dress

MAYA ANGELOU

The dress I wore was lavender taffeta, and each time I breathed it rustled, and now that I was sucking in air to breathe out shame it sounded like crepe paper on the back of hearses.

As I'd watched Momma put ruffles on the hem and cute little tucks around the waist, I knew that once I put it on I'd look like a movie star. (It was silk and that made up for the awful color.*) I was going to look like one of the sweet little white girls who were everybody's dream of what was right with the world. Hanging softly over the black Singer sewing machine, it looked like magic, and when people saw me wearing it they were going to run up to me and say, 'Marguerite (sometimes it was "dear Marguerite"), forgive us, please, we didn't know who you were,' and I would answer generously, 'No, you couldn't have known. Of course, I forgive you.'

Just thinking about it made me go around with angel's dust sprinkled over my face for days. But Easter's early morning sun had shown the dress to be a plain ugly cut-down from a white woman's once-was-purple throwaway. It was old-lady-long too, but it didn't hide my skinny legs, which had been greased with Blue Seal Vaseline and powdered with the Arkansas red clay. The age-faded color made my skin look dirty like mud, and everyone in church was looking at my skinny legs.

Wouldn't they be surprised when one day I woke out of my black ugly dream, and my real hair, which was long and blond, would take the place of the kinky mass that Momma wouldn't let me straighten? My light-blue eyes were going to hypnotize them, after all the things they said about 'my daddy must have been a Chinaman' (I thought they meant made out of china, like a cup) because my eyes were so small and squinty. Then they would understand why I had never picked up a Southern accent, or spoke the common slang, and why I had to be forced to eat pigs' tails and snouts. Because I was really white and because a cruel fairy stepmother, who was understandably jealous of my beauty, had turned me into a too-big Negro girl, with nappy black hair, broad feet and a space between her teeth that would hold a number-two pencil.

* American spelling

Explanations –

Autobiography

An autobiography is a book a person writes about his or her own life, so it is written from the point of view of that person. This piece is from the first book of Maya Angelou's seven autobiographies.

Descriptive language

We can say that a writer is using descriptive language when the writing appeals to our emotions and our senses. For example, words like 'growling' or 'fizzy' convey a particular sound to us. Similarly, if something is described visually, such as 'red' or 'shimmering', we can see it in our mind's eye and we can smell something that is described as 'musty' or 'fishy'.

Maya Angelou is a very descriptive writer. A good example of this can be found in the very first line when she uses 'rustling' to describe the sound her dress makes when she moves. Look out for other examples as you read.

Thinking about the text

1 How does the writer think people will react when she wears her new dress?

2 Use your own words to say what actually happened.

3 Use these statements to think about this piece of writing.

> What I liked best about this story was …

> What I didn't like was …

> What I'd like to know more about is …

4 'Just thinking about it made me go around with angel's dust sprinkled over my face for days.' Explain in your own words what you think the writer means by this.

5 What do you understand Maya to mean when she writes about waking from her 'black ugly dream'?

6 Re-read the piece and pick out any words that suggest that she is not happy with how she looks. Write out a list of these and share them with a partner.

7 What clues in the piece tell you that it is an autobiography?
(See Explanations above.)

Oral Language

1 What if this story were written from Momma's (her grandmother's) point of view? How would it be different? Write down some thoughts and then discuss with a partner.
Or:

2 Underline all the descriptive words or phrases that appeal to you in the piece. Swap your lists with a partner and have a conversation to choose your favourite three for sharing with the rest of the class. Be ready to explain the reasons for your choices.

Research

Maya Angelou was an internationally known and highly decorated American author who died in May 2014. Use the internet to find out something about her life and works. For example, see if you can find out more information about *I Know Why the Caged Bird Sings*, one of her autobiographies, which tells of her life up to the age of 17. (This piece is taken from the book.) Also try to find a poem she wrote that you like and be able to say why you like it. Use an interesting and colourful method to present your findings to a small group or to your class.

Writing Task

Are there times when you would like to swap places with another person? Have you ever said something like, 'Oh, I really wish I was … even for one day!'? Now you have an opportunity to do this in your writing.

Find a photograph of someone you'd like to be for a day. You can choose anyone you like – the President of Ireland, the Queen of England, a famous sports star or film star …

Complete this task in your portfolio, p. 25.

Groupwork

Working in groups of three or four, compile lists of words describing sound, sight and smell that you can use to make your own writing more colourful. As a group, agree on about ten really good words under each heading and share them with the rest of the class.

Use the graphic organiser to help you. A couple have been filled in to give you a start.

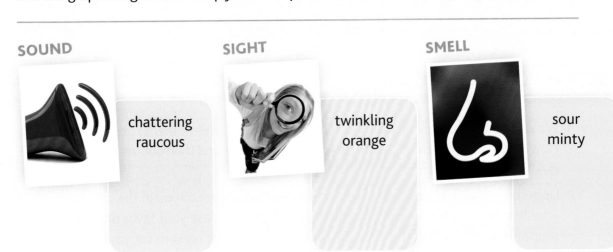

SOUND	SIGHT	SMELL
chattering raucous	twinkling orange	sour minty

Language Alert

Punctuation

Is punctuation important? Yes, punctuation is important because it shows the reader when to pause, when to stop, when a change of speaker occurs and what to expect next. Good punctuation is like good manners – it makes life easier for everyone. Here are some of the most important points of punctuation.

Capital letters and full stops

All sentences begin with a **capital letter** and end with a **full stop** (or an **exclamation mark** or **question mark**).

Capital letters are also used for:

> all proper names – the names of people, places or special pets (Maya, Dublin, Lassie)
> the days of the week and the months of the year (Tuesday, October)
> the names of lakes, rivers and seas (Lough Derg, the Shannon, the Atlantic)
> the main words in titles (*Private Peaceful, The Boy in the Striped Pyjamas*)
> the names of organisations, societies and products (Fine Gael, Friends of the Earth, Kellogg's)
> periods in history (First World War)
> the personal pronoun – 'I'.

Commas

Commas are used to do three basic things:

> to mark off one part of a sentence from another:
  As Jackie reached the boat, the moon grew bright.
> to separate items in a list: *Maya ate two oranges, an apple, a banana, a pear and two sandwiches.*
> to separate direct speech from the rest of the sentence:
  'Your new dress is ready,' said Maya's mother.

Groupwork

Working in pairs, rewrite this passage, putting in commas where you think they are needed. Explain your thinking to your partner.

As the moon rose the children got ready to leave. Maya picked up the heavy rucksack which had once belonged to her father. It held all her most treasured possessions – her diary her pen the comb her mother gave her for her last birthday and her copy of *The Secret Garden*.

'We'll have to hurry' said her brother.

(a) Do you know anyone who went to a boarding school? Would you like to go to boarding school and live away from your family for most of the year? How would you feel?

(b) Were you ever blamed for something you didn't do? What was the occasion and how did it make you feel?

Think about these issues and then exchange your feelings with a partner.

Roald Dahl was sent to boarding school when he was only nine years old. In this piece, he is giving us an insight into what life was like for him. Every evening all the boys would sit in the main hall for one hour to do Prep (schoolwork).

Captain Hardcastle

ROALD DAHL

The rules of Prep were simple but strict. You were forbidden to look up from your work, and you were forbidden to talk. That was all there was to it, but it left you precious little leeway. In extreme circumstances, and I never knew what these were, you could put your hand up and wait until you were asked to speak but you had better be awfully sure that the circumstances were extreme. [...]

Author Biography

Check out the *Be Inspired!* website for Roald Dahl's author biography.

Prep was in progress. Captain Hardcastle was sitting up on the dais in front of us, stroking his orange moustache, twitching his head and grunting through his nose. His eyes roved the Hall endlessly, searching for mischief. The only noises to be heard were Captain Hardcastle's little snorting grunts and the soft sound of pen-nibs moving over paper. Occasionally there was a *ping* as somebody dipped his nib too violently into his tiny white porcelain ink-well.

Explanation –
Creating characters

Creating interesting characters is a very important part of a good story. Readers must find them memorable and appealing. As you read, think about how this writer describes people.

Disaster struck when I foolishly stubbed the tip of my nib into the top of the desk. The nib broke. I knew I hadn't got a spare one in my pocket, but a broken nib was never accepted as an excuse for not finishing Prep. We had been set an essay to write and the subject was 'The Life Story of a Penny' (I still have that essay in my files). I had made a decent start and I was rattling along fine when I broke that nib. There was still another half-hour of Prep to go and I couldn't sit there doing nothing all that time. Nor could I put up my hand and tell Captain Hardcastle I had broken my nib. I simply did not dare. And as a matter of fact, I really *wanted* to finish that essay. I knew exactly what was going to happen to my penny through the next two pages and I couldn't bear to leave it unsaid.

I glanced to my right. The boy next to me was called Dobson. He was the same age as me, nine and a half, and a nice fellow. [...]

Dobson's desk was almost touching mine. I thought I would risk it. I kept my head lowered but watched Captain Hardcastle very carefully. When I was fairly sure he was looking the other way, I put a hand in front of my mouth and whispered, 'Dobson … Dobson … Could you lend me a nib?'

Suddenly there was an explosion up on the dais. Captain Hardcastle had leapt to his feet and was pointing at me and shouting, 'You're talking! I saw you talking! Don't try to deny it! I distinctly saw you talking behind your hand!'

I sat there frozen with terror.

Every boy stopped working and looked up.

Captain Hardcastle's face had gone from red to deep purple and he was twitching violently.

'Do you deny you were talking?' he shouted.

'No, sir, no, b-but …'

'And do you deny you were trying to cheat? Do you deny you were asking Dobson for help with your work?'

'N-no, sir, I wasn't. I wasn't cheating.'

'Of course you were cheating! Why else, may I ask, would you be speaking to Dobson? I take it you were not inquiring after his health?'

It is worth reminding the reader once again of my age. I was not a self-possessed lad of fourteen. Nor was I twelve or even ten years old. I was nine and a half, and at that age one is ill equipped to tackle a grown-up with flaming orange hair and a violent temper. One can do little else but stutter.

'I … I have broken my nib, sir,' I whispered. 'I … I was asking Dobson if he c-could lend me one, sir.'

'You are lying!' cried Captain Hardcastle, and there was triumph in his voice. 'I always knew you were a liar! *And* a cheat as well!'

'All I w-wanted was a nib, sir.'

'I'd shut up if I were you!' thundered the voice on the dais. 'You'll only get yourself into deeper trouble! I am giving you a Stripe!'

These words of doom. A Stripe! *I am giving you a Stripe!* All around, I could feel a kind of sympathy reaching out to me from every boy in the school, but nobody moved or made a sound. [...]

For exceptionally poor work or bad behaviour, you were given a Stripe, and that automatically meant a thrashing from the Headmaster. [...]

I got up from my desk and walked to the dais. He already had his book of Stripes on the desk and was filling one out. He was using red ink, and along the line where it said *Reason*, he wrote, *Talking in Prep, trying to cheat and lying*. He signed it and tore it out of the book. Then, taking plenty of time, he filled in the counterfoil. He picked up the terrible piece of green-blue paper and waved it in my direction but he didn't look up. I took it out of his hand and walked back to my desk. The eyes of the whole school followed my progress.

For the remainder of Prep I sat at my desk and did nothing. Having no nib, I was unable to write another word about 'The Life Story of a Penny', but I was made to finish it the next afternoon instead of playing games.

The following morning, as soon as prayers were over, the Headmaster called for [...] Stripes. I was the only boy to go up. The assistant masters were sitting on very upright chairs on either side of the Headmaster, and I caught a glimpse of Captain Hardcastle, arms folded across his chest, head twitching, the milky-blue eyes watching me intently, the look of triumph still glimmering on his face. I handed in my Stripe. The Headmaster took it and read the writing. 'Come and see me in my study,' he said, 'as soon as this is over.'

Five minutes later, walking on my toes and trembling terribly, I passed through the green baize door and entered the sacred precincts where the Headmaster lived. I knocked on his study door.

'Enter!' [...]

The Headmaster was sitting behind the desk holding my Stripe in his fingers. 'What have you got to say for yourself?' he asked me, and the white shark's teeth flashed dangerously between his lips.

'I didn't lie, sir,' I said. 'I promise I didn't. And I wasn't trying to cheat.'

'Captain Hardcastle says you were doing both,' the Headmaster said. 'Are you calling Captain Hardcastle a liar?'

'No, sir. Oh no, sir.'

'I wouldn't if I were you.'

'I had broken my nib, sir, and I was asking Dobson if he could lend me another.'

'That is not what Captain Hardcastle says. He says you were asking for help with your essay.'

'Oh no, sir, I wasn't. I was a long way away from Captain Hardcastle and I was only whispering. I don't think he could have heard what I said, sir.'

'So you *are* calling him a liar.'

'Oh no, sir! No, sir! I would never do that!'

It was impossible for me to win against the Headmaster. What I would like to have said was, 'Yes, sir, if you really want to know, sir, I *am* calling Captain Hardcastle a liar because that's what he is!', but it was out of the question. I did, however, have one trump card left to play, or I thought I did.

'You could ask Dobson, sir,' I whispered.

'*Ask Dobson?*' he cried. 'Why should I ask Dobson?'

'He would tell you what I said, sir.'

'Captain Hardcastle is an officer and a gentleman,' the Headmaster said. 'He has told me what happened. I hardly think I want to go round asking some silly little boy if Captain Hardcastle is speaking the truth.'

I kept silent.

'For talking in Prep,' the Headmaster went on, 'for trying to cheat and for lying, I am going to give you six strokes of the cane.'

He rose from his desk and crossed over to the corner-cupboard on the opposite side of the study. He reached up and took from the top of it three very thin yellow canes, each with the bent-over handle at one end. For a few seconds, he held them in his hands, examining them with some care, then he selected one and replaced the other two on top of the cupboard.

'Bend over.'

I was frightened of that cane. There is no small boy in the world who wouldn't be. It wasn't simply an instrument for beating you. It was a weapon for wounding. It lacerated the skin. It caused severe black and scarlet bruising that took three weeks to disappear, and all the time during those three weeks, you could feel your heart beating along the wounds.

I tried once more, my voice slightly hysterical now. 'I didn't do it, sir! I swear I'm telling the truth!'

'Be quiet and bend over! Over there! And touch your toes!'

Very slowly, I bent over. Then I shut my eyes and braced myself for the first stroke.

Crack! It was like a rifle shot! With a very hard stroke of the cane on one's buttocks, the time-lag before you feel any pain is about four seconds. Thus, the experienced caner will always pause between strokes to allow the agony to reach its peak.

So for a few seconds after the first *crack* I felt virtually nothing. Then suddenly came the frightful searing agonising unbearable burning across the buttocks, and as it reached its highest and most excruciating point, the second *crack* came down. I clutched hold of my ankles as tight as I could and I bit into my lower lip. I was determined not to make a sound, for that would only give the executioner greater satisfaction.

Crack! ... Five seconds pause.

Crack! ... Another pause.

Crack! ... And another pause.

I was counting the strokes, and as the sixth one hit me, I knew I was going to survive in silence.

'That will do,' the voice behind me said.

I straightened up and clutched my backside as hard as I possibly could with both hands. This is always the instinctive and automatic reaction. The pain is so frightful you try to grab hold of it and tear it away, and the tighter you squeeze, the more it helps.

I did not look at the Headmaster as I hopped across the thick red carpet towards the door. The door was closed and nobody was about to open it for me, so for a couple of seconds I had to let go of my bottom with one hand to turn the door-knob. Then I was out and hopping around in the hallway of the private sanctum.

Directly across the hall from the Headmaster's study was the assistant masters' Common Room. They were all in there now waiting to spread out to their respective classrooms, but what I couldn't help noticing, even in my agony, was that *this door was open*.

Why was it open?

Had it been left that way on purpose so that they could all hear more clearly the sound of the cane from across the hall?

Of course it had. And I felt quite sure that it was Captain Hardcastle who had opened it. I pictured him standing in there among his colleagues snorting with satisfaction at every stinging stroke.

> ***Reminder –***
> ## Adjectives
>
> Adjectives describe a person or thing, e.g. 'an **old, lined** hand', 'a **big, blue coat'**. As you read, notice how Roald Dahl uses adjectives to add depth and colour to his descriptions.

Thinking about the text

1 What were the rules of Prep, according to the writer?

2 In your own words tell the story of the 'disaster' that struck him. What happened, and what caused the master to notice him?

3 Use these sentence starters to write your thoughts about this story.

> › What surprised me was …
> › What I found unfair was …
> › What I thought was cruel was …
> › What I was most sorry about was …

4 What adjectives (see Reminder above) would you use to describe the master, Captain Hardcastle? Either choose some of these adjectives below (look up any you don't know in a dictionary) or use a thesaurus to find your own:

unkind	cruel	vicious	mean
nasty	malicious	inhuman	sadistic

5 '... and the white shark's teeth flashed ...' This is how the writer describes the Headmaster's teeth. What does this tell us about him? Do you think this is a good indication of the character of the headmaster? Explain.

6 In your own words, recount what happened in the headmaster's study, capturing a sense of the terror the boy felt.

7 Examine closely Dahl's description of Hardcastle, underlining all the words and phrases he uses to influence our thinking about the character. Choose two such instances that you think are particularly suggestive. Discuss your choices with a partner and pick the one you both agree is the best example.

Oral Language

Examine the text and underline what stood out for you as the most powerful example of (a) Hardcastle's lack of mercy *or* (b) the headmaster's cruelty. Write a short oral presentation (about two minutes) that you will give either to a small group or to the full class on your thoughts.

Writing Task

Imagine that you are Dobson in this piece and that you post a blog (an online diary that invites comments from others) about your time in boarding school. Write a blog about this day.

Or:

Write the letter about life at school that the young Roald Dahl would write home to his mother the next day. When you are deciding on the content, bear in mind that he might not want to worry her by telling her about the previous day's episode.

Groupwork

Imagine that your school is running a competition to find the best original book cover to accompany an article about the importance of reading on the school website.

In a small group of three or four students, decide on one image from this piece that best captures the theme and use this to illustrate your entry for best book cover. Create an interesting title.

Research

'An autobiography is a book a person writes about his own life and it is usually full of all sorts of boring details ...' Roald Dahl makes this statement on the back cover of *Boy: Tales of Childhood*, the book from which this story comes. Do some research into the subject of autobiographies in your local library, in a bookshop or on the internet. See if you can find one that is not 'full of all sorts of boring details' that you think you might like to read. Prepare a two-paragraph report for your class. The first paragraph should include the title, author and some information about the book, and the second paragraph should explain your reasons for choosing this particular autobiography.

Language Alert

Punctuation

Apostrophes

The **apostrophe** is a punctuation mark that seems to confuse many people. It is used to do two basic things:

(a) to show that letters have been left out of a word, as in these examples:

| I'll (I will) | they're (they are) | it's (it is) | who's (who is) |

(b) to show ownership or possession. If the noun ends in **s**, just add the apostrophe after the **s**. If the noun does not end in **s**, add **'s**. The following examples show the rules in operation:

the tail of the dog (singular)	→	the dog's tail
the tails of the dogs (plural)	→	the dogs' tails
the books of the teacher (singular)	→	the teacher's books
the books of the teachers (plural)	→	the teachers' books
the handbag of the woman (singular)	→	the woman's handbag
the handbags of the women (plural)	→	the women's handbags

Groupwork

Rewrite the following phrases using the apostrophe:

> the schoolbag of the girl
> the toys of the boys
> the eyes of the wolf
> the tails of the cats
> the shed of the gardener.

Be careful!

It is easy to confuse **it's** and **its**.

> **it's** means 'it is', as in the sentence 'It's a beautiful day.'
> **its** means 'belonging to', as in the sentence 'The cat licked its paw.'

Wrapping up

In this chapter you met four writers who wrote about episodes and memories from their own lives. Along the way, you gathered some hints about describing characters, writing from different points of view, and using significant moments in your life as a stimulus to write. You also got a chance to try some of these features for yourself.

Here are two tasks to bring this chapter to a close:

1 In your portfolio, p. 26, you will find a table with questions which is intended to help you gather together details about your own life in preparation for writing your own life story later on. You might not use everything you write down now, but having it all there to hand will be very helpful when you come to making some choices about what you will reveal about yourself in your story.

2 Compose a letter to yourself aged about eighteen years old. You will be doing your Leaving Certificate and you will probably have made decisions about what you would like to do with the rest of your life. The letter should contain some of these hopes and dreams for yourself in the future. Pretend you have been given a magic wand and you can make all your wishes come true.

Young Writer's Toolkit

Here are some tools to help you to write diaries, blogs, letters and emails.

Diaries

A diary entry is very like a personal letter in which you write about things that happen to you, your feelings, your hopes and your plans. Because it is personal and informal there are a number of ways it can be written. Here is one example of a format:

Date:	*13 March 20xx*
Address to:	*Dear Diary,*
Introduction:	(Some thoughts on the kind of day you have had or how you are feeling)
	Today was a wonderful day …
	or
	I'm feeling very sad right now …
Main part:	(You can write about what happened, how you feel or felt about it …)
Conclusion:	(Some final thoughts or a remark about the day, or about your thoughts)
	I feel better now that …
	or
	I have to switch off the light now because …
Closing signature:	(if you wish)

Some entries will be long, others short. You are in control and you can decide how you want your diary to look and how you would like to record your thoughts. Here is one example from a young Bosnian girl named Zlata Filipović, who started to keep a diary of her life in Sarajevo during the siege of that city.

Monday, 30 March 1992

Hey Diary! You know what I think? Since Anne Frank called her diary Kitty, maybe I could give you a name too. What about: ASFALTINA, SEFIKA, SEVALA, PIDZAMETA, HIKMETA, MIMMY or something else??? I'm thinking, thinking, I've decided! I'm going to call you MIMMY. All right, then. Let's start.

Dear Mimmy,

It's almost mid-term. We're all studying for our tests. Tomorrow we're supposed to go to a classical music concert at the Skenderija Hall. Our teacher says we shouldn't go because there will be 10,000 people, pardon me, children, there, and somebody might take us as hostages or plant a bomb in the concert hall. Mummy says I shouldn't go. So I won't.

Love,

Zlata

Thursday, 9 April 1992

Dear Mimmy,

I'm not going to school. All the schools in Sarajevo are closed. There's danger hiding in the hills above Sarajevo. But I think things are slowly calming down. The heavy shelling and explosions have stopped. There's occasional gunfire, but it quickly falls silent. Mummy and Daddy aren't going to work. They're buying food in huge quantities. Just in case, I guess. God forbid!

Still it's very tense. Mummy is beside herself, Daddy tries to calm her down.

Zlata

Tuesday, 14 April 1992

Dear Mimmy,

People are leaving Sarajevo. The airport, train and bus stations are packed. I saw sad pictures on TV of people parting. Families, friends separating. Some are leaving, others staying. It's so sad. Why? These people and children aren't guilty of anything.

Zlata

Blogs

A blog is like an online diary. Like a diary, it contains the personal thoughts and comments of either one person or a group of people. The main difference is that we write our diaries for ourselves and like to keep them very private, whereas blogs are written for our friends and others to read online. Some bloggers write about themselves in very personal ways, but choose to stay anonymous. Like diaries, blogs can be written about anything we feel strongly about and people who feel the same can 'follow' the blog and comment on what has been written. Here is a sample of a comment on a blog entry by another blogger:

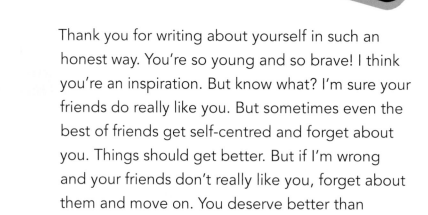

Thank you for writing about yourself in such an honest way. You're so young and so brave! I think you're an inspiration. But know what? I'm sure your friends do really like you. But sometimes even the best of friends get self-centred and forget about you. Things should get better. But if I'm wrong and your friends don't really like you, forget about them and move on. You deserve better than people who ignore you or forget about you.

Letters

You will have to write many different kinds of letter. But, even though they are different, they all share a basic shape and format, which it is important to get right.

The **personal** or **informal letter** is the easiest to write as you can just be yourself and use casual language. The following is a sample informal letter.

Your address goes here

49 Bushy Lane
Forthgate

Date

13 July, 20xx

The greeting

Dear Cheryl,

Introductory paragraph (the reason for the letter)

It feels like a very long time since we last talked. I know it's only been two weeks since we met in the shopping centre but it feels longer. The holidays have been great so far!

The weather has been amazingly good so I spend most days at the beach. You won't believe how tanned I am — you won't be able to say I'm whiter than you any more! As well as some of the old crowd, I've met a great bunch of new friends and we spend lots of time playing beach volleyball so I'm keeping fit as well.

Body of letter (usually has a number of paragraphs)

Last weekend I was offered a job in the local newsagent's for two afternoons a week. I didn't want to take it but I need the money so I said yes. At least I will have more pocket money to spend with my new friends. Some of them are so cool but I'll wait until I see you to tell you all about them!

I hope the holidays have been going well for you too. There's only a month and a half left and then it's back to school. Yuck! I can't wait to meet up and tell you all my news.

Closing statement (usually 'Yours ...')

Yours with love,

Sarah

Postscript (if you want to add anything)

PS Gareth O'Connor says hi.

Formal letters are different in a number of ways.

> The name, title and address of the person you are writing to will also go on the letter. This is placed on the left side just above the greeting (see below).

> You can also include your phone number and email address if you wish.

> The language is more formal.

> The greeting and closing statements are also more formal. For example, you might say 'Yours sincerely' or 'Yours faithfully'.

54 Port View
Blackrock
Co. Dublin

051 894237
jonosaunders@email.com

7 April 20xx

Ms M. T. Powell
Human Resources
Northridge and Foley Books
Forthgate

Dear Ms Powell,   The greeting

Introductory paragraph

I am writing in connection with the advertisement you placed in 'The Dunderry Express' on Thursday last about a part-time job in your bookshop.

Body of letter

Could you please send me an application form so that I can apply for this position? I feel that I would be very well suited for the job you are offering as I love reading and enjoy a wide range of different kinds of books and magazines. In addition, I have some experience as I worked for six weeks in a newsagent's shop during my summer holidays this year.

Final paragraph/ closing statement

I look forward to hearing from you and hope that you will give me an opportunity to tell you more about myself.

Yours sincerely,

Signature

Jonathan Saunders

Emails

Email (electronic mail) is a system for sending and receiving messages from one computer to another and, nowadays, it often replaces a letter. Both letters and emails are similar in that they share the same purpose, content and tone and they can be either informal or formal. The main difference is that the computer automatically formats the email and the sender can simply fill in some details such as the receiver's email address and the subject of the email. See an example of a chatty email below from a dad to his daughter who is away at school.

Dearest Lal,

I hope you are OK and not crying into your new pillows every night! I know it's hard, but try your best to settle and get down to some serious study. Please, for all our sakes, do your very best and stay out of trouble. Of course, I miss you very much and Tillie is not happy – she scratches and meows at your bedroom door every night.

Please, please, please try to get on with your mother. I know you spark off each other but that is because you are alike in so many ways. And remember that she loves you very much.

With a bit of luck, I will be down to see you soon. In the meantime don't pine too much and study hard.

Lots of love,

Dad

Check Your Understanding!

Match each of these terms, all of which were used in this chapter, with the correct meaning.

autobiography	paragraph	blog	adjective
simile	sentence	apostrophe	email
adverbial	conjunction	point of view	punctuation

Term	Meaning
	Describes when, where or how the action takes place in a sentence
	A statement that makes grammatical sense and that contains a subject and a verb
	A system for sending messages from one computer to another
	Shows the reader when to pause, when to stop, when a change of speaker occurs and what to expect next
	An online diary where personal thoughts and comments are recorded for others to read
	Describes a person or a thing
	The stance from which a story is told in a piece of writing
	A phrase using 'like' or 'as' to make a comparison between two things
	A punctuation mark used to show ownership or to show where letters have been omitted from a word
	A group of sentences on a single point or idea
	A book a person writes about his or her own life
	A link word that can be used to make one longer sentence from two simple ones

Chapter Four
MEDIA A & B

Media A: Advertising

In this section you will learn about advertising. Advertising is when we use words and images to change the way people think. The aim of advertising is usually to get people to spend their money on a product. Sometimes it aims to change people's behaviour to make the world a better place.

Communicating
> You will read and watch a number of advertisements.
> You will work with others to share and compare opinions about the meaning of the advertisements.
> You will choose the best words to speak on your own or with others in a short presentation to your classmates.

Exploring and Using Language
> You will use a number of reading strategies to find information, to make links to what you already know and to interpret advertisements.
> You will discuss the ads using appropriate language.

> You will also understand how an ad is enhanced by examining the choice of words and images and their effect on the audience.

Understanding Language
> You will use language to analyse and explain, to convince and persuade and to tell a good story.
> You will write for a variety of audiences and in a wide range of forms.
> You will enjoy writing for your own pleasure, discovering your own unique writing voice.

Wrapping Up
> You will wrap up the section by creating a campaign to persuade your school principal to allow you to organise a fundraising event.

www.edco.ie/beinspired

Advertisements

Paint it Pink

Thinking about the ad

1 What connection do you see between the words written in this advertisement and the picture?

2 Why is colour so important in this advertising campaign?

3 Two very different organisations appear in this ad. Name them. Why is each one mentioned?

4 Describe the audience this advertisement is aiming to reach.

Explanation – Audience

Audience is the word we use for the group of people who see or hear a performance.

A **target audience** is the type of people an advertisement is aimed at, e.g. 'a rural audience'.

Research

Advertisements often include a *url* address as a prompt for the audience to find out more about a product or issue. Check out the information at www.paintitpink.ie. Make some notes and present your findings to your class.

Oral Language

Why do you think a supermarket chain like Centra chose to sponsor 'Paint it Pink'? Think about the possible reasons and then discuss your ideas with a partner. Share your views with the entire class as part of a group discussion.

BE INSPIRED!

New Balance

Before you read ...

Conduct a short class survey about sport. You can use the following statements or design a survey with your own questions. Tick the statements you agree with:

- ☐ Sport is for boys and girls
- ☐ Boys are better at football
- ☐ In team games the sexes should be kept apart
- ☐ Sport is for fun
- ☐ Only boys are aggressive
- ☐ Sport is about winners

Oral Language

1 Discuss the results of your survey as a class. Do you all share a common view of sport?

2 What areas do you disagree about?

3 Compile a list of Irish women sporting heroes. Is it a long list?

Thinking about the ad

1 What product is this ad helping to sell?

2 Write a short paragraph describing the woman in the picture.

3 Explain why the colour of her singlet and shorts is significant.

4 Where is the slogan in this ad? Explain how the slogan is linked to the picture.

5 How do you feel about the image of women shown in this ad?

> ### Explanation – Slogan
> A short phrase used in an ad is called a slogan. Slogans sum up the message of an ad in a catchy motto, for example 'I'm lovin' it'.

Research

Now that you have discussed your own opinions of women in sport, check out the This Girl Can campaign. Sport England set up the campaign to encourage girls and women to take part in sport. Find out all about the This Girl Can campaign through links in the *Be Inspired!* weblinks document.

Groupwork

Working in pairs, design your own #ThisGirlCan poster using the This Girl Can app. You can download the app to your phone or tablet by visiting the This Girl Can homepage link provided in the *Be Inspired!* weblinks document.

IKEA

Free home delivery now! **IKEA**

Thinking about the ad

1 What do you notice when you look at this advertisement for the IKEA furniture store?

2 How do you explain the slogan 'Free home delivery now!'?

3 Look carefully at the variety of colours used in the picture. Suggest a reason for the choice of colours on the bedspreads, pillows and curtains.

4 Who is the advert meant to appeal to most?

> Adults
> Children
> Parents of young children
> Both parents and children

Explain your choice.

Explanation – Logo

At the bottom right-hand corner of the ad, we see the word IKEA in bold blue writing against an oval yellow background. This symbol is the **logo**; it represents the brand and appears on all IKEA's ads and packaging.

Writing Task

Imagine you were offered the chance to give your own room a makeover. In your portfolio, p. 31, describe in detail your ideal bedroom. You might like to refer to:

> Decor   > Furniture   > Lighting   > Storage

Kit Kat

Before you read ...

If you were choosing a snack, what product would you buy? Discuss your favourite snack with a partner.

Explanation – Graphic

A graphic is a picture or drawing used as an illustration in an ad.

#blackfriday

H4VE 4 8RE4K

Thinking about the ad

1 Can you find the product in this advert?

2 There is a visual joke in this ad. Explain it.

3 There is a combination of letters and numbers along the bottom of the ad. Where do you usually find this style of writing?

4 Describe the type of audience who might be amused by this advertisement.

Explanation – Humour

Humour makes ads memorable. Funny ads also give the audience a positive feeling because they make them laugh.

Kleenex Cottonelle

Lab tested for learners

KLEENEX® COTTONELLE® Flushable Wipes for Kids give a fresh, superior clean and all the bathroom confidence they need.
kleenexpuppy.com.au

Care in every square

Thinking about the ad

1 The slogan in this ad has several possible meanings. How do you explain it?

2 Words are often repeated in ads. What ideas are repeated in this advert?

3 Kittens and pups are common in ads for toilet paper. Do you agree with this approach? Explain your point of view.

4 What buzzwords are used in the ad? What effect do they have?

Explanation – Buzzwords
Buzzwords are words or phrases that give the reader a happy feeling or emotion, e.g. 'fresh'.

Oral Language

Kleenex, the makers of Cottonelle, claim to 'look after the environment'. Check out the meaning of the word 'sustainable' in your dictionary. Now have a class discussion about how a company like this can contribute to a better world.

Research

Find out about sustainable forestry. You might like to begin by looking up suggested websites from the *Be Inspired!* weblinks document.

World Wide Fund for Nature and Snapchat

Before you read ...

1 Have you ever taken a selfie with your phone camera? Talk to a partner about the first time you took a selfie.

2 Where were you at the time?

3 Who else was there? Was it a special occasion?

4 Did you share the photo?

Thinking about the ad

1 What do the three species of animal in the posters have in common?

2 What happens to a Snapchat picture in 60 seconds?

BE INSPIRED!

Oral Language

1. Conduct a quick survey to find out how many people in your class use Snapchat or Instagram.

2. Watch the video of '#LastSelfie' on the *Be Inspired!* website.

3. Do you agree that Snapchat is a 'mirror of real life'? Explain your answer.

4. Who are the target audience for this advert?

5. Is this advertising campaign a good way to help protect endangered species?

Research

Find out more about the World Wide Fund for Nature at the link provided in the *Be Inspired!* weblinks document.

Groupwork

In small groups, choose one of the following species and give a presentation to your class about the species and why it is in danger. In your presentation you might like to suggest what actions teens can take to help.

> Giant panda
> Elephant
> Rhinoceros
> Gorilla

> Sea turtle
> Polar bear
> Whale
> Tiger

World Health Organisation

CLIMATE CHANGE HURTS

Besides environmental and economic damage, the ultimate impact of climate change represents a toll on our most precious resource - human lives and health.

Protecting health from climate change

World Health Organization

www.who.int/phe   www.who.int/globalchange

BE INSPIRED!

Climate Reality Project

The Climate Reality Project encourages young people to question their politicians about climate change. Look at the two images below. Write a caption for each image in the form of a question to a politician. For example:

Why have you let this happen?

Why not act now to save the world for us?

Thinking about the images

1 What kind of world is shown in the first photo?
2 How old do you think the two girls in the second photo are?
3 Do you think politicians should ask children their views on climate change?
4 At what age should people be allowed to vote? Explain your answer.

Research

Watch the Climate Reality Project video through the link provided in the *Be Inspired!* weblinks document.

Writing Task

Use the format from the Climate Reality Project to write your own set of questions for the world's leaders at the United Nations. Complete your questions in the space below.

Why _____

_____?

Why not _____

_____?

ISPCC

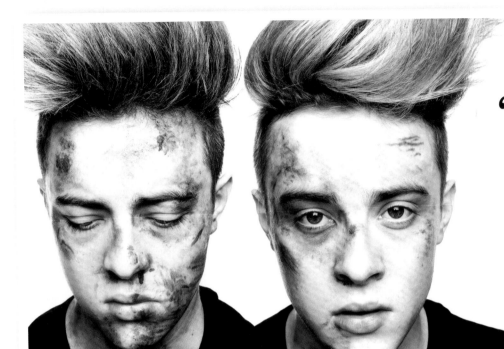

> **"Imagine if every child knew that nothing can ever happen that can't be fixed by someone who cares."**

JOIN THE FIGHT FOR CHILDREN'S RIGHTS
ISPCC.I

Thinking about the ad

1 Which of the following best describes your first reaction to this poster?
   Choose one or two sentences and complete them in your copybook.

   > I feel shocked because …
   > I feel afraid because …
   > I feel amused because …

   > I feel curious because …
   > I feel concerned because …

2 Who appears in this advertisement? Why, do you think, were these two celebrities chosen to appear in the advertisement?

3 What do the initials ISPCC stand for?

4 Describe the kinds of people who might notice this advertisement.

Explanation – Endorsement
An endorsement is when a famous person shows his/her support for a product or media campaign, e.g. Rory McIlroy endorses Nike equipment.

Writing Task
Write a paragraph about a person or a group of people you think should appear in a similar advert for the ISPCC. In your paragraph, explain why you think the individual or group would be a good choice of celebrity to endorse the campaign.

BE INSPIRED!

Thomson

Thinking about the ad

1 How often does a smile appear in this ad?

2 What sense can you make of the main slogan, 'Escape from Reality this Summer'?

3 Why do you think the slogan 'Discover your smile' is printed in handwriting style instead of regular print?

Explanation – **Repetition**

Repetition is when the same words or images are used many times in an ad.

Oral Language

1 The video uses the words from a famous song. Can you name it?

2 Do you agree that this is a funny ad? Explain your answer.

 Watch the video 'A Film about a Smile' on the *Be Inspired!* website.

Writing Task

Write a short essay about the best holiday you ever had. You might like to make a plan by thinking about some of the following:

> Where did you go on the holiday?
> Who else went on holiday with you?
> What new sights did you see?

> What was your favourite moment of the holiday?
> Did you make any new friends?
> How did you feel when you returned home?

Public Service Messages

An advertisement usually tries to encourage us to buy particular goods or make use of a company's services. The skills of persuasion can also be used to get us to change our behaviour. We call this type of advertisement a public service message.

Health and Safety Authority

Thinking about the ad

1 Describe the setting of this advertisement.
2 What is unusual about the tractor? Why was it chosen to appear here?
3 Explain the link between the slogan 'Children Don't See the Danger' and the graphic.

Oral Language

Talk to a partner about how you feel when you think about this advert. Try to sum up the moral or lesson of this prize-winning public service message.

BE INSPIRED!

Research

Check out the Health and Safety Authority website at www.hsa.ie. There are many important public service messages about health and the workplace on the website. Find out as much as you can about the hazards or dangers involved in one type of work.

Writing Task

Write out a list of safety instructions for a modern farm or any other workplace you know well.

Wrapping up

Let's recap on what you have learned in this section on advertising. You have:

> looked closely at advertisements
> explained in your own words the messages they express
> learned about some of the ways advertisements try to persuade us.

Now, to bring all your knowledge and skills together, work in a small group on the following creative task.

Imagine you are part of a group of students who wish to hold a charity fundraising event in your school. You have three minutes to persuade your school principal that it is a good idea.

The first thing you must decide is what cause or issue you hope to raise money for. Think of some of the issues raised in this unit. Your project might be local or it might be in aid of a national or international problem.

When you have chosen a project to promote, think about how you will convince the principal to let you run:

> a penalty shoot-out competition

   or

> a bring and buy sale.

Your presentation might include some of the following:

> catchy phrases
> clever use of colour
> exaggeration
> rhyming words

When you are ready, present your pitch. Your teacher or another student can play the part of the school principal and adjudicate on the pitches. At the end, the teacher will point out the clever techniques used by the various teams.

Young Writer's Toolkit

Explaining

Here you will find tools that will help you to explain your answers – both written and oral.

1 Brainstorming
2 Contributing to a class discussion
3 Debating

1 Brainstorming

This is a very good way of gathering lots of ideas about an issue or task that you've been asked to do – a story you've been asked to write, a class debate and so on. Brainstorming is best done with a large group, such as the whole class, because the more ideas and thoughts that are generated the better.

Someone needs to take charge of the session. This person, who could be the teacher or a student, encourages everyone to participate and also writes down all the ideas on a large sheet of paper or a whiteboard. No idea should be rejected, because brainstorming is all about opening up as many ideas as possible. They can be evaluated for their usefulness at the end of the session and formed into a proper plan.

The model below should help you to organise your ideas/thoughts. Each 'raindrop' can hold one idea and you can add as many raindrops as you like.

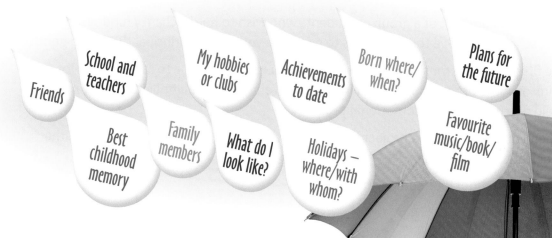

2 Contributing to a class discussion

The purpose of a discussion is to allow different opinions to be heard. This is a great way of helping you to think about a topic or an issue from different points of view before you make up your own mind.

One simple way to organise ideas is to put all the positives that you can think of about the topic into the **YES** triangle, and all the negative things into the **NO** triangle. The ideas that could be either positive or negative go in the **MAYBE** triangle.

BE INSPIRED!

3 Debating

Debating is really arguing, but it's a very formal approach to argument because there is a structure to it and there are rules to follow.

1 The subject of a debate is called a topic or a motion.

2 In class, there are usually two teams who take opposite sides, i.e. one team argues in favour of the topic or motion under debate and the other team argues against the motion.

3 Depending on which team you are on, you may have to argue for something you do not believe in or against something you do believe in.

4 As well as making points for your side of the debate, you will also have to criticise what the opposing team say – this is called **rebuttal**.

5 The rules include formal ways of addressing participants in the debate. You open your speech by addressing your audience and making it clear which side you are on.

For example, 'Chairperson, judges, fellow debaters and members of the audience, I firmly believe that … and I will now persuade you to …'

> The chairperson is the person in charge of keeping order and calling on debaters to speak.
> Judges/adjudicators decide which team wins the debate.
> Fellow debaters are the members of the two debating teams.
> Members of the audience are the rest of your class or school.

It is important to be really well prepared. Plan and prepare your points in favour or against the motion. Normally you will be working in a team, so you are likely to prepare the content/material together.

You may like to use the model below. Put the topic in the triangle and then all the ideas for the motion above the line and all the ideas against the motion below the line. It can be very helpful to think about both sides of the topic in advance as this will help you to plan your rebuttal.

Media B: News and Social Media

In this section you will learn about news and the way social media influences how we get news and how we make news. You will also get a chance to think about how teenagers like you use social media.

Communicating

> You will work with others in pairs and small groups to listen actively, and express your thoughts and feelings about all aspects of the news. You will read for a variety of purposes – knowledge, research and comparison of the variety of news outlets.

> You will get a chance to carry out many of the duties of editors and journalists as you learn about what makes the news.

Exploring and Using Language

> You will read to understand and appreciate what makes the news, and the different methods used to convey news to the public.

> You will read and learn from examples of newspaper articles to improve your own writing.

> You will collaborate with others to reach agreement and understanding of various aspects of the news media.

> You will complete a quiz on the *Be Inspired!* website that focuses on media terms.

Understanding Language

> You will understand how word choice, syntax and text structure may vary depending on the purpose of the newspaper.

> You will use language resources – dictionary, thesaurus and online resources – to help your own language development.

> You will learn to make appropriate choices as you work alone and with others to create a variety of written texts, including: compiling a news report, writing a letter to the editor, devising captions, inventing horoscopes. You will compose texts for newspapers that are clear and accurate.

Wrapping Up

To wrap up:

1 You will work alone to assess your own learning by completing:

   (a) a wordsearch

   (b) a checklist in your portfolio

2 You will work in groups to put some of your learning into practice by creating a front page for a novel or film the class is studying.

www.edco.ie/beinspired

Before you read ...

Before beginning this section, you should try to collect as many different kinds of newspaper as possible.

> Concentrate on the newspapers that are sold in Ireland.
> Collect both daily and weekly papers, including Sunday issues.
> Possible sources: home, neighbours, friends, local library and local newsagents.

News! News! News!

Everyone loves news! Whether it's news about our family, sports results or the latest fashion trends, we all love news.

Research

Following the News

An international survey asked people why they follow the news. You might like to ask yourself the questions or conduct a class survey. Tick three of the boxes and then put them in order of importance from 1 (most important) to 3 (least important).

I follow the news because:

> I want to know what's going on ☐
> I want to understand things that might affect me ☐
> I just do ☐
> I have a duty as a citizen to stay informed ☐
> I can discuss with friends the stories of the day ☐
> It's a good way to pass the time ☐

Newspapers and the News

Many people still get their news from newspapers; some people read the printed versions and others read the versions published online. These newspapers contain local and international news stories, commentary, analysis, factual information and advertising.

Newspapers in Ireland

Here in Ireland, as well as national papers, which are distributed all over the country, there are many local newspapers that are specific to a locality. In some areas free newspapers are also available. See some examples below:

National newspapers	Local newspapers	Free newspapers
Irish Times	Kilkenny People	Kenmare News
Irish Independent	Donegal News	Northside People (Dublin)
Irish Examiner	Western People	Dublin City Gazette
Sunday Independent	Longford Leader	Dublin Informer
Sunday World	Meath Chronicle	Waterford Today

Research

1 How many newspapers are you familiar with? What newspapers are available in your own local area?

2 In groups of four, carry out some research by visiting local newsagents. Find the answers to the following questions:

> What newspapers do they stock?
> What are their bestsellers?

Present the information from your group as clearly as you can on a large A3 sheet of paper that can be displayed on the classroom wall for all the class to see.

Front Pages: Broadsheet and Compact

Broadsheet (serious or 'quality')	Compact (popular or tabloid)
Irish Examiner	*Irish Independent*
Sunday Business Post	*Irish Daily Mail*
Irish Times	*Irish Sun*

Explanations –
Front pages
This is where we find out what kind of paper we are about to buy and what purpose that paper serves.
Format
Newspapers are usually in one of two formats: broadsheet or compact (see the table for some examples).

Note: Compact newspapers used to be known as tabloids or 'red tops', a term which implied lesser quality. However, increasingly, more serious newspapers are being printed in the compact format. A good example of this is the *Irish Independent*.

Thinking about newspaper formats

Work with a partner for this exercise.

1 Look at the front pages and see if you can list the principal differences between broadsheets and compact newspapers. Take some or all of the following into account in your analysis:

size of print   colour   title (masthead)   headlines

number of articles   list of contents   advertisements

names of journalists (bylines)

2 Draw a Venn diagram like the one here on a large sheet of paper, and put all the differences you found under the correct heading in the outside spaces. Then highlight all the similarities that you found and write these in the centre section of the diagram.

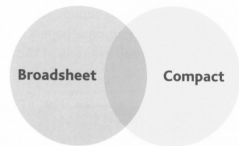

3 Join up with another pair to swap ideas and add to your own diagrams.

Styles of Writing

As well as the differences in the size and the content that you found between serious and popular newspapers, there are also contrasts in the styles of writing they use and the way they report the news.

Broadsheet/serious	Compact/tabloid
Balance between images and text	*Pictures often more prominent than text*
Objective reporting that lacks bias/favouritism	*Selective reporting, often for shock value*
Tone of headlines/articles tends to be neutral	*Attention-grabbing headlines*
Focus on major national and international events	*Focus on famous people, private lives and scandal*
Complex or multi-syllable language (words of more than five or six letters)	*Simpler, more straightforward language*
Longer sentences	*Shorter sentences*

Thinking about style

Examine the two lists of words below and say which list belongs to a serious paper and which to a popular paper. Give reasons for your answers.

cops	bash	losers	pics	axe
screwed	louts	gutter	pals	guy

historic	statistics	prominent	prosecute	indefensible
request	evidence	commence	vigilant	generosity

 Take a look at the Against the Clock quiz on the *Be Inspired!* website to check your knowledge of common media terms.

Headlines

Explanation – Headlines

Headlines are placed at the top of a news article and should be a clear and interesting indication of what's in the article. They are used to attract attention and also to act as a guide for the reader. Therefore, a good headline should:

› tell the reader what to expect in the article
› provoke interest and curiosity
› be short and economical – only use essential words
› be humorous and use word play or alliteration (depending on the subject).

The following are some popular devices used by journalists to capture attention in headlines.

Puns	Clichés	Alliteration	Hyperbole
A play on words, e.g. 'We're Barack for the craic' when the Obamas visited Ireland	*A one-liner or phrase which has lost its effect through over-use, e.g. 'as clear as mud'*	*When a number of words with the same first letter appear close together, e.g. 'whisper words of wisdom'*	*Exaggeration, to create comic effect or arouse strong feelings in the reader, e.g. 'skinny as a toothpick'*

Look at these headlines and write two sentences about each, saying (a) what kind of story you think will follow the headline and (b) which type of newspaper it is taken from.

Majority of public are law-abiding citizens

Reign in Spain has lately been a pain

Bullied at Ballot Box

Corrie Kev robbed on street

Theatre legend to join city orchestra

Jessie's on-set collapse drama

Parents warned on cyber bullying

Gardaí get new powers to check phones of motorists

It's a Kate crime!

5,000 leave each month in search of employment

Writing Task

Choose one of the following outlines that will appear as a story in the papers tomorrow and design two headlines, one to appear in a serious paper and one in a popular paper. Explain how you made your choices.

An Irish football striker named Stuart Dunne, who plays for a club in the Premier League, was caught speeding on the M1 motorway. When the case comes up in court the judge notes that this is the third time he has been charged for the same offence, so he decides that no leniency will be shown. He gives him a very heavy fine and also bans him from driving for one year, effective immediately.

or

A leading member of a girl band was charged with assaulting a fan who had approached her in a night club to ask for her autograph. When the case comes to court the judge decides that, since the fan had been polite and well-mannered, there were no mitigating circumstances. Therefore, she finds the celebrity guilty and she sentences her to 40 hours' community service.

BE INSPIRED!

Making News Reports: Compiling a Report for Printed or Online News

Writing a news report is different from writing a normal story. When you are writing a story you would usually save the really big news (or climax) until towards the end of the story, but in a news report the most important item goes near the beginning. This is done so that the casual reader can get the main points immediately without needing to read the full story.

The Inverted Pyramid

VITAL INFORMATION

Who? **What?** **When?** **Where?** **Why?** **How?**

This is where all the KEY information goes – what the reader MUST know to understand what the story is all about

EXPLANATION

Information that will answer any questions that readers may still have after reading the lead sentence/paragraph

LEAST IMPORTANT

Information it would be nice to include if space allows

Explanation – **Inverted pyramid**

The inverted pyramid is the format journalists use to help plan their stories. It means that all the really important information is at the beginning of the article and the least important information is at the end. It has two important advantages:

1 People can explore a story only as far as their interest or curiosity takes them.

2 It allows the editor to cut the story in a number of places, depending on what space he/she has on a page.

Explanations –

Byline

The name of the writer of an article usually appears after the headline and before the main body of the article. This is called the *byline*.

Lead

The main story or top story that appears on the front page of a newspaper is referred to as the *lead* story.

Writing Task

Complete this task in your portfolio, p. 32.

Imagine that a team in your school has just won a prestigious trophy in a major competition for the first time in ten years of trying. Choose a competition of your choice – debating, sports, drama or any other. In your portfolio you will find some ideas to help you create a news report for your school website or magazine.

Things to Remember

> As you move through the story from top to bottom, the information you present must get less and less crucial to the story.
> Write an eye-catching headline.
> Include a byline.
> Create a strong opening statement that contains as much relevant information as possible.
> Add other interesting but less important information, such as quotes from those involved.
> Finally, add the least important information, such as the background to the story.

Pictures and the News

Pictures are used to illustrate important news articles and stories. Sometimes the picture tells the entire story, but usually it works with the written text to convey information to the reader.

Explanation – Capturing attention

Pictures are great for grabbing attention, as they immediately draw your eye to them. Since newspapers are keen to sell as many copies as possible, the pictures on the front page are chosen to create an immediate and interesting effect.

Thinking about the photo

1 Use the following sentence starters to help you to analyse the photo opposite. Jot down the ideas you come up with.

> What I see is ...
> This makes me think ...
> So now I wonder ...

2 Examine the picture closely, paying particular attention to the clothes the people are wearing. Say what information this provides about the circumstances.

3 If you were the editor of a newspaper, where would you place the photo in (a) a serious newspaper and (b) a popular newspaper? Explain your reasons in each case.

Groupwork

Working with a partner, compose two captions for the photo:

1 To accompany the picture in a serious broadsheet newspaper. Remember that these papers try to present facts and use a neutral tone.

2 To accompany the same picture in a popular/tabloid newspaper. Remember that some of these papers appeal to readers' emotions and tend to play with language to accomplish their effect.

Writing Task

1 Write a thought bubble for any one of the three people near the front of the photo who appear to be still awake.

2 Imagine that this photograph appeared in the *Irish Times* alongside a two-paragraph story. Write the story and give it a title.

Groupwork

Currently there are approximately 16 million refugees worldwide (source: TV3 News, 19 August 2015). The images here all depict a story about this crisis.

1 Working in groups of three or four, make editorial decisions about how photographs should be used.

2 As a team, decide which of the following photos should accompany an article about the current crisis in (a) a serious broadsheet newspaper and (b) a popular tabloid newspaper. Explain your choice in each case.

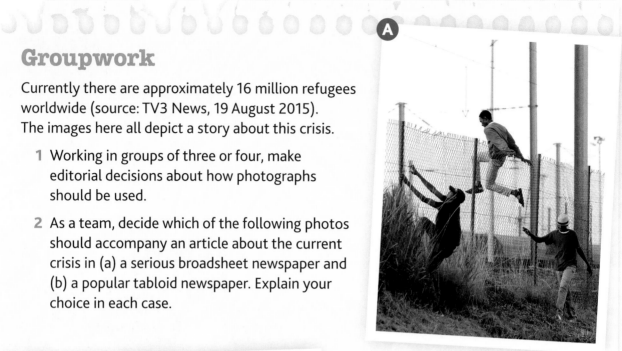

Letter to the Editor

Writing Task

Complete this task in your portfolio, p. 34.

Find your local newspaper and examine it to see if there is something happening locally that people in the community are worried or upset about. Write a letter to the editor of the paper expressing your feelings about the issue. (See YWT, p. 82, and your portfolio, p. 67, for help with writing formal letters.)

Horoscopes

Get into groups of four. Your task is to write the horoscopes for a 'popular' weekend newspaper.

1 Start by collecting some horoscopes from newspapers and magazines you may have at home so that you can get some ideas about content and layout.

2 Ensure that the horoscopes are general so that they can apply to anyone who reads them. Horoscopes in newspapers and magazines tend to make fairly vague statements so that all readers can see something in them that will apply to themselves. You could say something like, 'Take the advice you are offered about a health matter.' This could mean 'Listen to your dentist who tells you to stop eating sweets or your teeth will decay' or 'Pay heed to your mother who tells you to go out and get fresh air instead of watching TV', and so on.

3 You need to be careful not to give any bad news to readers, so you should write only positive and good things that readers will want to hear, for example 'This is a very good week for you.' Make a list of other positive things that you can say so that you do not have to use the same ones over and over again.

4 Many horoscopes are divided into different areas of life. For example, you could use sub-headings like **work**, **relationships**, **the week ahead** or any others you like (see the Leo example).

5 Before you begin, it would be useful to make some lists of the following:
 › vague, general statements that can apply to anyone
 › positive and non-threatening statements.

LEO

(23 July–22 August)

INFLUENCES

Partnership ideas of both a personal and professional nature dominate this week. There will be many things to talk about. At times people may not seem very co-operative, but stay cool and everything will work out.

WORK

All Leos, especially those born in August, should be asking questions about the quality of group members' commitment to hard work this week. Be prepared to ask questions to ensure that everyone else is contributing to the group's success.

LOVE

This is a good time to think about achieving a deeper level of understanding in a relationship. There may be some small misunderstandings, but these will be overcome, and it will all be worth it in the end.

Online Sites and the News

Smartphones are changing the way people, especially young adults, get the news. Although TV and radio news is still very popular, newspaper sales have declined. In response to this, most newspaper publishers produce an online version.

In Ireland, thejournal.ie is a new and popular online news outlet, designed to let users read and share the news, while BuzzFeed and the Huffington Post are two American-based digital news and entertainment sites that attract millions of users each day.

Online sites can use videos to report and illustrate the news, and they also allow readers to:

> post comments on what they read
> share stories on other platforms, such as Facebook, Twitter or WhatsApp.

They also mix serious news with celebrity and entertainment news. Readers like to share the lists, the celebrity gossip and the pictures, as well as the breaking stories.

In Ireland in 2014, the top social networks used to access news were:

> Facebook   46%
> YouTube   18%
> Twitter   14%
> Google+   5%
> WhatsApp   5%

Good News or Bad News?

Apart from online news sites, users of the internet post and share news items and gossip with each other. However, with so much news being shared across social media it can be hard to decide whether those who provide the news are reliable. Interestingly, many online users turn to TV and trusted television stations when they want news reports that they can trust as accurate and reliable, even though they use social media for keeping in touch with breaking news.

BE INSPIRED!

Here are some questions for you to speculate about with a partner:

> Are online news sites accurate in what they report?
> Are the reports unbiased and fair to people?
> Do they include a variety of opinions?
> And how can we know?

Smartphones and the News

Can Smartphones Bring about Real Change?

People use smartphones and social media to get the news, but both smartphones and social media can make the news.

More and more, smartphones and social media are used to launch, promote, sustain and co-ordinate social and political actions and campaigns. For example:

> During 2014 in Ireland, social media played a central role in the protest campaign against the introduction of water charges.

> In 2015 social media helped secure a Yes vote in the marriage equality referendum.

User-generated Content from Smartphones

In all kinds of disaster and conflict situations, people use their smartphones to record what is happening and share it with the world. Many news broadcasters, like RTÉ and the BBC, regularly use photos and videos recorded on smartphones in their news coverage. These images are not made by journalists or reporters but by ordinary people who are in the situation and who share their images online.

For example, 18-year-old Louis Cryer was on holiday with his family in Sri Lanka when they were caught up in a tsunami. His photos and videos were used by the BBC.

In many conflict situations, such as the war in Syria, user-generated or eye-witness content helps tell stories that otherwise could not be told. Journalists often use tweets or text messages sent by eye witnesses to get a clearer picture of what is happening in breaking-news situations.

Photos, videos, tweets, text messages and emails tell us what is happening. Good journalists and feature writers ask:

> 'Why did this happen?'
> 'How did it happen?'
> 'Can we prevent this happening again?'

Is Social Media Content Reliable?

There is a danger that some online content can be false. **Storyful** is a news agency that brings social media content to news broadcasters such as RTÉ and the BBC and has been called the site that keeps social media 'honest'! One of the main tasks of the agency is to monitor social media for breaking news and check the reliability of the information. As one of the editors explains: 'It is like being Superman, you can hear everyone's voices, but you need to know which ones you should listen to.'

For example, in 2014 the American Olympic athlete Kate Hansen posted a video of a wolf roaming the hallway outside her dormitory in the Olympic village of Sochi in Russia. The story was carried by many news outlets before it was revealed as a hoax.

Young People and Social Media

Of course, it's not all about news. Smartphones and social media are used for entertainment (watching videos, playing games, sharing funny photos, live tweeting ...) and for keeping in touch with friends and family.

A Central Statistics Office (CSO) survey of Irish teenagers found that the most popular reason for using social media was for keeping in contact with friends. Enjoying the content and finding out the latest gossip were also given as reasons.

Another survey found that:

> Almost 98 per cent of Irish youth audiences use Facebook on their smartphone.

> 'Texting' (66 per cent) is the top answer to the question 'If you could only do two things on your mobile, what would they be?' followed closely by 'Talking' at 50 per cent.

> Almost all young Irish people check their phone 'when they wake up' (90 per cent); 'on public transport' (87 per cent) and 'while watching TV' (84 per cent).

> 57 per cent are more likely to check their mobile when they are 'on the loo' than when they are 'at the cinema'. (*Source:* Think House)

This diagram shows the most popular social media platforms among American teenagers in 2015:

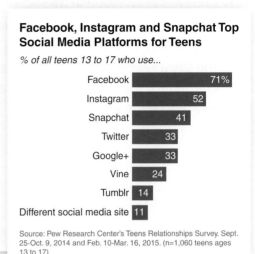

Facebook, Instagram and Snapchat Top Social Media Platforms for Teens

% of all teens 13 to 17 who use...

Facebook	71%
Instagram	52
Snapchat	41
Twitter	33
Google+	33
Vine	24
Tumblr	14
Different social media site	11

Source: Pew Research Center's Teens Relationships Survey. Sept. 25-Oct. 9, 2014 and Feb. 10-Mar. 16, 2015. (n=1,060 teens ages 13 to 17)

Research

Take six websites or apps that are popular with the students in the class. Conduct a survey to find out which websites are the favourites.

You might like to use the same social media platforms cited in the American research or substitute one or two with YouTube, WhatsApp or Viber.

Or:

Conduct a survey to find the most entertaining short videos as voted on by the class.

Twitter

Did You Know?

According to figures published by Twitter, in July 2015 the four tweeters with the most followers were:

> Katy Perry   72 million followers
> Justin Bieber   65 million followers
> Barack Obama   62 million followers
> Taylor Swift   60 million followers

The Irish tweeters with the most followers were:

> Niall Horan   23 million   > Rory McIlroy   2.6 million
> Great Minds Quotes   2.8 million   > The Script   2.2 million

Research

Find out who currently has the most followers on Twitter. You could start your research by going to www.statista.com. Summarise your findings in a paragraph.

Photos and the Internet

In research, Facebook consistently features as the most popular social platform. According to statistics from Facebook (2015) there are 1.5 billion Facebook users. At almost any moment of the day a Facebook user posts a photograph online. In fact, internet users upload and share nearly two billion photos per day!

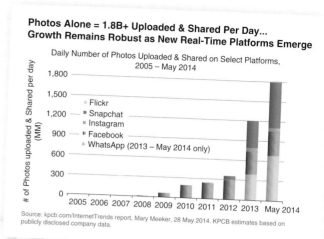

**Photos Alone = 1.8B+ Uploaded & Shared Per Day...
Growth Remains Robust as New Real-Time Platforms Emerge**

Daily Number of Photos Uploaded & Shared on Select Platforms, 2005 – May 2014

- Flickr
- Snapchat
- Instagram
- Facebook
- WhatsApp (2013 – May 2014 only)

Source: kpcb.com/InternetTrends report, Mary Meeker, 28 May 2014. KPCB estimates based on publicly disclosed company data.

Groupwork

Working in pairs, discuss the ways in which you create, view and share photographs.

Selfies

In 2013 the *Oxford English Dictionary* declared 'selfie' to be the new word of the year.

A survey in 2014 estimated that close to a billion selfies are taken each day on android phones alone! Some reasons for so much self-portraiture could be:

> The availability of front-facing phones

> The number of online platforms for sharing photos – Facebook, Instagram, SnapChat, Tumblr, and many more.

Some critics dismiss selfies as an unhealthy preoccupation with ourselves. The word is closely linked to 'selfish'. But there are many different kinds of selfie:

> political selfies
> joke selfies
> sports and activity-related selfies
> fan-related selfies
> illness-related selfies

> soldier selfies
> crime-related selfies
> selfies at funerals
> selfies at famous places or museums

Some selfies have made world headlines.

> When the then Danish Prime Minister Helle Thorning-Schmidt took a selfie with US President Barack Obama and UK Prime Minister David Cameron at Nelson Mandela's memorial service in December 2013, the behaviour of the three politicians was described as 'disrespectful', 'uncouth', 'bad-mannered' and 'childish'.

> The selfie taken by Ellen DeGeneres at the 2014 Oscars ceremony became the most shared tweet of all time. Within an hour of DeGeneres posting it on her Twitter account, the photo had been retweeted over a million times!

Research

With at least one other student, see if you can identify the actors in the photograph.

> In August 2013 a group of students visiting the Vatican took a selfie with Pope Francis, which went viral.

Serious Selfies

In many parts of the world, selfies are used for serious reasons.

> Selfies empower young people. In some slums in Brazil, selfies are used by teenagers to highlight violence in their communities, to document their lives and to let their families know they are safe.

> Posting selfies can also help teenagers and young adults to express solidarity with like-minded others through viral campaigns. An example is #BlackLivesMatter, a campaign set up in response to the unlawful killing of black youths by police in America. The campaign has become an important and powerful way of allowing young people to stand up for their rights and feel part of a community.

> In Beirut in Lebanon, a car bomb, whose driver was targeting a politician, killed an innocent sixteen-year-old boy, Mohammad al-Chaar. A few moments before the blast, he and his friends had posted a group selfie online. The bomb was planted in a car in the background.

Many of Mohammad's peers were angered by his senseless death. They were also angered by press reports that referred to him as a martyr – to his friends he was a victim of violence. Hundreds protested by posting selfies holding messages about what they wanted for their country on Twitter and Facebook, using the hashtag #NotaMartyr.

> When over 200 schoolgirls were kidnapped by the militant group Boko Haram in northern Nigeria in May 2014, Michelle Obama expressed her outrage and tweeted a picture of herself holding a placard with the #BringBackOurGirls campaign hashtag.

> However, not everyone was impressed by her gesture. One critic, Christine Sisto, wrote:

This trend (online activism) is the perfect blend of the social-media generation's laziness and the need to belong to something … If Michelle Obama had held up that sign and then scheduled a trip to Nigeria, or spoken to the families of the kidnapped students, or met with President Jonathan, urging him to take action, or donated some of her personal money to a Nigerian non-profit, her gesture might have been credible.

Others saw it as an important mark of solidarity with poor families in an African country.

Oral Language

What do you think of Michelle Obama's action? Do you agree with Christine Sisto? Discuss with a partner before joining with another pair (or the entire class) to:

> share your views on the Obama tweet
> discuss the degree to which posting a selfie under a hashtag campaign is a real act for change or a desire to be trendy.

Research

Carry out some research to find five selfies that have made the news.

Writing Task

In your portfolio, p. 35, write a short report explaining the background of the selfies you found in the Research task.

Me: My Social Media Self

> How much time do you spend online?

> What kind of online presence do you have?

> Is your online self any different from your offline self? If yes, what are the differences?

> What social media do you use to communicate with others? Do you tweet or blog? Do you have a Facebook page? Do you send text messages? Do you use email? Do you post photos? Are you part of a conversation or chat group?

> Do you subscribe to any websites or follow people online? If yes, who?

> Do you watch TV programmes while communicating with friends on what you are watching?

> Do you play video games online?

> Do you have a favourite website? What makes it your favourite? Do you participate in conversations on that website?

Writing Task

To conclude this section, you might like to make a portrait of your social media self. Write a portrait of your social media self. You can use the questions above to prompt you.

Wrapping up

1 Wordsearch

Find the following words:

Broadsheet
Caption
Compact
Facebook
Headline
Photos
Report
Selfies
Snapchat
Twitter

K	X	U	T	A	Z	O	T	M	X	B	P	D	R	U
P	O	O	K	V	F	S	C	R	P	R	C	E	U	M
H	Y	O	C	V	E	H	A	G	A	O	S	Y	R	Z
O	S	J	B	I	H	Q	P	L	Z	A	J	D	E	L
T	Z	Z	F	E	H	B	M	Q	N	D	L	L	T	K
O	I	L	I	E	C	S	O	N	T	S	H	L	T	H
S	E	T	O	X	K	A	C	L	H	H	A	T	I	L
S	T	U	W	V	N	I	F	E	V	E	T	X	W	M
C	A	P	T	I	O	N	A	O	J	E	F	R	T	L
I	P	Y	F	Q	T	D	J	W	D	T	E	O	H	P
A	E	H	R	C	L	T	A	H	C	P	A	N	S	H
I	M	H	F	I	R	V	E	J	O	T	X	Y	T	O
S	F	E	N	K	T	S	T	R	P	F	M	S	O	O
L	S	E	J	D	J	G	T	E	P	T	K	X	V	S

2 You have gained a lot of knowledge about the newspaper business in this section and you have had the chance to try your hand at some tasks essential to preparing a newspaper for publication. To wrap up this section you are going to put all your new knowledge into practice in a final activity.

Divide into groups of four and use a novel or film that you are studying in class as a subject for this project.

Create a front page for the novel or film that you are reading and studying in class.

Include all these elements:

> Masthead (newspaper's title and logo)
> Banner headline (main headline)
> Byline (author)
> Lead article (answering the five Ws and one H –
   Who? What? When? Where? Why? How?)
> Picture(s)
> Caption
> Choose story or stories
> Indicate further content on inside pages
> Advertisement(s).

For example, if you are reading or watching *Private Peaceful* (by Michael Morpurgo) you would make sure that everything you put on the front page relates to something from the book or film. So you might have *Peaceful Times* or *Wartime Express* as your title. Your banner headline would be chosen to match an episode in the book, such as 'Conditions in the Trenches', and you would write the accompanying story for the front page. You might also indicate some of the contents to be found inside the paper. Examples might be a feature article on 'Colonel's Wife Chokes on Scone' or a diary written by Tommo from No-man's Land and so on.

Alternatively if you have read *In Pieces* by the Trinity Comprehensive Writers you might think of a title connected to the ghosts and some content with connections to the Dead Zoo and/or cemeteries.

The Ghostly Gazette
by Trinity Comprehensive Writers
Magic in the Dead Zoo

Wartime Express
by Thomas Peaceful
Conditions in the Trenches

Chapter Five
DRAMA

Drama is all about making things up and acting them out. For over 2,000 years, audiences have been going to see actors play at make-believe. The reason is simple – we all love imagining new worlds and situations.

In this chapter you will be introduced to a well-known playwright, Mr William Shakespeare, and you will read four dramatic scenes and a short play.

Communicating

> You will use a variety of oral language strategies as you perform and improvise scripts.
> You will engage actively in class discussions and groupwork on the meaning of the dramatic texts.
> You will give your opinion and express your thoughts and feelings.
> You will write for a variety of purposes in your voice and in the voices of characters.
> You will discuss your writing with other students.
> You will use the language of theatre in responding to the texts.
> You will use what you have learned from the drama texts in your own writing and performance.

Exploring and Using Language

> You will listen actively to interpret and respond to the drama texts.
> You will practise speaking lines from the texts, including the plays of William Shakespeare.
> You will explore ways of expressing the meaning of words through movement and gesture.
> You will think and write about the thoughts and feelings of the characters, the settings and the key moments in the plays.

> You will examine and respond to the writers' use of language.
> You will respond in imaginative ways to the texts and discover the pleasure of playing a part.
> You will complete a quiz on the *Be Inspired!* website that relates to the witches' scene from *Macbeth*.

Understanding Language

> You will write accurately, paying attention to spelling, punctuation and grammar.
> You will choose your words carefully as you create characters.
> You will show your understanding of how speakers and writers change their language in different contexts.
> You will evaluate your own and others' written and oral work.
> You will read an author biography on the *Be Inspired!* website and research topics online.

Wrapping Up

> To wrap up the chapter, you will have a chance to work in a group and devise your own short play. So go on – 'Break a leg!'

www.edco.ie/beinspired

123

Introducing Mr Shakespeare

Before you read ...

Answer the five questions below by ticking the correct boxes.

	YES	NO
1 Did you ever think that your lost property 'vanished into thin air'?	☐	☐
2 Have you ever refused to 'budge an inch'?	☐	☐
3 Was there ever a time when you insisted on 'fair play'?	☐	☐
4 Did you ever 'laugh yourself into stitches'?	☐	☐
5 Have you ever suspected 'foul play'?	☐	☐

Whenever you use one of these phrases you are repeating an expression first used by William Shakespeare hundreds of years ago. He is one of the most famous writers of plays for the stage. His stories have been performed all over the world and translated into more than 80 different languages. He lived from 1564 to 1616 – four hundred years ago – but his work continues to entertain audiences of all ages. In this chapter you will sample some of his writing to find out just why Shakespeare remains such a popular author.

Speaking Lines of Dialogue

Oral Language

In this exercise you will find 12 lines taken from different Shakespeare plays. These short phrases were written to be spoken out loud by an actor on a stage. All of Shakespeare's stories were written in this way.

> ### Explanation – Dialogue
>
> Spoken lines in a play are called dialogue. A well-known example is the opening line from Shakespeare's *Hamlet* which opens with the question, 'Who's there?'

1. Match each line of dialogue in column A with a suitable 'feeling' word in column B. You can do this in pairs by choosing a line and speaking it out loud in different ways.

2. Listen carefully to how the words sound when they are spoken in an 'angry' voice or a 'stubborn' voice.

One way of discovering the emotion of a line is to speak the words aloud, making every word count. For example, to test the first line, begin by saying 'Death' on its own, thinking about the meaning of the word. Then you add 'is' and say 'Death is', noticing how each individual word adds something new to the line until you end up with 'Death is a fearful thing.'

Column A	Column B
Death is a fearful thing.	angry
Disobedient wretch.	apologetic
He has eaten me out of house and home.	delighted
I have not slept one wink.	disappointed
I like this place and willingly could waste my time in it.	disgusted
I'll not budge an inch.	exhausted
I must be cruel only to be kind.	frightened
I was adored once too.	generous
Off with his head!	relieved
Out of the jaws of death.	sad
The game is up.	stubborn
What's mine is yours, and what's yours is mine.	vicious

Writing Task

Now choose one of these lines of dialogue and write a short description of the type of character who might say those words in a play.

The text below makes up most of a famous sonnet 'Sonnet Number 18' by William Shakespeare. You will notice that there are 14 words missing from the poem. Look at the words in the box and write each one in the correct space to complete the lines of the poem.

But	By	fade

gold	his	life	long

more	see	short

shines	summer's	too	winds

Shall I compare thee to a _____ day?
Thou art more lovely and _____ temperate:[1]
Rough _____ do shake the darling buds of May,
And summer's lease[2] hath all too _____ a date:
Sometime ____ hot the eye of heaven _____,
And often is his _____ complexion dimm'd;
And every fair[3] from fair sometime declines,
__ chance or nature's changing course untrimm'd:
___ thy[4] eternal summer shall not _____
Nor lose possession of that fair thou owest;[5]
Nor shall death brag thou wanderest in ___ shade,
When in eternal lines to time thou growest:
So ____ as men can breathe, or eyes can ____,
So long lives this, and this gives _____ to thee.

_____

[1] **temperate:** mild
[2] **lease:** period of time
[3] **fair:** beauty
[4] **thy:** your
[5] **owest:** own

> **Explanation –**
> **Sonnet**
>
> A sonnet is a poem made up of exactly 14 lines. Sonnets usually have a pattern of rhyming words at the ends of the lines.

Now compare your completed sonnet with the original and correct any mistakes you made.

Sonnet Number 18

Shall I compare thee to a summer's day?
Thou art more lovely and more temperate:
Rough winds do shake the darling buds of May,
And summer's lease hath all too short a date:
Sometime too hot the eye of heaven shines,
And often is his gold complexion dimm'd;
And every fair from fair sometime declines,
By chance or nature's changing course untrimm'd:
But thy eternal summer shall not fade
Nor lose possession of that fair thou owest;
Nor shall death brag thou wanderest in his shade,
When in eternal lines to time thou growest:
So long as men can breathe, or eyes can see,
So long lives this, and this gives life to thee.

Thinking about the poem

1 In the first line the speaker wonders how the person he loves would compare to a 'summer's day'. He flatters her, telling her that she is more beautiful and that a 'summer's day' can often be disappointing. Find a number of different ways he is disappointed by summer weather.

2 How does the poet compare the sun to a person?

3 In this love poem the person speaking says lots of pleasant things about his lover. What is the highest compliment he pays her? Rate the following from 1 to 3 with number 1 as the highest.

☐	She is 'more lovely' than a 'summer's day'.
☐	Her beauty 'shall not fade'.
☐	His poem 'gives life' to her for ever.

4 Write a short paragraph explaining your choice.

5 How would you feel if someone wrote a poem like this for you? Explain your answer using some of the words from the poem to clarify your points.

Oral Language

Choose one line in the poem that you like and speak it out loud for the class, expressing the feeling that you think is contained in that line.

The Dumb Show in *Hamlet*

This dumb show is taken from one of Shakespeare's most popular plays. *Hamlet* is the tragic story of a young prince who is mourning the death of his father.

Explanation –
Dumb show

A short, silent piece of action or mime included in a play is called a dumb show. It is a type of silent storytelling using simple human movement to tell a tale. In a dumb show exaggerated actions and gestures, as well as facial expressions and posture, are the main ways of communicating the story.

Groupwork

Read the following set of stage directions and try to figure out how best to mime it for your class. Clear a space in the room to perform in. You will need to work in groups of five or six. The parts are:

> King
> Queen
> Poisoner
> two or three companions.

When you are miming, remember to:

> keep the actions simple
> move slowly
> make one gesture at a time.

Each member of the group can help to direct by coming up with suggestions for how the actions should be performed. This is the story and the sequence of movements to be performed.

1 Enter a King and a Queen very lovingly, embracing each other.
2 She bows down before him.
3 He takes her up, and rests his head upon her neck.
4 He lies down on a bank of flowers.
5 She, seeing him asleep, leaves him.
6 In comes the Poisoner, takes off the King's crown, kisses it, pours poison in the King's ear, and exits.
7 The Queen returns, finds the King dead and is very upset.
8 The Poisoner, with two or three companions, comes in again, seeming to mourn with her.
9 The dead body is carried away.
10 The Poisoner offers the Queen many gifts.
11 She seems unwilling to accept them for a while, but in the end accepts his love.
12 All leave.

Oral Language

1 When you have decided how to perform your mime, each group can present the show to the class. Your teacher can take nominations for the 'Class Oscars' in the following categories:

Best King | Best Companion(s) | Best Queen | Best Poisoner | Best Director

2 Propose someone for a 'Class Oscar'. You must state the reason why you think his/her performance was very good.

Let's review your work so far in this chapter.

> You have spoken lines of dialogue, expressing a distinct feeling in each line.
> You have performed a short mime show.

You will combine the skills you have learned for the following exercises.
Each scene is taken from the work of William Shakespeare.

Juliet is a teenage girl who plans to elope with her new boyfriend, Romeo.
In this scene she has been waiting at home to find out if the wedding will go ahead.
Her nurse returns with news from a secret meeting with the priest and Romeo.

Juliet and the Nurse

FROM *ROMEO AND JULIET*

Enter Nurse

Juliet	O honey nurse, what news?
Nurse	I am weary ... how my bones ache!
Juliet	Speak; good, good nurse, speak.
Nurse	Do you not see that I am out of breath?
Juliet	How art thou out of breath, when thou hast breath
	To say to me that thou art out of breath?
	Is thy news good, or bad? Answer to that;
	Let me be satisfied, is't good or bad?
Nurse	You know not how to choose a man: Romeo! No, not he; though his face be better than any man's, yet his leg excels all men's; and for a hand, and a foot, and a body, though they be not to be talked on, yet they are past compare. What, have you dined at home?
Juliet	No, no: but all this did I know before.
	What says he of our marriage? What of that?
Nurse	Lord, how my head aches! What a head have I!
	It beats as it would fall in twenty pieces.
	My back o' t' other side, – O, my back, my back!
	A curse on you for sending me about,
	To catch my death with jaunting up and down!

Juliet	I am sorry that thou art not well.
	Sweet, sweet, sweet nurse, tell me, what says my love?
Nurse	Your love says, like an honest gentleman, and a courteous, and a kind, and a handsome, and, I warrant, a virtuous, – Where is your mother?
Juliet	Where is my mother! Why, she is within;
	Where should she be? How oddly thou repliest!
	'Your love says, like an honest gentleman, Where is your mother?'
Nurse	O God's lady dear! Are you so hot? Henceforward do your messages yourself.
Juliet	Come, what says Romeo?
Nurse	Have you got leave to go to shrift* to-day?
Juliet	I have.
Nurse	Then get you hence to Friar Laurence's cell;
	There stays a husband to make you a wife.

---

* **shrift:** confession

Thinking about the scene

1 How is Juliet feeling when the nurse arrives?

> Is she angry?
> Is she excited?
> Is she impatient?

Explain your choice.

2 The nurse talks about Romeo. Does she like the look of him? How do you know?

3 How does the nurse tease Juliet in this scene?

4 Did you enjoy acting out this scene from *Romeo and Juliet*?

Writing Task

From what you have seen so far, do you think you would like to see the full play? Write a paragraph outlining your views.

In this scene, Macbeth pays a visit to the three witches who have helped him become King of Scotland. Now he is looking for their protection. The three weird sisters are brewing a magic potion, the strange ingredients for which are associated with evil or bad luck. You will notice that there are lines for each character to speak alone and also several lines to be said in unison – all together.

Check out the Against the Clock quiz about the witches' brew on the *Be Inspired!* website.

Witches' Brew

A SCENE FROM *MACBETH*

Groupwork

In groups of four, read through the script together. Pay attention to the rhythm of the lines and the order in which the different characters speak.

Talk about:

> how the lines should sound
> where the characters could be positioned on the stage
> the movements of the characters.

Oral Language

1 Listen to each other as you speak the lines. Have a brief discussion about what type of voice is best suited to each character. Think about the four characters and talk about who would look best in each part. Make a decision about who will play each of the three witches and Macbeth. This is called 'casting the play'.

2 Rehearse the scene for ten minutes and then review the performance, making any changes that you think will help to improve it.

3 For homework, learn your lines. Any word you find confusing can be checked in a dictionary or online.

First Witch	Round about the cauldron go;
	In the poisoned entrails throw.
	Toad, that under cold stone
	Days and nights has thirty-one
	Swelter'd venom sleeping got,
	Boil thou first i'the charmed pot.
All Three	Double, double, toil and trouble;
	Fire burn and cauldron, bubble.

Second Witch	Fillet of a fenny snake,
	In the cauldron boil and bake;
	Eye of newt and toe of frog,
	Wool of bat and tongue of dog,
	Adder's fork and blind-worm's sting,
	Lizard's leg and howlet's wing –
	For a charm of powerful trouble,
	Like a hell-broth boil and bubble.
All Three	Double, double, toil and trouble;
	Fire burn and cauldron bubble.
Third Witch	Scale of dragon, tooth of wolf,
	Witch's mummy, maw and gulf
	Of the ravined salt-sea shark,
	Root of hemlock digged i'the dark [...]
	Add thereto a tiger's chaudron,*
	For the ingredients of our cauldron.
All Three	Double, double, toil and trouble;
	Fire burn and cauldron, bubble.
Second Witch	Cool it with a baboon's blood,
	Then the charm is firm and good [...]
Second Witch	By the pricking of my thumbs,
	Something wicked this way comes:
	Open, locks, whoever knocks!
	Enter Macbeth.
Macbeth	How now, you secret, black, and midnight hags!
	What is't you do?
All Three	A deed without a name.

* **chaudron:** entrails

Writing Task

Complete this task in your portfolio, p. 38.

Imagine that you are putting on this play in a theatre and you have been asked to design the show. What suggestions would you make about costumes, make-up, props and sound effects?

Research

In groups, see what you can find out about Shakespeare. Look up information about:

> the period of history he lived through
> his family background and personal life
> the number and type of poems and plays he wrote
> the Globe Theatre.

Think about how you would like to communicate this information to your class. When you have finished gathering the facts, give a short presentation.

You might like to start your research by visiting some of the websites listed in the weblinks document on edcodigital. Your teacher can access this document and recommend links.

Wrapping up

Finally, let's take a look at what you have learned in this section.

> You have spoken various lines from Shakespeare out loud and in different voices.
> You have worked together to perform a silent mime.
> You have helped to act out and direct a number of short scenes from the poetry and plays of Shakespeare.
> You have completed a research project on the life and work of William Shakespeare.

To wrap up your introduction to Mr William Shakespeare, look back over your work in this chapter and choose the line or phrase you like best from the Shakespeare texts covered here.

On a large sheet of paper, write the words using plenty of colour and any other illustrations you think are suitable for this quotation. When your work is done, find a space on the classroom wall to display it.

Four Short Scenes for Reading on Your Feet

We all love stories, and drama is another way of telling a story, with the added excitement of characters we can watch and hear as they bring the story to life. Because drama was written to be performed, you will have the chance to be active participants in the scripts that you are going to read.

Lucy is an ordinary young teenager, absolutely fed up with her family who are too preoccupied with their own lives to bother about her place in the school swimming team. In protest, Lucy resorts to her childhood fantasy friend, Zara, who not only materialises in the play, but also introduces her own ideal family and shows Lucy how to make her family vanish.

Before you read ...

Did you have a 'pretend' friend when you were young, or do you know anyone who did? Can you think of a reason why you or someone else might do this? Share your thoughts with a partner.

FROM ...

Invisible Friends

ALAN AYCKBOURN

Author Biography
Check out the *Be Inspired!* website for Alan Ayckbourn's author biography.

Time: *The present. In Lucy's house.*

Lucy   (*as she goes upstairs, to audience*) Come with me, if you will. Upstairs. If you listen very carefully you can just hear the distant sounds of the greater spotted Grisly Gary, my unbelievably talkative brother. Grisly Gary is doing a building course at the technical college, training to be a bucket. (*She reaches the door of Gary's room. The music is louder now.*) Here we go. I'll just have a quiet word with him. Cover your ears.

Lucy opens Gary's door. The heavy metal music comes up to a deafening level. Lucy, when she speaks, is quite inaudible. Gary, lying on the bed with his eyes closed, fails to notice her at all.

(*Mouthing, swiftly.*) Hallo, Grisly. It's your loving sister, Lucy. Just to tell you I've been picked for the school swimming team.

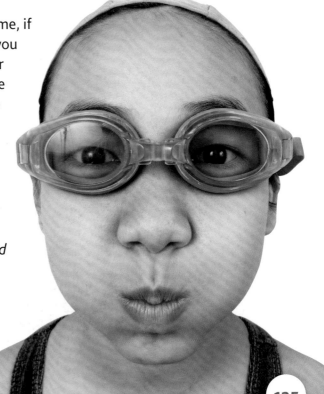

Thought you'd like to know. Bye, Grisly. (*Lucy closes the door again. The music goes down to a lower level.*) I enjoyed that chat. (*She opens the door of her own room and goes inside.*) This is my room. No one's allowed in here, except me.

I'm a very tidy sort of person. Which is a bit extraordinary in this house. I think I must be a freak. I actually like to know where I've put my things. This is my bed. That's my desk. And up there on the shelf. Those are my special, most favourite books. (*The music pounds through the wall.*) Actually, one of the reasons I keep it tidy is because my very, very best friend, Zara, also likes things tidy. Oh yes, I ought to explain to you about Zara. You may have heard my mum talking about my invisible friend. Do you remember? Well, that's my invisible friend, Zara. (*Introducing her.*) This is Zara. I want you to meet Zara. Zara say hallo. That's it. Will you say hallo to Zara, my invisible friend? I invented Zara – oh, years ago – when I was seven or eight. Just for fun. I think I was ill at that time and wasn't allowed to play with any of my real friends, so I made up Zara. She's my special friend that no one can see except me. Of course, I can't really see her either. Not really. Although sometimes I … It's almost as if I could see her, sometimes. If I concentrate very hard it's like I can just glimpse her out of the corner of my eye. (*She is thoughtful for a second.*) Still. Anyway. I've kept Zara for years and years. Until they all started saying I was much too old for that sort of thing and got worried and started talking about sending for a doctor. So then I didn't take her round with me quite so much after that. But she's still here. And when I feel really sad and depressed like I do today, then I sit and talk to Zara. Zara always understands. Zara always listens. She's special. Aren't you, Zara? (*She listens to Zara. Pause.*) Oh, Zara, did I tell you I've been picked for the school swimming team? Isn't that exciting? Yes. Thank you. I'm glad you're excited, too. Good. (*Pause. Shouting.*) IF ANYONE IS INTERESTED AT ALL, I WAS PICKED FOR THE SCHOOL SWIMMING TEAM TODAY. WHAT ABOUT THAT, FOLKS? (*She listens. No reply.*) Great. Thanks for your support, everyone. (*Tearful.*) They might at least … They could have at least … Oh, Zara … I know you're always here, but sometimes I get so … lonely …

She sits on her bed, sad, angry and frustrated.

Explanations –

Opening scenes

Opening scenes give us the context and set the tone and atmosphere of a play. The audience also gets an idea about whether the play will be funny or sad. We meet the characters during the opening scenes and get our first impressions of how they interact with each other. This extract is part of the opening sequence of the play *Invisible Friends*.

Characters

Characters in plays are very different from characters in short stories or novels. Because we see them on stage, we can read their body language and facial expressions, and we can see how they move and hear how they interact with others.

Monologue

Monologue is when a character shares his/her inner thoughts and feelings.

Thinking about the scene

1 What does Lucy tell us about her brother Gary?

2 Why does Lucy think she might be 'a freak'?

3 Lucy also gives the audience some other information about herself. List all these details in your own words.

4 Lucy refers to her brother as 'Grisly'. Look up this word in a dictionary and say what it tells you about the kind of relationship she has with him.

5 What do you expect the rest of the play to be like? Look at the statements below and choose an answer. Explain your choice.

> The play will have a happy ending.
> The play will have a sad ending.
> This is how I think things will turn out: ... and; this is why ...

Oral Language

In the Explanations above, you learned about the importance of opening scenes. Do you think this opening scene is a good one? Prepare a one-minute explanation of your opinion to share with either a small group or the whole class.

Groupwork

1 With a partner, read the section beginning at *Hallo, Grisly. It's your loving sister...* and ending, *I enjoyed that chat*, and discuss the kind of expression you think Lucy has on her face as she is speaking. Together, try out different expressions as you speak the words to each other. When you are happy that you have captured her expression, join up with another pair and speak the lines, demonstrating your ideas.

2 **Hot-seating a character:**

Work in groups of four for this exercise. Place a chair in a central position in the group. This is the 'Hot Seat' and it will help you to learn more about Lucy.

Begin by discussing why Lucy invented Zara and the reasons why Zara is so important in her life.

Following the discussion, one of the group takes on the role of Lucy and sits in the Hot Seat.

The other group members ask Lucy about her life and her reasons for inventing Zara. It's a good idea to start with easy questions like:

> Is your name Lucy?
> What is your brother's name?
> Where do you live?
> Who are your friends?

Then the group can start asking more searching questions about Lucy's motivation for inventing Zara and so on.

As a follow-up exercise you might also like to 'hot-seat' Zara to find out more about her. You should prepare questions relating to where she lives, how she met Lucy, what she thinks of Lucy and so on.

Writing Task

Write an account of what you learned about Lucy, both from the discussion in the group and from the Hot Seat exercise.

Research

Imaginary or fantasy friendships have featured in many films and TV series in recent years, the Irish sitcom *Moone Boy* being a recent example. Do a little research online and find the titles of some of these films or programmes. Have you seen any of them? Is there one in particular you would like to see? Prepare a short report on your findings to share with your class.

This play is set in wartime Germany. Three sisters, Monika, Maria and Heidi, have disguised Mike, an English RAF pilot, and are hiding him in a barn.

Before you read ...

Think about the title of this piece. If someone is described as a 'chicken', what possible meanings could this have? Exchange ideas with a partner.

FROM ...

Nobody Here But Us Chickens

STEPHANIE MILLER

Scene: *A disused barn.*

Set: *Bales of straw, sacking, a pile of boxes and crates, overturned chairs, and a 'scarecrow' dressed in a very large coat and a huge hat.*

Action: *Voices offstage. Marching feet. Monika runs to the door.*

Monika	Oh hurry! Hurry! They're here!
Sergeant	(*Offstage*) Squad halt! (*Marching stops.*) Corporal!
Corporal	Sir!
Sergeant	Take one man. Guard the back entrance.
Corporal	Sir! (*Feet marching away.*)
Sergeant	You others. Cover this door. I'll search inside.
Maria	Quickly! Make a circle. (*The girls join hands round the 'scarecrow'.*) Now then, look HAPPY. Sing and dance. (*They dance round the 'scarecrow' in a circle, singing.*)
	The sergeant enters noisily, with rifle and fixed bayonet at the ready. The singing stops. The sergeant advances slowly, looking threatening.
Sergeant	You there! Have you girls seen anyone here today?
Maria	No one! Only us! Us and the chickens!
Sergeant	Just you three?
Monika	Why? Are you ... Are you looking for someone?
Sergeant	Yes! And I'll find him. An enemy. Hiding out.
	He prowls round, searching. Jabs bayonet savagely into bales. And into sacks. Crosses to crates, kicking them over. Sees 'scarecrow'.
Sergeant	So. A scarecrow! You made him?
Maria	Yes! Yes! We did.
	The sergeant stares at the 'scarecrow'. The three girls hold their breaths. Then the sergeant smiles, speaking in a softer tone.

Sergeant	When we were small we used to make scarecrows. (*He walks round the 'scarecrow' inspecting it.*) Not bad. Not bad at all – but we made better ones. (*His mood changes back to the hard soldier.*) Shall I tell you what the Army uses a scarecrow for?
Heidi	(*Fearfully.*) What?
Sergeant	Bayonet practice! (*The girls gasp.*)
	The sergeant, holding bayonet in position, prepares to jab the 'scarecrow'.
Sergeant	Would you like a demonstration … like this!

Explanations –
Tension and suspense

Good drama has a sense of tension. *Tension* develops when there is some mystery or uncertainty about what might happen next in a play. When we do not know what is going to happen, we, the audience, are held in suspense. *Suspense* is a feeling of uncertainty or worry when we do not know how something is going to work out.

Lighting and sound

Lighting helps to create the mood and atmosphere of a scene. Dark lighting can create a scary mood, whereas bright lighting can create a happy one. Lighting is used to direct our attention to one part of the stage or one character on stage. It is also used to suggest the time of day: blue light suggests night-time; an orange glow suggests sunlight.

Sound effects, which include music as well as other kinds of sound, are also used to create mood or atmosphere. Sometimes sound effects are used to mirror what's happening on stage. For example, the sounds of a storm might be used when two characters are arguing on stage.

Thinking about the scene

1 Where have the girls hidden the pilot?

2 **a)** What was the *very first* sign of tension you noted?

  b) List all the places in the script where you think tension or suspense is created. Explain each of your choices.

3 What do you think happens after the sergeant jabs the 'scarecrow' with the bayonet?

4 Are there clues in the scene to suggest the sisters have different kinds of personalities? For example, does anyone take the lead? Is one more fearful than the others? Give reasons for your choices.

5 Would you agree that we are left in suspense at the end of the scene? Give reasons for your view.

6 Watch the video 'Most Shocking Second a Day' on the *Be Inspired!* website. As with 'Nobody Here But Us Chickens', the video shows a child in a war situation. Which piece do you find the most frightening? Give reasons for your answer.

Video

Writing Task

Write out the script of the next three or four lines of dialogue you think might take place between any one of the girls and the sergeant.

Or:

A newspaper reporter hears about the incident later and interviews Heidi, who was very quiet, about her experiences. Write a series of questions and answers appropriate to the situation.

Oral Language

Work in groups of five to (a) **set up the stage** and (b) **act out the scene.**

(a) Take a large sheet of paper and mark out the stage area. Now mark out where you would put all the items listed in the set instructions at the start of the scene: bales of straw; sacking; a pile of boxes and crates; overturned chairs; and a 'scarecrow' dressed in a very large coat.

Now create a space in your classroom or on the stage area in your school and set it up using your design and whatever objects you have to hand. (You can mark out the space using masking tape.)

(b) Each group member will take on the role of one of the people in the scene and act out the scene in full. The other groups will be your audience. Each group will get feedback about their performance from the rest as follows:

> › The best thing about your performance was …
> › You could improve your performance by …

Groupwork

Work in a small group of three or four for this exercise on **lighting** and **sound**.

Your class is staging this scene and your group is responsible for looking after any lighting and sound that are required. Using the information in the Explanations above, think about the lighting you would use and the sounds you might add in this scene. Agree on your reasons for doing so.

Make notes so that you can report back to the class.

This is a series of short extracts from Lovers *by Brian Friel, a play in two sections. The first section, entitled 'Winners', follows the story of two 17-year-old lovers, Joseph Michael Brennan and Margaret Mary Enright, more commonly known as Joe and Mag respectively. They are about to do their Leaving Certificate in a school in Northern Ireland. In this scene it is a lovely June morning three weeks before their exams begin and they are sitting, studying, on a hilltop.*

FROM ...

Lovers

BRIAN FRIEL

Joe	Look, Mag: we came up here to study. What are you going to do first?
Mag	French. And then maths. And then Spanish. And then English language and literature. After lunch geography and history of the world. I have planned a programme for myself. The important thing about revising for an examination is to have a method. What are you starting with?
Joe	Maths.
Mag	Then what?
Joe	That's all.
Mag	Only maths?
Joe	Huh-huh.

She considers this absurd idea for a second. Then, because Joe is wiser in these things than she, she readily agrees with him.

Mag	Then that's what I'll do too. (*Really worried*) My God, if the volume of a cone doesn't come up, I'm scootrified! Not that I care – I can afford to go down in one subject. (*Pause*) Joe …
Joe	What?
Mag	What's the real difference between language and literature?
Joe	You're not serious, Maggie!
Mag	Don't – don't – don't tell me … I remember now … One is talking and the other is … books!
	[…]
Joe	Honest to God, the stories that you come up with – juvenile, that's the only word for them. And I'm trying to work at integration. So will you shut up?
Mag	(*With dignity*) I will. I certainly will. And the next time I break breath with you, you'll be a chastened man. (*Brief pause*) But before I go silent for the rest of the day, there's something I want to get clear between us, Joseph Brennan. (*Pause*) Joe.
Joe	What?
Mag	You never proposed to me.
Joe	Huh?
Mag	You haven't *asked* me to marry you.
Joe	What are you raving about?
Mag	Propose to me.
Joe	God!
Mag	Now.
Joe	You really are – !
Mag	Ask me.
Joe	Will-you-marry-me. Now!
Mag	Thank you, Joseph. I will.
	He goes back to his books.
Joe	Bats! Raving bloody bats!
	[…]
Joe	See the sun glinting on the headstones beside the chapel.
Mag	Some day we'll be buried together.
Joe	You're great company.
Mag	I can't wait for the future, Joe.
Joe	What's that supposed to mean?
	Maggie suddenly leaps to her feet. Her face is animated, her movements quick and vital, her voice ringing.
Mag	The past's over! And I hate this waiting time! I want the future to happen – I want to be in it – I want to be in it with you!

Joe	You've got sunstroke.
	She throws her belongings into her case.
Mag	Come on, Joe! Let's begin the future now!
	Not comprehending, but infected by her mood, he gets to his feet.
Joe	You're nuts.
Mag	Where'll we go? What'll we do? Let's do something crazy!
Joe	Mad as a hatter.
Mag	The lake! We'll dance on every island! We'll stay out all night and sing and shout at the moon! (*Joe does a wolf howl up at the sky*) Come on, Joe! While the sun's still hot!
	[...]
	She catches his hand and begins to run.
Mag	We're away!
Joe	Easy – easy –
Mag	Wheeeeeeeee –
Joe	Aaaaaaaaah –
	They run down the hill, hand in hand. At the bottom Joe takes her bicycle. Their voices fade slowly.

Explanations –
Relationships in drama

Relationships in drama are the connections that characters form with each other. These connections or relationships can be very diverse; some can be affectionate and warm, while others can be cold and uncaring.

Body language

Body language is an important part of communication; it refers to the signals we give off when we are speaking to another person. Anyone watching will usually be able to read how one person relates to another by reading those signals – facial expressions, tone of voice, body posture, eye movement and so on.

Props

Props are anything movable on a stage that can be used by an actor during the performance. Some examples are: chairs, tables, telephones, newspapers, glasses.

Thinking about the scene

1 From what you read here, what adjectives would you use to describe the characters? Choose at least three adjectives from the list below and/or use your thesaurus to find your own and insert them into the relevant boxes.

loving	self-centred	affectionate	insensitive	endearing
immature	warm	passionate	childish	serious
charming	silly	caring	indifferent	enthusiastic

Mag	Joe

2 When Mag says she will be 'scootrified' if the volume of a cone does not appear on the exam paper, what does she mean? Choose one of the options below and explain your choice.

> In deep trouble
> Disappointed
> Other – suggest your own definition

3 Which character – Joe or Mag – do you think is the better student? Give reasons for your answer.

4 Explain in your own words what kind of relationship you think Mag and Joe have. Is it a good relationship? (See Explanations above.)

5 When Mag tells Joe that she can't wait for the future, explain in your own words what you think she means.

6 Why does Joe tell Mag she is 'mad as a hatter' at the end of the scene?

7 Which teenager would you like to play in a production of this scene? Explain your decision in two or three sentences.

1 With a partner, role-play the second extract, beginning *Honest to God ...* as far as *Bats! Raving bloody bats!* Try to capture the correct tone of voice and body language the characters would use in this scene (see Explanations above). When you are happy with your parts, perform your role-play for at least one other group or for the class.

Or:

2 With a partner, script the conversation you both agree might take place between Mag and her mother when she tells her that Joe has proposed to her. Role-play your scene for at least one other pair and give each other feedback about your script as follows:

> One thing we really liked about your script was ...
> One way we think you could make your scene better is ...

Writing Task

Based on your reading of these extracts, write a character sketch of Mag. (Complete this task in your portfolio, p. 39.)

Or:

Imagine that Joe keeps a personal diary. Write two entries he might make (a) the evening before this scene and (b) immediately after this scene.

Groupwork

In small groups of three or four, imagine that your group has been asked to find the props to be used in this scene (see Explanations above). Give reasons for your choice of each prop.

Research

Do some research in your library or online to find out all you can about this play. For example, you might like answers to some of the following questions.

> What happens after this extract?
> Do Joe and Mag get married?
> How does the play end?

Prepare a short summary for sharing with a group in your class.

This play is set in the 1920 War of Independence, a particularly vicious war played out between the IRA (the 'Shinners') and the British forces in Ireland (the 'Auxies' or 'Black and Tans'). The play centres on the mistaken identity of a poet called Donal Davoren, who is sharing a room in a poor Dublin tenement slum with Seamus Shields. Donal is thought to be an IRA gunman on the run.

In this scene, which comes at the end of the play, the Black and Tans are carrying out a raid in search of 'Shinners' in the tenement building. Earlier, Minnie Powell had taken a bag of bombs from Shields and Davoren's room and brought them to her own room.

Before you read ...

Have you ever been to the theatre to see a play or watched a play on television? What was the title? Did you like it or not? Why/why not? Swap stories with a partner.

FROM ...

The Shadow of a Gunman

SEAN O'CASEY

Mrs Grigson	They're gone, Mr Shields, an' here's poor Dolphie an' not a feather astray on him. Oh, Dolphie, dear, you're all right, thanks to God; I thought you'd never see the mornin'.
Adolphus Grigson	(*entering without coat or vest*) Of course I'm all right; what ud put a bother on Dolphie Grigson? – not the Tans anyway!
Mrs Grigson	When I seen you stretched out on the bed an' you … singin' a hymn …
Adolphus Grigson	(*fearful of possible humiliation*) Who was singin' a hymn? D'ye hear me talkin' to you – where did you hear me singin' a hymn?
Mrs Grigson	I was only jokin', Dolphie, dear; I …
Adolphus Grigson	Your place is below, an' not gosterin' here to men; down with you quick!
	Mrs Grigson hurriedly leaves the room.
	(*Nonchalantly taking out his pipe, filling it, lighting it, and beginning to smoke*) Excitin' few moments, Mr Davoren; Mrs G. lost her head completely – panic-stricken. But that's only natural, all women is very nervous. The only thing to do is to show them that they can't put the wind up you; show the least sign of fright an' they'd walk on you, simply walk on you. Two of them come down – 'Put them up', revolvers under your nose – you know, the usual way. 'What's all the bother about?' says I, quite calm. 'No bother at all,' says one of them, 'only this gun might go off an' hit

somebody – have you me?' says he. 'What if it does,' says I. 'A man can only die once, an' you'll find Grigson won't squeal.' 'God, you're a cool one,' says the other; 'there's no blottin' it out.'

Seamus That's the best way to take them; it only makes things worse to show that you've got the wind up. 'Any ammunition here?' says the fellow that come in here. 'I don't think so,' says I, 'but you better have a look.' … 'I don't know of any clause,' says I, 'in the British Constitution that makes it a crime for a man to speak in his own room,' – with that, he just had a look around, an' off he went.

Adolphus Grigson If a man keeps a stiff upper front – Merciful God, there's an ambush!

Explosions of two bursting bombs are heard on the street outside the house, followed by fierce and rapid revolver- and rifle-fire. People are heard rushing into the hall, and there is general clamour and confusion. Seamus and Davoren cower down in the room; Grigson, after a few moments' hesitation, frankly rushes out of the room to what he conceives to be the safer asylum of the kitchen. A lull follows, punctuated by an odd rifle-shot; then comes a peculiar and ominous stillness, broken in a few moments by the sounds of voices and movement. Questions are heard being asked: 'Who was it was killed?' 'Where was she shot?' which are answered by: 'Minnie Powell'; 'She went to jump off the lorry an' she was shot'; 'She's not dead, is she?'; 'They say she's dead – shot through the buzzom!'

Davoren (*in a tone of horror-stricken doubt*) D'ye hear what they're sayin', Shields, d'ye hear what they're sayin'? – Minnie Powell is shot.

Seamus	For God's sake speak easy, an' don't bring them in here on top of us again.
Davoren	Is that all you're thinking of? Do you realize that she has been shot to save us?
Seamus	Is it my fault; am I to blame?
Davoren	It is your fault and mine, both: oh, we're a pair of dastardly cowards to have let her do what she did.
Seamus	She did it off her own bat – we didn't ask her to do it.
	Mrs Grigson enters. She is excited and semi-hysterical, and sincerely affected by the tragic occurrence.
Mrs Grigson	(*falling down in a sitting posture on one of the beds*) What's goin' to happen next! Oh, Mr Davoren, isn't it terrible, isn't it terrible! Minnie Powell, poor little Minnie Powell's been shot dead! They were raidin' a house a few doors down, an' had just got up in their lorries to go away, when they was ambushed. You never heard such shootin'! An' in the thick of it, poor Minnie went to jump off the lorry she was on, an' she was shot through the buzzom. Oh, it was horrible to see the blood pourin' out, an' Minnie moanin'. They found some paper in her breast, with 'Minnie' written on it, an' some other name they couldn't make out with the blood; the officer kep' it. The ambulance is bringin' her to the hospital, but what good's that when she's dead! Poor little Minnie, poor little Minnie Powell, to think of you full of life a few minutes ago, an' now she's dead!

Explanations –

Closing scenes

Ideally a closing scene should give the audience the feeling that events are coming to a satisfactory conclusion and that all loose ends have been tied up. This helps them to decide whether they liked the play or not. It does not matter whether the outcome is happy or sad as long as it feels right.

Costume

The costumes that characters in a play wear tell us something about them. For example, we are inclined to think differently about characters who dress fashionably in a modern way and those whose clothes are old-fashioned or worn.

Oral Language

In pairs, take a part each and practise a role-play of the first part of this scene, from 'They're gone, Mr Shields ...' to '... down with you quick!'

Pay particular attention to movement, gesture, facial expression and tone of voice when preparing. Perform for one other pair. Then, as a group of four, have a discussion about which of the two characters you are more likely to believe.

1 Choose an adjective from the list below (or find your own) to help you explain your overall opinion of this scene. Explain your choice.

| funny | sad | comical | serious | dark |

| optimistic | depressing | cheerful | disheartening | humorous |

2 Do you agree that there is a big difference between what characters say and how they act? Back up your answer with evidence from the scene.

3 What impression of Minnie Powell have you gathered from reading this scene? How do you imagine her character?

4 Would you agree that Adolphus Grigson's name suits him perfectly? Is there a sense in which O'Casey is poking fun at him? Explain your view.

5 Imagine that this scene is to be staged and you are the director. What instructions would you issue with regard to costume? Choose any two of the characters and describe the costumes you would dress them in.

6 Having studied this scene *and* the stage directions, use the table below to place the characters into categories. Include Minnie Powell in your analysis.

Weak or cowardly characters		Strong or heroic characters	
Character	Reason	Character	Reason

7 The 'Guardian Open Journalism' video on the *Be Inspired!* website raises the issue of victims. Watch the video and take note of the newspaper headlines that are written about the wolf. Write a similar headline for Davoren.

8 In 'Explanations' you read that what matters about closing scenes is that they 'feel' right. Does this scene feel right to you? Are you happy that it's a good ending to a play? Explain your view.

Groupwork

A **freeze-frame** is like pushing the pause button on a DVD player to freeze the action at a particular moment in time.

> *If a man keeps a stiff upper front – Merciful God, there's an ambush!*

In groups of three, create a still image of this moment when Grigson, Shields and Davoren hear the explosions outside. The rest of your group or class will have to 'read' what you are showing through your frozen action.

Thought-tracking: have a one-sentence thought in your head to be able to say how you, as the character, are feeling at this moment.

Writing Task

Complete this task in your portfolio, p. 40.

'… oh, we're a pair of dastardly cowards …'. If you were given an opportunity to spend time in the company of either Davoren or Shields, based on the evidence here which one would you choose and why?

Research

This scene comes from the closing section of the play. Join with three other students to carry out some research into the story behind this scene. Each of you should take one of the following areas to research and prepare a summary report for your group.

1 Find out what life was like in Dublin for people who lived in a tenement building at the time of the play. You might find the website of the National Archives helpful. Your teacher can find this link in the *Be Inspired!* weblinks document on edcodigital.

2 Who was Minnie Powell and how important was her part in the play?

3 Find out about the other characters in the play – their names and a little about each of them.

4 Research a short piece about the political situation at the time and the story of the play itself.

A Full Play

This play is set in the children's ward of a large modern hospital in the 1990s. Four boys share a ward in the hospital.

The Children's Ward

ELLEN DRYDEN

Characters: Patrick, Chris, Marcus, Valerie, Keith

A six-bedded ward in a bright modern hospital. It is a children's ward. There are three beds on each side. Each bed has a locker beside it, and one or two plastic chairs. There is a door, left, to the playroom and another, right, to the corridor, the offices, etc. The windows have cards, cut-outs, and brightly coloured pictures and posters pasted up on them, including one of Postman Pat. The window-sill is full of cards and books. Five beds are empty. The bed nearest to the window has been transformed into a small 'living area'. There are cartons of juice, packets of biscuits, crisps, mousse and yoghurt cartons and coke bottles on the locker, together with a Sony Walkman, some comics and a few books. Carefully placed on a wooden drawing board on the bed is an intricate cardboard model of an Elizabethan house. On the window-sill, in the corner beside the bed, are several other models – all beautifully made. The house on the bed is unfinished. A cardboard shoebox of pens, glue, etc. stands beside it.

The bed next to it is bare by comparison. A simple cardboard sign saying 'Nothing by mouth' hangs over the bed. The locker has a jug and glass on it. A tall, pale-faced boy is lying, in dressing gown and pyjamas, on the bed, staring into space. Patrick – aged thirteen – has the air of someone passing through. But he looks worried, even a little frightened.

The bed opposite him has been carefully made, the sheets tightly tucked in. There is a pile of books on the locker. The window-sill beside the bed is full of brightly coloured 'get well soon' cards. The other four beds in the ward have obviously been recently vacated, the bedclothes tumbled, comics, books, toys lying higgledy-piggledy all over them.

Patrick gets up and crosses to the bed with the 'get well' cards. He picks up one of the cards and stands reading it.

Chris enters quietly and sees Patrick with the card. Chris is a delicate-looking boy with a permanently 'closed in' expression on his face, a suggestion of long-term pain. He is fifteen. He walks with a pronounced limp.

Chris	That's Darren. They took him this morning. He's having a big heart operation.
	Patrick, embarrassed, puts the card back carefully and scoots back to his bed and sits down rather self-consciously.
Patrick	Oh. I was just looking …
Chris	He's been here ages. His heart's pretty well knackered. He keeps going blue.

Patrick	Oh.

Chris limps back to his bed, sits down and looks speculatively at Patrick.

Chris	When did you get in?
Patrick	(*A touch of pride*) Half past four this morning. They thought I had a burst appendix. (*Lamely*) But it's not that bad now.
Chris	I didn't hear you.
Patrick	No. You were all asleep. The boy in that corner bed shouted out something. Well, sort of screamed. I didn't hear what he said. I'd been in Emergency – or whatever it is – since one o'clock. Then they brought me here. They just ignored him …
Chris	Wayne. Yeah they would. He's a real nuisance. He's always shouting in his sleep. They ought to move him. Keeping everybody awake. They take your appendix out?
Patrick	No. I don't know whether they're going to. They're going to do some tests. But I don't think that's for appendix …
Chris	Well, that's all you get in here. Tests. Tests. Tests. Never bother to tell you what for. Nothing by mouth for twelve hours. No liquids, no solids, no nothing. Needles up your bum. Tubes down your throat … then just when you think you're gonna get a bit of peace they whip you down to the theatre, cut you open, have a rummage round inside, then sew you up again and send you back up here. You don't feel like eating for a week after that.
Patrick	(*Looking worried*) Oh … Are you here for – have you got something the matter with your leg?
Chris	No. I've just broken a bone in my ankle. I did that in here. I've got a liver disease.

He is very dismissive as if he does not wish to discuss this.

I broke this skateboarding down the corridor.

Patrick	(*Amazed and quite impressed*) Is that allowed?
Chris	No.

He settles himself on his bed and begins to work on his model. There is a silence. Patrick watches him. Chris examines one piece of the model, sets it down, and looks round angrily.

Chris	Have you been messing about with this?

Patrick   No. I haven't touched it. Honest. I wouldn't.

Chris   (*Unconvinced*) Hmmmm. (*He carries on working*) This isn't just messing, what I'm doing. This is complicated work. It's not a toy. I'll have a whole village when I've finished. I've got the Church and the pub and a row of cottages done already. This is the Manor House.

Patrick   It's brilliant. I'm useless at that sort of thing.

Chris   You need practice ... But it's not a toy. My stupid Auntie Kathleen came in last Sunday. 'Oh! Aren't you a clever boy? Isn't that fantastic? I think it's a great idea to have something to play with in here. Gives you an interest.' Then she sat down on a whole dry-stone wall I'd got drying on a chair. Stuck to her stupid dress. She didn't bother to apologise! No, just moaned about the glue on her skirt. Kept on and on. 'Does it show? Has it marked it? I'm going on from here you know! I've got a function this evening at the hotel.' Stupid cow! Do you know what she brought me? Action Man and his Jungle Campaign! I told her, 'Auntie Kathleen, I am sixteen next birthday.' My Dad told me not to be so cheeky or he'd give me a dig. I love visitors. At least I've been here so long they only come once a week. It was terrible at first. Every day! How long will you be here?

Patrick   Just a couple of days I think.

Chris   Kid with kidney failure had that bed last.

He looks suspiciously at his model.

Somebody's definitely been messing with this. Look. This is all bent back. Shouldn't be like that.

Patrick   There was a little kid running round in here earlier. Come to visit that boy with the glasses. I didn't take much notice of him. I was – I was – (*Selecting his words carefully*) They'd just brought me back – I was – reading. He was playing with a little car. His Mum took him to the Playroom.

Chris   Oh ... Dominic! Marcus's brother. He's a real pest. Came up to me last week and grabbed hold of the box I keep all the Pentels and glue and stuff in. I told him to bring it back. He wouldn't. So I took it. He screamed the place down. His Mum just sat there. Then she turned on me! 'Oh, couldn't he just play with them for a while? He likes the colours. He loves drawing.' So I told her it wasn't a toy and they were mine. She just said, 'Oh he won't damage anything. I'll see you get them back.' Then she let him throw them all over the floor.

Patrick   What did you do?

Chris   Well, I picked them all up and took them away. I said I needed them. He screamed blue murder and Sister came in and his Mum said, 'He just wants to borrow the crayons for a minute but I'm afraid we're being a bit dog-in-the-manger!'

Patrick	Oh.
Chris	Sister was great. She just said, 'Christopher has been making his models for a long time, and there's a Stanley knife in that box. I don't think it's a very suitable toy for a small child. There's lots of toys in the Playroom.'
Patrick	She seems nice. The Sister …
Chris	Yeah. She's all right. They're all grand here.
	He becomes absorbed in his model and suddenly seems to have no further interest in Patrick, who watches him a little apprehensively.
Patrick	Er –
	He stops. Chris is taking no notice of him at all.
Chris	Mmmmm?
Patrick	Nothing.
	He picks up a book and attempts to read it. But he is not really seeing the words on the page.
	Marcus comes in. He is lively, energetic, bright, a long-stay patient. He is much more middle-class than his accent (which he adopts to be one of the crowd) would suggest. He looks at Patrick and decides to ignore him for the moment.
Marcus	Hi Chris.
	He goes and sits on his bed which is opposite Patrick's.
Chris	Hello.
	He carries on with his model.
Marcus	Where's Keith?
Chris	Dunno. (*Looking up suddenly*) Your little brother's here. He's in the Playroom.
Marcus	I know. That's why I came in here. He's screaming the place down. He wants the little house, he says. My Mum keeps shovelling him into the Wendy House and he keeps kicking the other kids. I wish she wouldn't keep bringing him.
Chris	(*Quite detached, concentrating on his model*) It must be embarrassing to have a brother like that.
Marcus	My Mum spoils him rotten. I tell her not to bring him but she thinks he might get what I've got so she wants him to get used to hospital.
	He gets up and crosses to Chris's bed, staring openly at Patrick.
Chris	He's been messing with my models again. Your Mum's got no control over him.
Marcus	I know. (*To Patrick, flatly*) What's your name?
Patrick	Patrick.
Marcus	What's the matter with you?
Patrick	(*Putting his book down and swinging his legs down onto the floor*) Suspected appendicitis. I've got to have some tests though. Would you like to sit down?
Marcus	No thanks.
	He moves nearer to Chris's bed. A young nurse, Valerie, appears in the doorway. She is friendly and easy-going but very junior – scarcely older than the boys.

Valerie	Oh there you are, Marcus! What are you doing here? Your Mum and your little brother are in the Playroom. (*Knowing exactly what he is up to*) What are you up to, running off when they've come all this way to see you?
Marcus	(*Sliding towards the door furthest from the playroom*) I was just going to the toilet. I won't be a minute.

He darts off before Valerie can say anything else to him.

Chris	(*Amused*) You're wasting your time. He hates his brother. Mind you, I don't blame him. If that horrible little –
Valerie	(*Warning*) Chris! Language!
Chris	What did I say?
Valerie	Ah! It's what you were going to say though, isn't it? Can't have you using bad language in front of our new patient, can we?

She smiles sunnily at Patrick who has, however, wandered off into a world of his own.

Chris	I was only going to say that if that little darling touches my models again I'll rearrange his face for him.

Valerie has noticed Patrick's abstracted, worried air and crosses and sits on the end of his bed.

Valerie	Come on now! Let's have some sort of smile! You look as if you'd lost a fiver and found 5p! You've still got your appendix, haven't you?
Patrick	(*With an attempt at a grin*) Yeah!
Valerie	Well then! We're not going to eat you!
Patrick	That's another thing. When can I eat? I'm starving!
Valerie	Not just yet. When the Doctor's been around.
Chris	That's what they're like here. First three days they don't let you have any food. It's the Government cuts. Then, if they don't reckon your chances are too good they don't bother to feed you at all – saves money on the catering.
Valerie	(*Laughing*) That'll do, Chris!
Chris	You've got to be fighting fit to keep the food down they give you here, anyway. God! I don't know where they get it from. I'm going to use some of the fish fingers to do the thatched roofs on my cottages … Paint 'em black and put dots on 'em. You could play dominoes with 'em!

Valerie and Patrick give a slight laugh. Chris cuts out a further section of his model. There is a slight pause.

Chris	(*Casually*) How's Darren?
Valerie	(*Carefully*) I don't know. He's still in the Theatre.

Silence. Keith comes in. He is a sullen, suspicious boy who does not grasp things very quickly and suspects people are trying to make fun of him. He goes straight to his bed which is in the corner, next to Marcus's bed.

Valerie	Hello, Keith. What've you been up to?
Keith	(*Aggressively*) Watching the telly. Trying to. Can't you tell Marcus's Mum to go home with that kid? He kept running in and changing the channel and screaming.

Valerie	(*Wearily*) Oh dear ...
Keith	He's been here since this morning. I don't think they should let people who come to visit you in hospital be a nuisance.
Chris	What are you worried about? Your Mum hasn't been here since Christmas!
Keith	I don't want her to come, do I? Being a nuisance to everybody.
Valerie	(*Hastily*) Is Marcus in the Playroom?
Keith	No. Nor his Mum. Just his brother. The little black kid from the baby ward scratched his face, 'cause he took his lorry from him. You should have heard him scream. And he kicked him.
Valerie	(*Getting up from the end of Patrick's bed*) Oh dear! No rest for the wicked! Roll on tea-time. Tracy'll be on again then.
	She begins to go out of the door to the playroom.
Chris	You can bring me my tea at four o'clock. I'm feeling a bit low. I need looking after. I'll have cucumber sandwiches, and tea with lemon, and strawberries and cream please.
Valerie	Private patient are we? You'll get bread and marge and plum jam and a bit of angel cake if you're lucky!
	She goes out, back to the playroom. Keith, making sure that no-one can see what he's doing, takes a chocolate bar from his locker and lies down on his bed with his back to the rest of them.
Chris	They do the teas in the Playroom. You can load up and bring it back here if you want 'cause there's always loads of little kids throwing jam about. I always bring mine back here. Not that it's worth eating. I've got a load of my own stuff in my locker. Do you want a bit of Twix?
Patrick	I'm not allowed yet. Thanks.
Chris	Oh no, better not, then. They might trace it back to me. Take a bar of Twix out in the playroom and you've had it. They swarm all over you – smelly nappies and all. I can't stand little kids.
Patrick	I wouldn't mind something to eat. I'm starving. I haven't had anything since six o'clock yesterday. That's over twenty hours. When do the doctors come round?
Chris	About three usually. This glue's rubbish.
	He gets up irritably, limps across to the window and stares disgustedly at the vividly coloured poster taped up on the window.
Chris	I am sick and tired of Postman bleedin' Pat.
	He takes a Pentel and draws a large curly moustache on the poster.
Patrick	How long are you staying? I mean – when are you going out? Do you have to have an operation?
Chris	(*Briefly*) 'Spect so. I dunno. They keep changing their minds.
Patrick	(*Carefully*) I expect you get a bit bored.

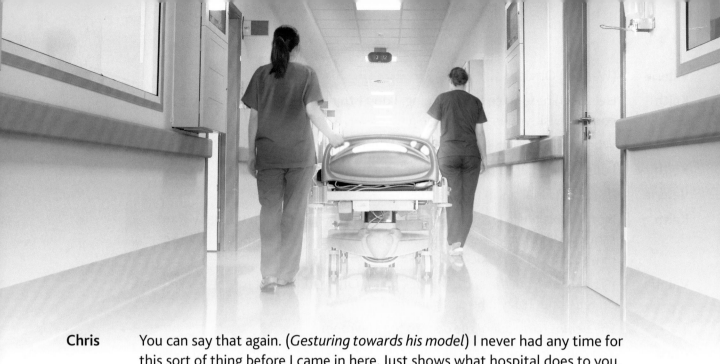

Chris	You can say that again. (*Gesturing towards his model*) I never had any time for this sort of thing before I came in here. Just shows what hospital does to you. I've spent hours on it … When I do go home my Mum'll shove it all in a carrier bag and crumple it all up. Then after a while she'll put it out for the dustman. 'Oh Christopher we can't have that cluttering the place up – collecting dust!'
Patrick	Won't she let you set it up in your room?
Chris	(*Jeering*) My room! My cupboard you mean. Get the bed in my room and you can't shut the door. I have to stand on the window-sill to get dressed – I'll get arrested one of these days. I suppose you've got a lovely big room with a train set and a snooker table and your own telly.
Patrick	(*Quickly*) No – (*Muttering*) It's not that big.
Chris	I bet! … At least there's a bit of space in here … I was in the Men's Ward for a couple of weeks before Christmas. That was terrible. All these old men coughing and spitting! There was one in the bed next to me, he'd had gallstones – and he kept them in a jam-jar on his locker. Disgusting! Just like little pebbles they were, and he kept showing them to everybody. Then there was another one in the corner bed who kept smoking his pipe under the covers when nobody was around. I reckon it was shredded underpants he was smoking – the smell! It was terrible.
Patrick	Is that why you came back here?
Chris	Not really. They decided it was bad for me to be there. They kept snuffing it, you see, in the Old Men's Ward. You know, you wake up in the morning and there's another set of curtains drawn –
Patrick	(*Shuddering*) Oh that's horrible. Do they leave the bodies behind the curtains?
Chris	Nah! Take them out on trolleys when nobody's looking. The last night I was in there I was fast asleep, and this old guy – really small he was – came over to my bed and got hold of my wrist and shook me and he kept saying, 'I'm going … I'm going!' Scared the life out of me. I'm not joking.
Patrick	What did you do?
Chris	I said, 'Well go on then!' and shoved him on the floor. Then I screamed blue murder for the night nurse … He was another curtain case by the morning.

Patrick	I couldn't stand that.
Chris	It's because I was fifteen. They thought I was too old for this ward, but after that, they decided I'd get psychologically disturbed if I stayed there so I came back here. Valerie – that nurse that was here just now – she says they ought to have teenage wards. They did where she comes from.
Patrick	Where's that?
Chris	Oh some dump up North.
	Marcus returns, peering round the door cautiously to make sure that the coast is clear.
Marcus	Has she gone?
Chris	Valerie? Yes.
Marcus	Good.
	He comes into the ward and crosses and sits on the end of his bed and looks cheerfully at Chris and Patrick.
Chris	She'll be back though … She's madly in love with me.
	As he speaks he is reading the instructions on his model and his mind is on that.
	She can't keep away from me … I have this problem with all the nurses … (*He looks across at Marcus*) Anyway she'll be looking for you. Leroy's scratched your brother's face open.
Marcus	(*Unimpressed*) Oh, he does that to everybody … Mind you, it's a brilliant idea when it comes to my brother. There's some horrible kids in this place but he's worse than any of them. My Mum doesn't believe in violence so she never hits him – she goes berserk when I do. And she sits up all night with my Dad discussing my aggressive tendencies and where she's gone wrong.
	He chuckles delightedly.
Chris	Your Mum's a nutcase.
Marcus	(*Sighing*) Yeah, I know. She goes to consciousness raising groups … She's going veggie as well. She cooks these great big panfuls of beans and stuff. Looks like puke. She reckons that my diet is the reason I'm in here. My Dad stops off at McDonald's on the way home from work and says he's not too hungry when he gets in. So she saves up all the bean stuff and puts some lentils in it and gives it to him the next day. Do you know, she won't let me or my brother have any aggressive toys or anything. She's trying to find a Save the Whale game for my computer. I can't have nasty War games because she's trying to breed a better sort of boy … My brother's the most violent little devil ever. I hate him. He got thrown out of his playgroup last week.
Patrick	What for?
Marcus	He set fire to the Wendy House.
	They laugh. Keith turns over angrily to face them.
Keith	I wish you'd shut up. I'm trying to get to sleep.
Marcus	That's all you ever do. It's half past two in the afternoon, you know, not midnight.

Keith	Well, I get tired. When are they bringing Darren back?
Chris	Dunno.
Marcus	They were all rushing about with bottles of blood when I was down the corridor. But I couldn't see anything.
Keith	You're not supposed to go down there. Sister'll murder you!
Marcus	I crawled past the office on my hands and knees. She didn't see me. Nobody saw me. I hid in that little alcove by the lifts to Casualty. I had a look in. There's hardly anyone there today.
Keith	I've been to Casualty.
Marcus	What for?
Keith	I stuck a wax crayon up my nose and I couldn't get it out.

Marcus roars with laughter.

Chris	When was this? Last week?
Keith	No! I was in the Infants!
Marcus	I thought you still were.
Keith	It was awful. They pushed these long steel things up my nose and twisted them round. It took four nurses to hold me down.
Marcus	What did you do a stupid thing like that for?
Keith	I don't know. It was a green crayon. This other kid wanted it. So I just stuck it up my nose and it broke off and got stuck.
Marcus	They should have shoved a wick up your nose and set fire to it and then all the wax would have melted and dripped out.
Keith	(*Puzzled*) No. They couldn't do that. It would be too hot.
Marcus	(*Jeering*) No–o–o–o! Oh go back to sleep.

Valerie returns, looking distressed and unwilling to talk. Marcus sidles across to the door, ready to disappear.

Chris	There he goes! Stop him! What's the little monster done now?
Valerie	What? Oh … No. I haven't come for Marcus. Your brother's all right, I think … I've just … Sister's sent me to collect these …

She crosses to Darren's bed and collects up his 'get well' cards. Marcus stands stock-still in the doorway; Keith watches her, puzzled; Patrick, with dawning realisation. He opens his mouth as if to speak, thinks better of it and picks up his book and stares unseeingly at it. It is as if the shutters have come down on Chris. Blank-faced, he goes to his bed and picks up his model, apparently absorbed in it.

Keith	What are you taking them for?
Valerie	(*Carefully*) Darren's Mum will be here – er – later. I'm just tidying up. Sister wants these in the office …

She stops. There is a tense pause.

Chris	How is Darren?

He does not look up from his model. He drops the words delicately, like pebbles into a pool. The only possible emotion he expresses is a kind of repressed anger.

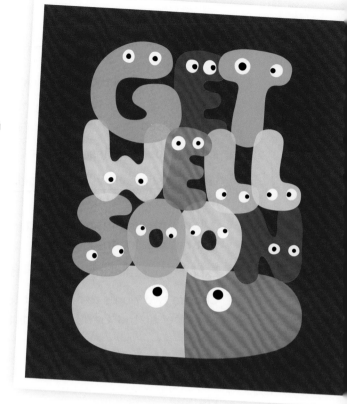

	Valerie bites her lip. She is too inexperienced to handle this situation very successfully.
Valerie	Oh. He's – fine. It's just he's being taken elsewhere. (*Hurriedly*) Sister will be along in a minute. She can tell you all about it. I've got to go and see to the little ones' teas …
	She goes out, left, towards the playroom, glad to escape. The four boys are quite still.
Keith	What's she mean, elsewhere? Why's she taken his cards away? Marcus!
	Slowly, Marcus crosses and sits on the end of Darren's bed. Keith takes a step towards him.
Keith	Marcus. What does she mean? What's happened to Darren? Why are they taking him somewhere else?
	Chris puts aside his model and limps angrily across to Keith.
Chris	(*In a ferocious undertone*) Shut up, shut up your stupid fat face! Go back to bed and stop driving everybody spare! I'm sick of your stupid voice, moaning on. Do you hear me, you stupid git!
	Patrick watches anxiously, Marcus lowers his head, Keith sits down abruptly. Chris limps back to his own bed, and sits down becoming absorbed, apparently, in his model.
Keith	(*Whining*) What have I done? What did I say? You've got no right to talk to me like that, Christopher Greenway. You're not the boss of this ward.
	But no-one is paying him any attention. He lies down on his bed with his back to them all, hunched up and angry. The others are all silent and still.
Chris	(*Singing tunelessly under his breath*) Postman Pat – Postman Pat – Postman Pat and his black and white cat …
	The four boys are all quite still as the lights fade.

The End

Thinking about the play

1 Chris has been on the ward a long time and has strong opinions on life in hospital. Write one full sentence for each of the following.

This is what Chris thinks about:

> the medical care in the hospital
> the food given to patients
> visitors

> going home
> children

2 How was Chris affected by his move to the men's ward? Explain your answer.

3 Choose the word that you think best describes Patrick's attitude to Chris:

> wary
> impressed

> nervous
> careful

> afraid
> sympathetic

Explain your thinking.

4 Here are some views of what being in hospital has done to Chris. Which one is nearest to your own view?

> It has made Chris more adult.
> It has made Chris kinder.

> It has made Chris impatient.
> It has made Chris angry.

Explain your thinking as clearly as possible.

5 Choose two words to describe the reaction of each of the boys when Valerie comes to gather up the 'Get Well' cards for Darren.

Chris	Patrick
Marcus	Keith

6 Chris is the most developed character in the play. Think of four or five words to describe Chris and place them in one or other of the columns below.

Positive	Negative

Now write a paragraph describing Chris, using the words you have placed in the columns.

7 Here are some views on the theme of the play. Say what you think of each view and then suggest which is the most important.

> It's about fear and not being able to talk about it.
> It's a play about growing up.
> It's about loneliness.
> It's about rivalry and wanting to be top dog.

> It's about friendship.
> It's about sickness and death.
> It's about bravery.

Writing Task

Complete this task in your portfolio, p. 41.

Imagine you are Chris. Write four diary entries describing your stay in the men's ward. Each entry should refer to a different part of the night, for example 10 p.m., 2 a.m., 4 a.m., 6 a.m. You can use the YWT guidelines on writing a diary entry (p. 78) and on describing a place (p. 244) to help you.

Research

The 2014 feature film *The Fault in Our Stars* was a big success with audiences and critics alike. Write a short report on the film and its treatment of teenage illness. You could begin your research by looking on the Internet Movie Database site, www.imdb.com.

Oral Language

Working in pairs, improvise the following scene:

> Valerie meets Chris on the corridor outside the children's ward two days after the final scene in the play. They haven't seen each other since.

> What Valerie wants: she wants to speak to Chris, offer her sympathy and find out how he is feeling.

> What Chris wants: he wants to avoid talking about Darren and about his own feelings.

Or:

Valerie is not much older than the boys in the ward. Complete a short monologue in which she expresses her thoughts and feelings at the end of the play and perform it for your class. Begin with *Sister's down there now. She's breaking the news to Darren's mother. I couldn't do that ...*

Groupwork

Working in groups of six, with one person acting as the director, and the other five speaking the parts of the characters, prepare a dramatised reading of the play.

> Decide what props, if any, you think are essential.

> Think about the space you will use to stage the reading.

> Rehearse the reading a number of times.

> When you are ready, read the play for your classmates. If possible, make a recording of the reading.

Wrapping up

To wrap up this chapter on Drama, devise your own three- to four-minute play.

Working in groups of five, write or improvise a short script from the following scenario. There are parts for four of the five members of the group. The fifth member acts as the director.

Scenario

Four first-year students are in their post-primary school. It is break time. The four are discussing whether they want a fifth student, who is new to the school, to be part of their group. They have to be careful – they don't want other students or the teacher on supervision to overhear what they're saying.

> **Student A** is full of confidence and wants to include the other student in the group.
> **Student B** is suspicious of new people and doesn't want anyone else in the group.
> **Student C** enjoys teasing Student B.
> **Student D** is very bright but is jealous that Student A is the most popular one in the group.

Task

> Assign the parts. Assign a name to each character.
> Discuss how you think the conversation might develop.
> Discuss what each person wants and how that will influence what he or she says.
> Discuss how the scene might end.
> Improvise the scene, remembering that it will last for no more than three or four minutes.
> Make sure that everyone speaks at least three times, though some characters might speak more than the others.

After the improvisation, the director leads a discussion on how well the scene worked. After this review, rehearse again. When you are ready, act out your play for the class. If you can, make a recording of your play.

Chapter Six
STORIES B

In these stories you'll meet characters with their own hopes, fears and dreams. Some cope well in their world; others less so.

Communicating

› You will listen actively and take part in class discussion.
› You will give your opinions and express your feelings.
› You will work in pairs and groups.
› You will speak and write with purpose about the stories and each other's work.
› You will write in a range of forms.

Exploring and Using Language

› You will edit your work and learn from the stories to improve your own writing.
› You will talk about the key moments in the stories and write about them in thoughtful ways.
› You will use your imagination to respond to the stories.
› You will develop your own personal way of writing.
› You will complete a quiz on the *Be Inspired!* website to check your knowledge of story terms.

Understanding Language

› You will learn about and be reminded of the importance of writing and speaking accurately.
› You will think about and talk about the purpose of your spoken and written texts.
› You will experiment with language.
› You will make language choices to match both your purpose and your audience as you perform a script, hot-seat a character, write a letter, plan and write a short story.
› You will make judgements about your own writing and think about how to improve it.
› You will read an author biography online on the *Be Inspired!* website.

Wrapping Up

› To wrap up you will write your own story.

www.edco.ie/beinspired

Sometimes other people don't always see who we are on the inside. Sometimes even we don't see who we really are.

Author Biography

Check out the *Be Inspired!* website for Helen Dunmore's author biography.

My Polish Teacher's Tie

HELEN DUNMORE

I wear a uniform, blue overall and white cap with the school logo on it. Part-time catering staff, that's me, £3.89 per hour. I dish out tea and buns to the teachers twice a day, and I shovel chips on to the kids' trays at dinner-time. It's not a bad job. I like the kids.

The teachers pay for their tea and buns. It's one of those schemes teachers are good at. So much into a kitty and that entitles them to cups of tea and buns for the rest of the term. Visitors pay, too, or it wouldn't be fair. Very keen on fairness, we are, here.

> *Explanation –*
> **Irony**
>
> Irony is saying one thing but meaning the opposite. One example of irony in the story is when Carla says: 'Very keen on fairness, we are, here.'

It was ten-forty-five when the Head got up to speak. He sees his staff together for ten minutes once a week, and as usual he had a pile of papers in front of him. I never listen to any of it as a rule, but as I was tipping up the teapot to drain I heard him mention Poland.

I am half-Polish. They don't know that here. My name's not Polish or anything. It was my mother, she came here after the war. I spoke Polish till I was six, baby Polish full of rhymes Mum taught me. Then my father put a stop to it. 'You'll get her all mixed up, now she's going to school. What use is Polish ever going to be to her?' I can't speak it now. I've got a tape, a tape of me speaking Polish with Mum. I listen, and I think I'm going to understand what we're saying, and then I don't.

'... long-term aim is to arrange a teacher exchange – several Polish teachers are looking for penfriends in English schools, to improve their written English ... so if you're interested, the information's all here ...'

He smiled, wagging the papers, and raised his eyebrows. I wrung out a cloth and wiped my surfaces. I was thinking fast. Thirteen minutes before I was due downstairs.

The meeting broke up and the Head vanished in a knot of teachers wanting to talk to him. I lifted the counter-flap, tucked my hair under the cap, and walked across. Teachers are used to getting out of the way of catering staff without really seeing them.

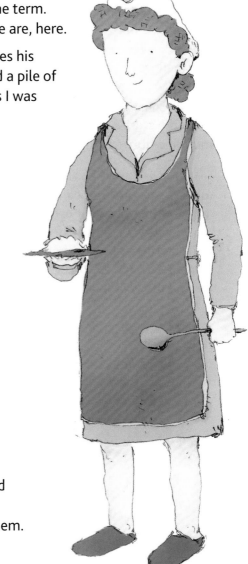

'Excuse me,' I said, pushing forward, 'excuse me' and they did. Then I was in front of the Head. 'Excuse me,' I said again, and he broke off what he was saying. I saw him thinking *trouble*. The kids chucking chips again. He stitched a nice smile on his face and said, 'Oh, er – Mrs, er – Carter. Is there a problem?'

'No,' I said. 'I was just wondering, could I have that address?'

'Address?'

'The Polish one. You said there was a Polish teacher who wanted an English penfriend.'

'Oh. Ah, yes. Of course.' He paused, looking at me as if it might be a trick question. 'Is it for yourself?'

'I'd like to write to a Polish teacher.'

'Oh,' he said. 'Yes. Of course, Mrs Carter.'

I took the address and smiled at him.

When Steve's first letter came I saw he'd taken it for granted I was a teacher. The person he had in his head when he was writing to me was an English teacher, a real professional. This person earned more money than him and had travelled and seen places and done things he'd never been able to do. He was really called Stefan, but he said he was going to call himself Steve when he wrote to me.

Jade saw the letter. 'What's that, Mum?'

'Just a letter. You can have the stamp if you want.'

In the second letter Steve told me that he wrote poetry.

> *I have started a small literary magazine in our department. If you want, I am happy to send you some of our work.*

I told him about Jade. I told him about the songs my mother taught me in Polish, the ones I used to know but I'd forgotten. I didn't write anything about my job. Let him think what he wanted to think. I wasn't lying.

The first poem he sent me was about a bird in a coal mine. He sent me the English translation. This bird flew down the main shaft* and got lost in the tunnels underground, then it sang and sang until it died. Everyone heard it singing, but no one could find it. I liked that poem. It made me think maybe I'd been missing something, because I hadn't read any poetry since I left school. I wrote back, '*Send me the Polish, just so I can see it.*' When the Polish came I tried it over in my head. It sounded a bit like the rhymes my mother used to sing.

At first we wrote every week, then it was twice. I used to write a bit every day then make myself wait until the middle of the week to send it. I wrote after Jade was in bed. Things would suddenly come to me. I'd write, '*Oh, Steve, I've just remembered ...*', or '*... Do you see what I mean, Steve, or does it sound funny?*' It made it seem more like talking to him when I used his name.

---

* **main shaft:** a vertical passageway in a mine

He wrote me another poem. It was about being half-Polish and half-English, and the things I'd told him about speaking Polish until I was six and then forgetting it all:

> Mother, I've lost the words you gave me.
> Call the police, tell them
> there's a reward, I'll do anything …

He was going to put it in the literary magazine, *'if you have no objection, Carla'.* That was the way he wrote, always very polite. I said it was fine by me.

One day the Head stopped me and said, 'Did you ever write to that chap? The Polish teacher?'

'Yes,' I said. Nothing more. Let him think I'd written once then not bothered. Luckily, Mrs Callendar came up to talk about OFSTED.

'Ah, yes, OFSTED. Speaking of visitors,' said the Head, raising his voice the way he does so that one minute he's talking to you and the next it's a public announcement, 'I have news of progress on the Polish teachers' exchange. A teacher will be coming over from Katowice next month. His name is Stefan Jeziorny, and he will be staying with Mrs Kenward. We're most grateful to you for your hospitality, Valerie.'

Mrs Kenward flushed.* The Head beamed at nobody. Stefan Jeziorny, I thought. I had clicked, even though I was so used to thinking of him as Steve. Why hadn't he said he was coming?

I dropped Jade off to tea with her friend. There was a letter waiting when I got home. I tore it open and read it with my coat still on. There was a bit about my last letter, and poetry, and then the news.

> You will know from your school, Carla, that I will come to England. I am hoping to make many contacts for the future, for other teachers who will also come to English schools. I hope, Carla, that you will introduce me to your colleagues. I will stay with an English family who offer accommodation.

I felt terrible. He sounded different, not like Steve. Not just polite any more, but all stiff, and a bit hurt. He must have thought I'd known about his visit from the other teachers, and I hadn't wanted to invite him to stay with me. But what was worse was that he was going to expect to meet me. Or not me, exactly, but the person he'd been writing to, who didn't really exist. *'I have been corresponding with a colleague of yours, Carla Carter,'* he'd say to the other teachers. Then he'd wait for someone to say, *'Yes, of course, Carla's here, she's expecting you.'*

Colleagues don't wear blue overalls and white caps and work for £3.89 an hour. Somebody'd remember me asking the Head for his address, and there'd be a whisper running all round, followed by a horrible silence. They'd all look round at the serving-hatch and there I'd be, the big teapot in my hand and a plate of buns in front of me. And Steve'd look too. He'd still be smiling, because that's what you do in a foreign place when you don't know what's going on.

He'd think I was trying to make a fool of him, making him believe I was a teacher. Me, Carla Carter, part-time catering assistant, writing to him about poetry.

I could be off sick. I could swap with Jeannie. She could do the teachers' breaks. Or I could say Jade was ill.

---

* **flushed:** became red with embarrassment

No. That wouldn't work. Steve had my name, and my address. I sat down and spread out his letter again, then I went to the drawer and got all his other letters. I'd never had letters like that before and I was never going to again, not after Steve knew who I really was.

I didn't write, and Steve didn't write again either. I couldn't decide if it was because he was hurt, or because he knew he'd be seeing me soon anyway. The fuss Valerie Kenward made about having him to stay, you'd think the Pope was coming for a fortnight. I never liked her. Always holding up the queue saying she's on a diet, and then taking the biggest bun.

'If you're that bothered,' I said, 'he can come and stay in my flat, with me and Jade.' But I said it to myself, in my head. I knew he'd want to be with the other teachers.

I couldn't stop looking for letters. And then there was the poetry book I'd bought. It seemed a shame to bin it. It might come in handy for Jade, I thought.

A week went by, eight days, ten. Each morning I woke up and I knew something was wrong before I could remember what it was. It got worse every day until I thought, *Sod it, I'm not going to worry any more.*

The next morning-break the buns were stale. Valerie Kenward poked them, one after another. 'We ought to get our money back,' she said. But she still took one, and waited while I filled the teapot from the urn.

'How's it going?' Susie Douglas asked her.

'Hard work!' stage-whispered Valerie, rolling her eyes.

'He's not got much conversation, then?'

'Are you joking? All he wants to talk about is poetry. It's hell for the kids. He doesn't mean to be funny but they can't keep a straight face. It's the way he talks. Philippa had to leave the room at supper-time, and I can't say I blame her.'

You wouldn't, I thought. If ever anyone brought up their kids to be pleased with themselves, it's Valerie Kenward.

'And even when it's quite a well-known writer like Shakespeare or Shelley, you can't make out what he's on about. It's the accent.'

'He *is* Polish. I mean, how many Polish poets could you pronounce?' asked Susie.

'And his *ties!'* went on Valerie. 'You've never seen anything like them.'

I looked past both of them. I'd have noticed him before, if I hadn't been so busy. He was sitting stiffly upright, smiling in the way people smile when they don't quite understand what's going on. The Head was wagging a sheaf of papers in front of him, and talking very loudly, as if he was deaf. Steve. Stefan Jeziorny. He was wearing a brown suit with padded shoulders. It looked too big for him. His tie was wider than normal ties, and it was red with bold green squiggles on it. It was a terribly hopeful tie. His shoes had a fantastic shine on them. His face looked much too open, much too alive, as if a child Jade's age had got into an adult's body.

'Isn't that tea made *yet?*' asked Valerie.

I looked at her. 'No,' I said. 'It's not. Excuse me,' and I lifted the counter-flap and ducked past her while her mouth was still open. I walked up to where Steve was sitting. He looked round at me the way a child does when he doesn't know anyone at a party, hoping for rescue.

'Hello,' I said. He jumped up, held out his hand. 'How do you do?' he asked, as if he really wanted to know. I took his hand. It was sweaty, as I'd known it would be. He was tense as a guitar string.

'I'm Carla,' I said.

'Carla?' He couldn't hide anything. I saw it all swim in his eyes. Surprise. Uncertainty. What was he going to do? And then I saw it. Pleasure. A smile lit in his eyes and ran to his mouth.

'Carla! You are Carla Carter. My penfriend.'

'Yes.'

Then he did something I still can't quite believe. He stood there holding on to my hand right in the middle of the staffroom, his big bright tie blazing, and he sang a song I knew. It went through me like a knife through butter. A Polish song. I knew it, I knew it. I knew the words and the tune. It was one of the songs my mother used to sing to me. I felt my lips move. There were words in my mouth, words I didn't understand. And then I was singing, stumbling after him all the way to the end of the verse.

'Good heavens. How very remarkable. I didn't realise you were Polish, Mrs ... er ...' said the Head as he bumbled round us flapping his papers.

'Nor did I,' I said. But I wasn't going to waste time on the Head. I wanted to talk about poetry. I smiled at Steve. His red tie with its bold green squiggles was much too wide and much too bright. It was a flag from another country, a better country than the ones either of us lived in. 'I like your tie,' I said.

Thinking about the story

1 What is Carla's attitude to the teachers in the school? Find three things that Carla says which show her attitude.

2 Why did Carla's father stop her speaking Polish? Do you think he was right to do so?

3 Suggest two reasons why the letters from Steve stopped coming.

4 '... the person he'd been writing to, who didn't really exist ...' What does this thought suggest to you about Carla and how she feels about herself? Do you think the Carla of the letters does exist? Explain your answer.

BE INSPIRED!

5 'It was a terribly hopeful tie.' Complete this sentence: 'I think the tie was hopeful because …'

6 'Valerie Kenward will never know the real Carla because she is too much of a snob.' Do you agree with this statement? Explain your thinking.

7 What, in your view, is the main theme of the story?

> hope   > identity – knowing who you are   > other …

> class difference   > connections

In your portfolio, p. 44, write two paragraphs explaining your opinion. Use references to the story to support the points you make.

Oral Language

What makes people who they are? Is it their:

> job   > education   > personality

> hopes and dreams   > nationality   > family?

Organise your thoughts and make a short oral presentation to the class.

Writing Task

1 Write a letter that Steve might have sent to Carla; use everything Carla tells us about Steve's letters to make it sound as much like him as you can. (See the YWT, p. 81, for tips on writing informal or personal letters.)

Or:

2 Write the dialogue for a scene in which the Head tells his wife about something remarkable that happened in school between one of the canteen staff and a visiting Polish teacher. Try to catch his tone and attitude.

Groupwork

Hot-seat Carla and find out how she felt at the end of the day after her meeting with Steve. The student in the hot seat should try to convey the chatty, informal way Carla speaks. The student(s) asking the questions should act and think like the host of a TV talk show who wants to find out what the interviewee really thinks.

When his family is murdered, a little boy toddles up the street to a graveyard.

How Nobody Came to the Graveyard

FROM *THE GRAVEYARD BOOK*

NEIL GAIMAN

> ***Rattle his bones***
> ***Over the stones***
> ***It's only a pauper***
> ***Who nobody owns***
>
> Traditional nursery rhyme

Author Biography
Check out the *Be Inspired!* website for Neil Gaiman's author biography.

Chapter 1

There was a hand in the darkness, and it held a knife. The knife had a handle of polished black bone, and a blade finer and sharper than any razor. If it sliced you, you might not even know you had been cut, not immediately.

The knife had done almost everything it was brought to that house to do, and both the blade and the handle were wet.

The street door was still open, just a little, where the knife and the man who held it had slipped in, and wisps of night-time mist slithered and twined into the house through the open door.

The man Jack paused on the landing. With his left hand he pulled a large white handkerchief from the pocket of his black coat, and with it he wiped off the knife and his gloved right hand which had been holding it; then he put the handkerchief away. The hunt was almost over. He had left the woman in her bed, the man on the bedroom floor, the older child in her brightly coloured bedroom, surrounded by toys and half-finished models. That only left the little one, a baby, barely a toddler, to take care of. One more and his task would be done.

He flexed his fingers. The man Jack was, above all things, a professional, or so he told himself, and he would not allow himself to smile until the job was completed.

His hair was dark and his eyes were dark and he wore black leather gloves of the thinnest lambskin.

The toddler's room was at the very top of the house. The man Jack walked up the stairs, his feet silent on the carpeting. Then he pushed open the attic door, and he walked in. His shoes were black leather, and they were polished to such a shine that they looked like dark mirrors: you could see the moon reflected in them, tiny and half full.

The real moon shone through the casement window. Its light was not bright, and it was diffused by the mist, but the man Jack would not need much light. The moonlight was enough. It would do.

He could make out the shape of the child in the cot, head and limbs and torso.

The cot had high, slatted sides, to prevent the child from getting out. Jack leaned over, raised his right hand, the one holding the knife, and he aimed for the chest …

… and then he lowered his hand. The shape in the cot was a teddy bear. There was no child.

The man Jack's eyes were accustomed to the dim moonlight, so he had no desire to turn on an electric light. And light was not that important, after all. He had other skills.

The man Jack sniffed the air. He ignored the scents that had come into the room with him, dismissed the scents that he could safely ignore, honed in on the smell of the thing he had come to find. He could smell the child: a milky smell, like chocolate chip cookies, and the sour tang of a wet, disposable, night-time nappy. He could smell the baby shampoo in its hair, and something small and rubbery – *a toy,* he thought, and then, *no, something to suck* – that the child had been carrying.

The child had been here. It was here no longer. The man Jack followed his nose down the stairs through the middle of the tall, thin house. He inspected the bathroom, the kitchen, the airing cupboard, and, finally, the downstairs hall, in which there was nothing to be seen but the family's bicycles, a pile of empty shopping bags, a fallen nappy and the stray tendrils of fog that had insinuated themselves into the hall from the open door to the street.

The man Jack made a small noise then, a grunt that contained in it both frustration and also satisfaction. He slipped the knife into its sheath in the inside pocket of his long coat, and he stepped out into the street. There was moonlight, and there were street lights, but the fog stifled everything, muted light and muffled sound and made the night shadowy and treacherous. He looked down the hill towards the light of the closed shops, then up the street, where the last high houses wound up the hill on their way to the darkness of the old graveyard.

The man Jack sniffed the air. Then, without hurrying, he began to walk up the hill.

Ever since the child had learned to walk he had been his mother and father's despair and delight, for there never was such a boy for wandering, for climbing up things, for getting into and out of things. That night, he had been woken by the sound of something on the floor beneath him falling with a crash. Awake, he soon became bored, and had begun looking for a way out of his cot. It had high sides, like the walls of his playpen downstairs, but he was convinced that he could scale it. All he needed was a step …

He pulled his large, golden teddy bear into the corner of the cot, then, holding the railings in his tiny hands, he put his foot on to the bear's lap, the other foot up on the bear's head and he pulled himself up into a standing position, and then he half climbed, half toppled over the railing and out of the cot.

He landed with a muffled thump on a small mound of furry, fuzzy toys, some of them presents from relations from his first birthday, not six months gone, some of them inherited from his older sister. He was surprised when he hit the floor, but he did not cry out: if you cried they came and put you back in your cot.

He crawled out of the room.

Stairs that went up were tricky things, and he had not yet entirely mastered them. Stairs that went down however, he had discovered, were fairly simple. He did them sitting down, bumping from step to step on his well-padded bottom.

He sucked on his dummy, which his mother had just begun to tell him that he was getting too old for.

His nappy had worked itself loose on his journey on his bottom down the stairs, and when he reached the last step, when he reached the little hall and stood up, the nappy fell off. He stepped out of it. He was only wearing a child's nightshirt. The stairs that led back up to his room and his family were steep and forbidding, but the door to the street was open and inviting …

The child stepped out of the house a little hesitantly. The fog wreathed around him like a long-lost friend. And, uncertainly at first, then with increasing speed and confidence, the boy tottered up the hill.

The fog was thinner as you approached the top of the hill. The half-moon shone, not as bright as day, not by any means, but enough to see the graveyard, enough for that.

Look.

You could see the abandoned funeral chapel, iron doors padlocked, ivy on the sides of the spire, a small tree growing out of the guttering at roof level.

You could see stones and tombs and vaults and memorial plaques. You could see the occasional dash or scuttle of a rabbit or a vole or a weasel as it slipped out of the undergrowth and across the path.

You would have seen these things, in the moonlight, if you had been there that night.

You might not have seen a pale, plump woman, who walked the path near the front gates, and if you had seen her, with a second, more careful glance you would have realised that she was only moonlight, mist and shadow. The plump, pale woman was there, though. She walked the path that led through a clutch of half-fallen tombstones towards the front gates.

The gates were locked. They were always locked at four in the afternoon in winter, at eight at night in summer. A spike-topped iron railing ran around part of the cemetery, a high brick wall around the rest of it. The bars of the gates were closely spaced: they would have stopped a grown man from getting through, even stopped a ten-year-old child.

'Owens!' called the pale woman, in a voice that might have been the rustle of the wind through the long grass. 'Owens! Come and look at this!'

She crouched down and peered at something on the ground, as a patch of shadow moved into the moonlight, revealing itself to be a grizzled man in his mid-forties. He looked down at his wife, and then looked at what she was looking at, and he scratched his head.

'Mistress Owens?' he said, for he came from a more formal age than our own. 'Is that what I think it is?'

And at that moment the thing he was inspecting seemed to catch sight of Mrs Owens, for it opened its mouth, letting the rubber nipple it was sucking fall to the ground, and it reached out a small, chubby fist, as if it were trying for all the world to hold on to Mrs Owens' pale finger.

'Strike me silly,' said Mr Owens, 'if that isn't a baby.'

'Of course it's a baby,' said his wife. 'And the question is, what is to be done with it?'

'I dare say that is a question, Mistress Owens,' said her husband. 'And yet, it is not *our* question. For this here baby is unquestionably alive, and as such is nothing to do with us, and is no part of our world.'

'Look at him smile!' said Mrs Owens. 'He has the sweetest of smiles,' and with one insubstantial hand she stroked the child's sparse blond hair. The little boy giggled with delight.

A chilly breeze blew across the graveyard, scattering the fog in the lower slopes of the place (for the graveyard covered the whole of the top of the hill, and its paths wound up the hill and down and back upon themselves). A rattling: someone at the main gate of the graveyard was pulling and shaking it, rattling the old gates and the heavy padlock and chain that held them.

'There now,' said Owens, 'it's the babe's family, come to bring him back to the loving bosom. Leave the little man be,' he added, because Mrs Owens was putting her insubstantial arms around the toddler, smoothing, stroking.

Mrs Owens said, 'He dun't look like nobody's family, that one.' The man in the dark coat had given up on rattling the main gates and was now examining the smaller side gate. It, too, was well locked. There had been some vandalism in the graveyard the previous year, and the council had Taken Steps.

'Come on, Mistress Owens. Leave it be. There's a dear,' said Mr Owens, when he saw a ghost, and his mouth dropped open, and he found himself unable to think of anything to say.

You might think – and if you did, you would be right – that Mr Owens should not have taken on so at seeing a ghost, given that Mr and Mrs Owens were themselves dead and had been for a few hundred years now, and given that the entirety of their social life, or very nearly, was spent with those who were also dead. But there was a difference between the folk of the graveyard and *this:* a raw, flickering, startling shape the grey colour of television static, all panic and naked emotion which flooded the Owenses as if it were their own. Three figures, two large, one smaller, but only one of them was in focus, was more than an outline or a shimmer. And the figure said, *My baby! He is trying to harm my baby!*

A clattering. The man outside was hauling a heavy metal rubbish bin across the alley to the high brick wall that ran around that part of the graveyard.

'Protect my son!' said the ghost, and Mrs Owens thought it was a woman. Of course, the babe's mother.

'What did he do to you?' asked Mrs Owens, but she was not certain that the ghost could hear her. Recently dead, poor love, she thought. It's always easier to die gently, to wake in due time in the place you were buried, to come to terms with your death and to get acquainted with the other inhabitants. This creature was nothing but alarm and fear for her child, and her panic, which felt to the Owenses like a low-pitched screaming, was now attracting attention, for other pale figures were coming from all over the graveyard.

'Who are you?' Caius Pompeius asked the figure. His headstone was now only a weathered lump of rock, but two thousand years earlier he had asked to be laid to rest on the mound beside the marble shrine, rather than to have his body sent back to Rome, and he was one of the most senior citizens of the graveyard. He took his responsibilities extremely seriously. 'Are you buried here?'

'Of course she's not! Freshly dead by the look of her.' Mrs Owens put an arm around the woman-shape and spoke to it privately, in a low voice, calm and sensible.

There was a thump and a crash from the high wall beside the alley. The rubbish bin had fallen. A man clambered up on to the top of the wall, a dark outline against the mist-smudged street lights. He paused for a moment, then climbed down the other side, holding on to the top of the wall, legs dangling, then let himself fall the last few feet, down into the graveyard.

'But my dear,' Mrs Owens said to the shape, now all that was left of the three shapes that had appeared in the graveyard. 'He's living. We're not. Can you imagine … '

The child was looking at them, puzzled. It reached for one of them, then the other, finding nothing but air. The woman-shape was fading fast.

'Yes,' said Mrs Owens, in response to something that no one else had heard. 'If we can, then we will.' Then she turned to the man beside her. 'And you, Owens? Will you be a father to this little lad?'

'Will I what?' said Owens, his brow crinkling.

'We never had a child,' said his wife. 'And his mother wants us to protect him. Will you say yes?'

The man in the black coat had tripped in the tangle of ivy and half-broken headstones. Now he got to his feet and walked forward more carefully, startling an owl, which rose on silent wings. He could see the baby and there was triumph in his eyes.

Owens knew what his wife was thinking when she used that tone of voice. They had not, in life and in death, been married for over two hundred and fifty years for nothing. 'Are you certain?' he asked. 'Are you sure?'

'Sure as I ever have been of anything,' said Mrs Owens.

'Then yes. If you'll be its mother, I'll be its father.'

'Did you hear that?' Mrs Owens asked the flickering shape in the graveyard, now little more than an outline, like distant summer lightning in the shape of a woman. It said something to her that no one else could hear, and then it was gone.

'She'll not come here again,' said Mr Owens. 'Next time she wakes it'll be in her own graveyard, or wherever it is she's going.'

Mrs Owens bent down to the baby and extended her arms. 'Come now,' she said, warmly. 'Come to mama.'

To the man Jack, walking through the graveyard towards them on a path, his knife already in his hand, it seemed as if a swirl of mist had curled around the child, in the moonlight, and that the boy was no longer there: just damp mist and moonlight and swaying grass.

He blinked and sniffed the air. Something had happened, but he had no idea what it was. He growled in the back of his throat, like a beast of prey, angry and frustrated.

'Hello?' called the man Jack, wondering if perhaps the child had stepped behind something. His voice was dark and rough, and there was an odd edge to it, as if of surprise or puzzlement at hearing himself speak.

The graveyard kept its secrets.

'Hello?' he called again. He hoped to hear a baby cry or utter a half-word, or to hear it move. He did not expect what he actually heard, a voice, silky smooth, saying:

'Can I help you?'

The man Jack was tall. This man was taller. The man Jack wore dark clothes. This man's clothes were darker. People who noticed the man Jack when he went about his business – and he did not like to be noticed – were troubled, or made uncomfortable, or found themselves unaccountably scared. The man Jack looked up at the stranger, and it was the man Jack who was troubled.

'I was looking for someone,' said the man Jack, slipping his right hand back into his coat pocket, so the knife was hidden, but there if he needed it.

'In a locked graveyard, at night?' said the stranger drily.

'It was just a baby,' said the man Jack. 'I was just passing, when I heard a baby cry, and I looked through the gates and I saw him. Well, what would anyone do?'

'I applaud your public-spiritedness,' said the stranger. 'Yet if you managed to find this child, how were you planning to get out of here with it? You can't climb back over the wall holding a baby.'

'I would have called until someone let me out,' said the man Jack.

A heavy jingling of keys. 'Well, that would have been me, then,' said the stranger. 'I would have had to let you out.' He selected one large key from the key ring, and said, 'Follow me.'

The man Jack walked behind the stranger. He took his knife from his pocket. 'Are you the caretaker, then?'

'Am I? Certainly, in a manner of speaking,' said the stranger. They were walking towards the gates and, the man Jack was certain, away from the baby. But the caretaker had the keys. A knife in the dark, that was all it would take, and then he could search for the child through the night, if he needed to.

He raised the knife.

'If there *was* a baby,' said the stranger, without looking back, 'it wouldn't have been here in the graveyard. Perhaps you were mistaken. It's unlikely that a child would have come in here, after all. Much more likely that you heard a nightbird, and saw a cat, perhaps, or a fox. They declared this place an official nature reserve, you know, thirty years ago, around the time of the last funeral. Now think carefully, and tell me you are *certain* that it was a child that you saw.'

The man Jack thought.

The stranger unlocked the side gate. 'A fox,' he said. 'They make the most uncommon noises, not unlike a person crying. No, your visit to this graveyard was a misstep, sir. Somewhere the child you seek awaits you, but he is not here.' And he let the thought sit there, in the man Jack's head for a moment before he opened the gate with a flourish. 'Delighted to have made your acquaintance,' he said. 'And I trust that you will find everything you need out there.'

The man Jack stood outside the gates to the graveyard. The stranger stood inside the gate, and he locked it again, and put the key away.

'Where are you going?' asked the man Jack.

'There are other gates than this,' said the stranger. 'My car is on the other side of the hill. Don't mind me. You don't even have to remember this conversation.'

'No,' said the man Jack, agreeably. 'I don't.' He remembered wandering up the hill, and what he had thought to be a child had turned out to be a fox, that a helpful caretaker had escorted him back out to the street. He slipped his knife into its sheath. 'Well,' he said. 'Goodnight.'

'A goodnight to you,' said the stranger, whom Jack had taken for a caretaker.

The man Jack set off down the hill, in pursuit of the infant.

Reminders –

Creating an atmosphere

Neil Gaiman creates a ghostly atmosphere through the words he uses and the sound of those words. Read the first three sentences of the story out loud. Note how the 's' and 'h' sounds and the long vowel sounds create a sense of quiet dread, while the final 'd' and 't' sounds in 'sliced' and 'cut' capture the sharp action of the knife.

> *There was a hand in the darkness, and it held a knife. The knife had a handle of polished black bone, and a blade finer and sharper than any razor. If it sliced you, you might not even know you had been cut, not immediately.*

Setting

The setting of a story can be really important. This story is set in an old graveyard, which adds to the creepy atmosphere.

 Check out the Against the Clock quiz on story terms on the *Be Inspired!* website.

Thinking about the story

1 In no more than five sentences, tell what happened to the baby when Jack was in the house.

2 How does the baby end up in the graveyard?

3 In your view, which of the following words best describes the man Jack?

> cold-hearted   > frightening
> methodical   > creepy
> professional

Explain your choice.

4 a) Which of these statements is closest to your view of Mrs Owens?

> Mrs Owens is bossy.   > Mrs Owens is kind-hearted.   > Mrs Owens is determined.

Explain your thinking.

b) Watch the video 'Thank You Mom' on the *Be Inspired!* website and say what you think Mrs Owens has in common with the mothers portrayed on screen.

5 Make a list of ten words from the story which you think help to create the ghostly atmosphere. For two of these words say why you chose them.

6 'How Nobody Came to the Graveyard' is the opening of a novel. What questions raised by this extract would make you want to read on to find the answers?

7 In your view, is this a good opening to a novel? Explain your answer.

Writing Task

Write a piece (about 10 or 12 lines) describing an old house or a churchyard. The piece should create a ghostly atmosphere. Pay attention to the sounds of the words and use at least three of the words that Neil Gaiman uses in 'How Nobody Came to the Graveyard'.

Groupwork

You are the writer of the novel. You have just written the opening chapter. Now you have to come up with a plausible reason to explain why Jack murdered the family and is hunting for the baby. Working in pairs, come up with two suggestions.

Research

Working in small groups, make a list of five stories (from books or films) that feature an orphan as the main character. Write a short report to share with the rest of the class.

Oral Language

Prepare a reading of the six opening paragraphs for reading aloud to the class. Make sure your reading captures the atmosphere and suspense of the story.

Have you ever imagined what it would be like to live on another planet? In this story, the absence of sunlight makes life on Venus almost unbearable.

All Summer in a Day

RAY BRADBURY

'Ready?'

'Ready.'

'Now?'

'Soon.'

'Do the scientists really know? Will it happen today, will it?'

'Look, look; see for yourself!'

Author Biography
Check out the *Be Inspired!* website for Ray Bradbury's author biography.

The children pressed to each other like so many roses, so many weeds, intermixed, anxiously peering out for a look at the hidden sun.

It rained.

It had been raining for seven years; thousands upon thousands of days compounded and filled from one end to the other with rain, with the drum and gush of water, with the sweet crystal fall of showers and the concussion of storms so heavy they were tidal waves come over the islands. A thousand forests had been crushed under the rain and grown up a thousand times to be crushed again. This was the way life was forever on the planet Venus, and this was the schoolroom of the children of the rocket men and women who had come to a raining world to set up civilisation and live out their lives.

'It's stopping! It's stopping!'

'Yes, yes!'

Margot stood apart from them, from these children who could never remember a time when there wasn't rain and rain and rain. They were all nine years old, and, if there had been a day, seven years ago, when the sun came out for an hour and showed its face to the stunned world, they could not recall. Sometimes at night she heard them stir, in remembrance, and she knew they were dreaming and remembering gold or a yellow crayon or a coin large enough to buy the world with. She knew they thought they remembered a warmness, like a blushing in the face, in the body, in the arms and legs and trembling hands. Then they always awoke to the tatting drum, the endless shaking down of clear bead necklaces upon the roof, the walk, the gardens, the forests, and their dreams were gone.

All day yesterday they had read in class about the sun. About how like a lemon it was, and how hot. And they had written small stories or essays or poems about it:

> I think the sun is a flower,
> That blooms for just one hour.

That was Margot's poem, read in a quiet voice and in the still classroom while the rain was falling outside.

'Aw, you didn't write that!' protested one of the boys.

'I did,' said Margot. 'I did.'

'William!' said the teacher.

That was yesterday. Now the rain was slackening, and the children were crushed before the great thick windows.

'Where's teacher?'

'She'll be back.'

'She'd better hurry or we'll miss it!'

They turned on themselves, like a feverish wheel, all tumbling spokes.

Margot stood alone. She was a very frail girl who looked as if she had been lost in the rain for years and the rain had washed out the blue from her eyes and the red from her mouth and the yellow from her hair. She was an old photograph dusted from an album, whitened away, and if she spoke at all her voice would be a ghost. Now she stood, separate, staring at the rain and the loud wet world beyond the huge glass.

'What're you looking at?' demanded William.

Margot said nothing.

'Speak when you're spoken to.' He gave her a shove. But she did not move; rather she let herself be moved only by him and nothing else.

They edged away from her; they would not look at her. She felt them go away. This was because she would play no games with them in the echoing tunnels of the underground city. If they tagged her and ran, she stood blinking after them and did not follow. When the class sang songs about happiness and life and games, her lips barely moved. Only when they sang about the sun and the summer did her lips move as she watched the drenched windows.

Then of course, the biggest crime of all was that she had come here only five years ago from Earth, and she remembered the sun and the way the sun was and the sky was when she was four in Ohio. And they, they had been on Venus all their lives, and they had been only two years old when last the sun came out and had long since forgotten the colour and heat of it and the way it really was. But Margot remembered.

'It's like a penny,' she said once, eyes closed.

'No, it's not!' the children cried.

'It's like a fire,' she said, 'in the stove.'

'You're lying. You don't remember!' cried the children.

But she remembered and stood quietly apart from all of them and watched the patterning windows. And once, a month ago, she refused to shower in the school shower rooms, and clutched her hands to her ears and over her head, screaming the water mustn't touch her head. So after that, dimly, dimly, she sensed it, she was different, and they knew her difference and kept away.

There was talk that her father and mother were taking her back to Earth next year; it seemed vital to her that they do so, though it would mean the loss of thousands of dollars to her family. The children hated her for all these reasons of big and little consequence. They hated her pale snow face, her waiting silence, her thinness, and possible future.

'Get away!' The boy gave her another push. 'What're you waiting for?'

Then, for the first time, she turned and looked at him. What she was waiting for was in her eyes.

'Well, don't wait around here!' cried the boys savagely.

'You won't see nothing!'

Her lips moved.

'Nothing!' he cried. 'It was all a joke, wasn't it?' He turned to the other children. 'Nothing's happening today. Is it?'

They all blinked at him and then, understanding, laughed and shook their heads. 'Nothing, nothing!'

'Oh, but,' Margot whispered, her eyes helpless. 'But this is the day, the scientists predict, they say, they know, the sun …'

'All a joke!' said the boy, and seized her roughly. 'Hey, everyone, let's put her in a closet before teacher comes!'

'No,' said Margot, falling back.

They surged about her, caught her up and bore her, protesting, and then pleading, and then crying, back into a tunnel, a room, a closet, where they slammed and locked the door. They stood looking at the door and saw it tremble from her beating and throwing herself against it. They heard her muffled cries. Then, smiling, they turned and went out and back down the tunnel to the classroom, just as the teacher arrived.

'Ready, children?' She glanced at her watch.

'Yes!' said everyone.

'Are we all here?'

'Yes!'

The rain slackened still more.

They crowded to the huge door.

The rain stopped.

It was as if, in the midst of a film concerning an avalanche, a tornado, a hurricane, a volcanic eruption, something had, first, gone wrong with the sound apparatus, thus muffling and finally cutting off all noise, all of the blasts and repercussions and thunders, and then, second, ripped the film from the projector and inserted in its place a peaceful tropical slide which did not move or tremble. The world ground to a standstill. The silence was so immense and unbelievable that you felt your ears had been stuffed or you had lost your hearing altogether. The children put their hands to their ears. They stood apart. The door slid back and the smell of the silent, waiting world came in to them.

Reminder –
Situation and setting

This is another story in which the setting, and the situation of the character, are very important.

The sun came out.

It was flaming bronze, and it was very large. The sky around it was a blazing blue tile colour. And the jungle burned with sunlight as the children, released from their spell, rushed out, yelling into the springtime.

'Now, don't go too far,' called the teacher after them. 'You've only two hours. You wouldn't want to get caught out!' But they were running and turning their faces up to the sky and feeling the sun on their cheeks like a warm iron; they were taking off their jackets and letting the sun burn their arms.

'Oh, it's better than the sun lamps.'

'Much, much better!'

They stopped running and stood in the great jungle that covered Venus, that grew and never stopped growing, tumultuously, even as you watched it. It was a nest of octopi, clustering up great arms of fleshlike weed, wavering, flowering in this brief spring. It was the colour of rubber and ash, this jungle, from the many years without sun. It was the colour of stones and white cheese and ink, and it was the colour of the moon.

The children lay out, laughing, on the jungle mattress, and heard it sigh and squeak under them, resilient and alive. They ran among the trees, they slipped and fell, they pushed each other, they played hide-and-seek and tag, but most of all they squinted at the sun until tears ran down their faces. They put their hands up to that yellowness and that amazing blueness and they breathed of the fresh, fresh air and listened and listened to the silence that suspended them in a blessed sea of no sound and no motion. They looked at everything and savoured everything. Then wildly, like animals escaped from their caves, they ran and ran in shouting circles. They ran for an hour and did not stop running.

And then –

In the midst of their running one of the girls wailed.

Everyone stopped.

The girl, standing in the open, held out her hand.

'Oh, look, look,' she said, trembling.

They came slowly to look at her opened palm.

In the centre of it, cupped and huge, was a single raindrop.

She began to cry, looking at it.

They glanced quietly at the sky.

'Oh. Oh.'

A few cold drops fell on their noses and their cheeks and their mouths. The sun faded behind a stir of mist. A wind blew cool around them. They turned and started to walk back toward the underground house, their hands at their sides, their smiles vanishing away.

A boom of thunder startled them, and like leaves before a new hurricane, they tumbled upon each other and ran. Lightning struck ten miles away, five miles away, a mile, a half mile. The sky darkened into midnight in a flash.

They stood in the doorway of the underground house for a moment until it was raining hard. Then they closed the door and heard the gigantic sound of the rain falling in tons and avalanches, everywhere and forever.

'Will it be seven more years?'

'Yes. Seven.'

Then one of them gave a little cry.

'Margot!'

'What?'

'She's still in the closet where we locked her.'

'Margot.'

They stood as if someone had driven them, like so many stakes, into the floor. They looked at each other and then looked away. They glanced out at the world that was raining now and raining and raining steadily. They could not meet each other's glances. Their faces were solemn and pale. They looked at their hands and feet, their faces down.

'Margot.'

One of the girls said, 'Well …'

No one moved.

'Go on,' whispered the girl.

They walked slowly down the hall in the sound of cold rain. They turned through the doorway to the room in the sound of the storm and thunder, lightning on their faces, blue and terrible. They walked over to the closet door slowly and stood by it.

Behind the closet door was only silence. They unlocked the door, even more slowly, and let Margot out.

Thinking about the story

1. Describe the difference that the sun makes to the planet when it comes out.

2. 'Margot stood apart from them … Margot stood alone.' Suggest three ways in which Margot stands apart from the other children. Explain your thinking.

3. Locking Margot in the closet was a cruel thing to do. Why might the children have done it?

4. How, do you think, will Margot react to the children locking her in the closet? Why, in your opinion, will she react in this way?

5. Do the children, other than Margot, seem happy on Venus? Explain your thinking.

6. Which of the following statements do you think explains why the other children don't like Margot?

   > She remembers the sun.
   > She keeps to herself and isn't friendly.
   > She reminds them that their own lives are miserable.
   > She's a bit strange.
   > She might be going back to Earth with her family.

   Explain your choice as clearly as you can.

7. Pick the theme that best describes the theme of the story:

   > bullying
   > feeling sorry for what you've done
   > loneliness
   > remembering a better time.

   Explain your choice.

Writing Task

In your portfolio, p. 45, write a concluding paragraph to the story that describes what happened immediately after Margot stepped out of the closet.

Groupwork

Hot-seat the boy whose idea it was to put Margot in the closet and find out why he did it and how he feels now. The student(s) asking the questions should act and think like the host of a TV talk show who wants to find out what the interviewee really thinks.

Oral Language

You are the boy whose idea it was to put Margot in the closet. Your teacher insists you must apologise to her before the whole class. Make your apology.

Wrapping up

In this chapter you:

> read carefully and thought about the stories
> gave your interpretation and opinions
> explained your thinking and argued your point of view
> contributed to class discussion
> responded in imaginative ways to the characters and their situations
> learned about some important features of writing stories.

Here is the final task to wrap up this chapter.

In your portfolio, p. 48, write one of the following short stories:

Story 1

The central character is a young girl (or boy). The setting of the story is a cold, harsh world. The character's situation is an isolated one. She tries to make friends with a group of other children but they reject her. She runs away. In a chance encounter with a kind person, she learns something important about herself that changes her life for the better.

Or:

Story 2

The central character is an old person. She (or he) lives on her own. The setting of the story is a lonely valley. Her situation is an isolated one. One day a young boy (or girl) calls to her door. He is tired and upset. The old person invites him in and listens to his story. She cooks him a meal and advises him what to do. She tells him something she has never told anyone else before. It is too late to leave so the boy sleeps in a spare bedroom. He realises that the bedroom once belonged to one of the children of the old woman. He thinks over what the old woman said to him. In the morning, he leaves, promising the old woman he will return.

Young Writer's Toolkit

Spelling alert: most used words

Here is a list of some of the most used words in English.

Groupwork

Working with a partner, test each other on the spelling of the words in the list.

Nouns		Verbs		Adjectives		Other
animal	number	asked	said	able	last	about
babies	part	called	saw	bad	little	against
case	people	came	say	beautiful	long	always
child	person	feel	see	big	many	because
children	place	felt	started	different	new	between
clothes	point	found	stopped	early	next	even
company	problem	get	take	few	old	might
day	school	give	telling	first	other	often
eye	something	going	think	frightened	own	should
fact	thing	have	thought	good	public	such
friend	time	knew	took	great	right	through
government	way	know	tried	high	same	toward
hand	week	leave	try	important	small	under
life	woman	look	use	interesting	young	until
man	work	make	wanted	large		very
money	world	running	want			where
morning	year					which
mother						would

Spelling alert: commonly misspelled words

The following are some of the most commonly misspelled words.

These words are hard to spell. On the following page, there are two simple methods that will help you to learn them.

Correct spelling	Remember	Correct spelling	Remember
across	one c	forward	begins with for
appearance	ends with –ance	immediately	ends with –ely
argument	no e after u	piece	i before e
beginning	double n before the –ing	really	two ls
business	begins with busi–	remember	–mem in the middle
completely	ends with –ely	sense	ends with –se
disappear	one s, two ps	surprise	begins with sur
disappoint	one s, two ps	tomorrow	one m, two rs
finally	two ls	truly	no e

1 Look, Say, Cover, Write, Check

> **Look** at each word on the page. Can you see any letters that go together? Are there any smaller words within the word? For example, in the word 'disappoint' you might see 'dis' at the beginning and 'point' at the end.
> **Say** each word carefully and slowly to yourself. Listen for the sounds in the words.
> **Cover** the word. Picture the word in your mind. Repeat the word to yourself.
> **Write** the word.
> **Check** to see if it is correct. If the word is not right, try again.

Groupwork

Working with a partner, use **Look**, **Say**, **Cover**, **Write** and **Check** to learn the words on the list and then test each other.

2 Memory phrases

Sometimes the spelling of a word does not follow any logical pattern. This is where a memory phrase can help. A memory phrase is a phrase or a sentence that helps you to remember difficult spellings. There are a number of ways you can create your own.

> You can create a sentence where the first letter of each word spells out the complete word. For example, if you want to remember how to spell the word 'because', you could come up with this sentence:

> **BECAUSE** = **B**ig **E**lephants **C**an **A**lways **U**nderstand **S**mall **E**lephants.

> For the word 'rhythm', you could use a sentence like:

> **RHYTHM** = **R**hythm **H**elps **Y**our **T**wo **H**ips **M**ove.

> You can create a sentence where the first letters spell out the parts of the word you find hard. For example, in the word 'address', you have to remember that there are two ds at the start and two ss at the end. The following sentence will help you:

> **ADDRESS** = **D**irectly **D**elivered letters are **S**afe and **S**ound.

> You can create a short phrase that helps you to remember the part of the word you sometimes misspell. For example, for 'separate', where many people leave out the first 'a', you might say:

> **SEPARATE** = There is **A RAT** in separate.

> You can also use a short phrase to help you to distinguish between two easily confused words. Take the example of 'desert' and 'dessert'. The following phrase might help:

> **DESERT or DESSERT** = There are two **S**ugars in the sweet one.

Writing Task

Go through the lists of the most used and most misspelled words. Pick three words that you sometimes misspell. Create your own memory phrase to help you to remember the spelling of each. Funny and humorous phrases are always easier to remember.

Writing stories

Here are some tools to help you to write stories.

1 Developing characters
2 Finding a plot
3 Writing dialogue
4 Story openings
5 The parts of a story
6 Story map
7 Following the rules – fairy tales

1 Developing characters

Every story needs a strong central character, and it is worth your while putting time and energy into creating one. Let's imagine you are going to write about a female character.

Begin by picturing the character in your mind. What does she look like? What kind of clothes does she wear? (Seeing the character in your mind's eye will help you to think about her personality. If your imagination fails you, use a photograph as a starting point.)

Think of three positive adjectives and three negative adjectives to describe her personality, for example:

Positive	Negative
brave	cruel
determined	wilful
loyal	snobbish

Decide on the relationship(s) that matters most to her. It could be a relationship with a sister, a brother, a friend or a parent. Now think about the character's situation. Does she live with her family? Is she happy? Why? Why not? What atmosphere surrounds her?

Imagine the way the character speaks. Write down two things she might say, for example 'Don't blame me!' or 'It's always the same here.' Have you found your character's voice?

Think of the possession that means most to your character and why she treasures it.

Using your imagination in this way will help you to create an interesting character.

Creating a character – a brief summary:

› Picture the character.
› Think about the different aspects of the character's personality – both positive and negative.
› Put the character in a relationship.
› Decide on the character's situation.
› Capture the character's voice.
› Think of the character's most precious possession.

2 Finding a plot

There's one golden rule in short story writing: keep the plot (the story) simple. Most good stories are built around one or two key events and involve a small number of characters. Nearly all are about conflict. By the end of the story, the central character has changed in some important way.

Here are thirteen ideas for a short story.

1 The central character has a secret. When it is revealed it changes everything.

2 The central character learns someone else's secret and has to decide what to do.

3 The central character sets his/her heart on something but is let down by the person closest to him/her.

4 The central character longs for something and is surprised when someone unexpected makes the dream come true.

5 The central character finds out something that causes him/her to grow up.

6 The central character finds out that his/her hero is just an ordinary person.

7 The central character finds out that an ordinary person is really a hero.

8 The central character makes a decision that brings him/her into conflict with an authority figure.

9 The central character finds the courage to stand up for himself/herself.

10 The central character sees someone being mistreated but is afraid to act.

11 The central character comes to the defence of someone who is being bullied.

12 The central character is happy and this makes someone jealous.

13 The central character sees someone else's happiness and wants to destroy it.

Groupwork

Pick one of the above ideas and write an outline for a story. Share your idea with a partner before hearing ideas from the rest of the class.

Three things to remember:

1 Keep the plot of your short story simple.

2 Make sure that there is some kind of conflict.

3 Make sure that the central character changes as a result of what happens.

3 Writing dialogue

'Dialogue' refers to the words spoken by the characters in a story. Good dialogue sounds natural and tells your reader something important about the characters and their relationships. (Monologue is when characters speak to themselves.)

When you write dialogue, be sure to show the character's personality and capture the character's voice.

The layout of dialogue

The layout of dialogue is important. For stories, quotation marks (double inverted commas "..." or single inverted commas '...') are used to show the words spoken by each character. These guidelines will help you to lay out your dialogue.

> Only the words spoken by the speaker and the punctuation marks for those words are enclosed in the quotation marks: 'Did he eat the second little pig?'

> The first word spoken always starts with a capital letter.

> Commas are used to separate the words spoken from the rest of the sentence. The comma goes inside the quotation marks: 'That wasn't very nice of him,' said Granny.

> Start a new line for a change of speaker.

> These examples show you how the guidelines work in practice:

'I couldn't find my school blazer,' said John, 'so I put this old jacket on instead. Is it at all acceptable?'

'Certainly not,' said the teacher. 'You will have to stay at home until you can come to school properly dressed in your full uniform.'

Checklist for dialogue

☐ Are the words spoken by the speaker in quotation marks?

☐ Does the first word start with a capital letter?

☐ Have you used a comma to separate spoken words from the rest of the sentence?

☐ Did you start on a new line for each change of speaker?

4 Story openings

It's always a good idea to try to catch the attention of the reader from the first line of a story. Here are some examples.

> The *intriguing opening* raises questions that interest readers and makes us want to read on to find the answer, e.g. 'I never really liked my brother, Sonny.'

> The *direct opening* talks directly to the reader, e.g. 'Lots of sisters I had (said the old man), good girls too; and one elder brother.'

> The *drip-feed opening* gives the reader information bit by bit so that the reader has to put the pieces together, e.g. 'I am seven years old. My mum, my brother and I have just watched a cowboy and Indian film. I'm sad because the Indians have lost again, and I wanted them to win.'

> The *overheard opening* brings the reader right into the middle of a conversation, e.g.
> 'Ready?'
> 'Ready.'
> 'Now?'
> 'Soon.'

> The *setting of the scene opening* gives a clear picture of when and where things are happening, e.g. 'A hot September Saturday in 1959, and we are stationary in Cheshire.'

> You can also have an opening that is really atmospheric and descriptive (good for ghost stories) or you can have a humorous opening. In fact, you can have a mixture of the various approaches. The important thing is that the opening should catch the reader's attention and make him/her want to read more.

5 The parts of a story

Just like making a good cake, when you write a short story you must have the right ingredients. These include:

> an interesting central character
> a dramatic situation and conflict
> a problem or a crisis for the central character
> a moment of decision for the central character
> an ending or aftermath that is related to the decision made by the central character.

> **Remember!**
> Catch the attention of the reader from the opening words of your story.

Groupwork

Working in pairs, identify each of the above ingredients in the story 'My Polish Teacher's Tie'. These are the basic ingredients and we can find them in nearly every story.

6 Story map

Here is a story map for a short story that uses all the key ingredients.

Characters and relationships:

> John is nine years old. He is kind and is his mother's favourite.

> John's dad is full of himself and hates to be questioned. His temper is uncertain.

> John's mum is kind and tries to smooth things over.

Situation:

> John lives with his mum and dad. His relationship with his mum is good but he and his dad do not get on.

> John's dad has promised him a puppy for his birthday.

Conflict and crisis
John reminds his dad of the promise he made. His dad gets very angry.

Revelation
John discovers there is no dog.

Decision
John runs away and hides. He tries to think things through. He comes to a decision.

Opening
On the morning of his birthday, John is awake at dawn, mad with excitement, waiting to see his new dog.

End
John comes back but he is changed.

Writing Task

Using the information above, write the story. Remember to:

> introduce the central character
> outline the situation
> show the conflict
> describe the moment when the character makes his/her decision
> describe the aftermath of the decision.

7 Following the rules – fairy tales

Traditional fairy tales follow familiar patterns or 'rules'. You can follow these 'rules' or change one or two as you go along when you are composing your own fairy tale. Interestingly, many of the rules of fairy tales are used by modern writers of fantasy.

The setting

Fairy tales usually take place a long time ago in one or more of the following settings:

> castle or palace
> forest or enchanted garden
> simple cottage.

Characters

There is a predictable set of characters:

> kings and queens
> beautiful maidens
> princes and princesses
> dwarfs and giants
> heroes and warriors
> children
> fairy godmothers
> witches or wicked stepmothers
> woodcutters, cobblers or tailors.

Contrasts

Characters are often grouped into contrasting pairs:

> rich and poor
> good and evil
> kind and spiteful
> beautiful and ugly

> foolish and wise
> young and old
> huge and tiny.

Sometimes goodness and ugliness are combined in one character, as are beauty and evil. (Can you think of some examples?) At the end of the story, there is often a sudden reversal, when the ugly character is shown to be beautiful, and the beautiful character is shown to be evil and becomes ugly.

Magical powers

Whether good or evil, fairy-tale characters often have magical powers with which to solve problems or cause them.

Animals and nature

In fairy tales, animals can talk. Sometimes trees, plants and statues also have the power to talk. Certain animals are friendly – birds, deer, rabbits and squirrels. Others are not – bats, wolves and cats. Some, like the fox, can be either friend or foe.

Names

Apart from the hero and heroine, most of the characters in fairy tales are not given names. They are referred to as 'the witch', 'the children', 'the woodcutter' and so on.

The story

Many fairy tales are based upon one theme or idea:

> a dangerous journey
> a difficult task
> the lifting of an evil spell
> the release of a prisoner.

Special language

The language in fairy tales follows predictable patterns.

> Tales often begin 'Once upon a time' and end with 'happily every after'.
> Repetition is used: 'Granny, what big eyes/ears you have.'
> The conversations are often formal and polite, even when the villain is speaking: 'Mirror, mirror on the wall, who is the fairest one of all?'

Happily ever after

Fairy tales always end happily, with good triumphing over evil. The hero successfully completes the task; goodness is rewarded; and evil spells are broken. No wonder such stories are told to children – how comforting for them to know that the wicked witch or the big bad wolf will always be defeated!

Numbers

Certain numbers are used time and time again in fairy tales, especially three, seven and twelve. There are three little pigs, seven dwarfs and twelve dancing princesses.

The storyteller

In fairy tales, storytellers tell tales about others but never about themselves. There is no use of the first person 'I'. Storytellers never comment on or explain what happens. They simply tell the story.

Groupwork

Working in pairs, use the rules of fairy tales to compose your own fairy tale. Working together, tell the story to your class. You could make a podcast of your tale and make a class collection.

Chapter Seven
POETRY B

Poetry can explore many interesting subjects or topics. In this chapter you will read poems about weird and wonderful things, the changing seasons of the year and the thrill of exploring.

Communicating

> You will listen to and read a variety of poems so that you can say what they mean, compare them with other poems and judge how good they are.

> You will enjoy working with others to discover how poems sound when spoken out loud.

> You will speak about a variety of subjects and prepare a short talk for your classmates.

Exploring and Using Language

> You will read poems for your own enjoyment and express your response to them in various ways.

> You will discuss the reasons why poets chose certain words or phrases to express thoughts and feelings.

> You will use these poems as models for your own writing.

> You will complete a quiz on the *Be Inspired!* website to check your knowledge of poetry terms.

Understanding Language

> You will become better at speaking and writing, learning how to use the best words to express your thoughts and feelings.

> You will work on your own and with others to find suitable ways to improve your writing.

> You will discover that the words and sentences you use will change depending on who you are writing for and why you are writing.

> You will read author biographies on the *Be Inspired!* website and research topics online.

Wrapping Up

> To wrap up, you will put together your own class collection of poetry and read it aloud.

www.edco.ie/beinspired

Theme 1: Weird and wonderful

Before you read ...

Imagine you have to fill a treasure chest and hide it on some desert island for strangers to discover in the future. Think about the precious things you might put in this box. When you have thought about your own choices, listen to a partner tell you about what he/she might put in a treasure chest.

Now read Kit Wright's poem about what he would like to put in a magic box.

The Magic Box

KIT WRIGHT

Author Biography
Check out the *Be Inspired!* website for Kit Wright's author biography.

I will put in the box

the swish of a silk sari[1] on a summer night,
fire from the nostrils of a Chinese dragon,
the tip of a tongue touching a tooth.

I will put in the box

a snowman with a rumbling belly,
a sip of the bluest water from Lake Lucerne,
a leaping spark from an electric fish.

I will put into the box

three violet wishes spoken in Gujarati,[2]
the last joke of an ancient uncle,
and the first smile of a baby.

I will put into the box

a fifth season and a black sun,
a cowboy on a broomstick
and a witch on a white horse.

My box is fashioned from ice and gold and steel,
with stars on the lid and secrets in the corners.
Its hinges are the toe joints of dinosaurs.

I shall surf in my box
on the great high-rolling breakers of the wild Atlantic,
then wash ashore on a yellow beach
the colour of the sun.

---

[1] light dress   [2] language spoken in India

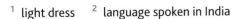

Thinking about the poem

1 Search through 'The Magic Box' to find something you could:

see	hear	smell	touch	taste

2 Look again at all the things the poet will put in the magic box. What does the list tell you about him?

3 Complete the sentence below, describing the feelings you have when you read the poem.

'When I read this poem I feel ...'

You might like to select some of the 'feeling words' from the following list:

> amused   > excited   > jealous
> annoyed   > frightened   > pleased
> curious   > inspired   > sad

4 Draw a picture to illustrate your favourite line from the poem.

Groupwork

What is this poem about?

> adventure   > excitement   > treasure
> beauty   > magic   > wonder

Discuss with a group of your classmates the themes in 'The Magic Box'. Is there one theme you all agree on or are there several possibilities? When you have listened to each other, tell the whole class what you discovered.

Writing Task

Complete this task in your portfolio, p. 53.

Write your own Magic Box poem using the shape of the original poem.

Before you read ...

Imagine you could be an animal for a day. Think about which creature you would choose to be. Talk to a partner about the animal and why you would like to become that creature. When you have listened to each other, explain your ideas to the class.

The Eagle

ALFRED, LORD TENNYSON

He clasps the crag with crooked hands;
Close to the sun in lonely lands,
Ring'd with the azure[1] world, he stands.

The wrinkled sea beneath him crawls;
He watches from his mountain walls,
And like a thunderbolt he falls.

_____

[1] bright blue

Explanation –
Tone
In poetry, *tone* is the attitude or feeling in the lines of the poem, e.g. a serious tone, a mocking tone.

Thinking about the poem

1 What words tell you about the place where the eagle lives?
2 To what is the eagle compared in the poem?
3 What do you notice about the rhyming words in this poem?

Oral Language

1 Listen again as the poem is read aloud and notice the sounds of the words. Which words do you like most? Say why.

2 With a partner, practise saying the poem in a variety of different tones. You might like to use the following list:

> admiring   > fearful   > respectful   > triumphant

3 With a partner, think of a single action or gesture to go with each of the six lines. Take turns saying the poem aloud as your partner does the actions.

Research

Choose a wild animal – an eagle or any other creature – and find out as much as you can about it. Use the following headings when you are making notes, and add any others you can think of.

> habitat
> appearance
> diet
> behaviour

Writing Task

When you have gathered your information, write a short talk for your class telling them what you found out. Aim to write about 300 words. Divide your writing into five or six short paragraphs. You could use the headings above for your paragraphs or come up with your own headings. Use information from your notes to tell your audience the facts about this animal. Don't forget to mention why you chose it, describing your own thoughts and feelings about why you find this animal interesting.

Groupwork

Work in pairs and read your short talk to a partner. Listen to any advice your classmate offers about speaking clearly. When you have both listened to each other's work, share your findings by giving a short talk to the whole class. Think about any pictures or props that might be useful for your talk. Don't forget to look up when you are speaking, to make eye contact with your audience.

Eagles are hunter birds; they catch and kill their own food. Vultures, in contrast, are scavengers; they feed off the remains of dead animals that they happen to find.

1 Look carefully at the photograph of the vulture.

2 Which of the following words best describes the bird?

> sad
> lazy
> funny
> frightening
> hungry
> peaceful

The Vulture

HILAIRE BELLOC

The Vulture eats between his meals,
And that's the reason why
He very, very, rarely feels
As well as you and I.

His eye is dull, his head is bald,
His neck is growing thinner.
Oh! what a lesson for us all
To only eat at dinner!

> **Reminder –**
> **Rhyme**
>
> Rhyme is when two or more words have the same sound. The rhyme here is *end rhyme*, where 'meals' rhymes with 'feels'.

Thinking about the poem

1 Explain the first line of the poem.

2 Manners or etiquette are the unwritten rules that influence our behaviour. Do you agree with the poet that people should 'only eat at dinner'? Explain your opinion on this subject.

Oral Language

1 Think about the poem 'The Vulture'. If the person in the poem could be heard speaking out loud, what tone of voice would he/she use? Choose from the following list or suggest a different word to describe the tone:

> angry
> serious
> jealous

> mocking
> disapproving
> warning

> snobbish
> admiring
> comical

2 Try reading the poem out loud in a variety of tones of voice. How does the tone change the way you think about the poem?

3 How do the rhyming words affect the way you feel about the vulture?

4 Learn this very short poem for homework.

Groupwork

Working in groups of four, write a set of instructions for teenagers under one of the following headings:

> How to behave in a hotel restaurant
> Eating meals at home
> A guide to dining in fast-food outlets
> Rules for school lunch break

Your set of instructions must include between five and ten sentences.
The tone of your guidelines may be serious or humorous.
Remember, you are writing rules for a group of teenagers.

Writing Task

1 Now compare 'The Vulture' and 'The Eagle'. Write a list of …

… differences between the poems	… ways in which they are alike

2 Use the points from the grid above to write two paragraphs. Your first paragraph will be about how the two poems are similar to each other. The second paragraph will be about the ways they are different.

What do you imagine might happen in a house like this?
Talk about what you expect to happen in the poem the picture illustrates.

The Listeners

WALTER DE LA MARE

'Is there anybody there?' said the Traveller,
    Knocking on the moonlit door;
And his horse in the silence champed the grasses
    Of the forest's ferny floor.
And a bird flew up out of the turret,[1]
    Above the Traveller's head:
And he smote[2] upon the door again a second time;
    'Is there anybody there?' he said.
But no one descended to the Traveller;
    No head from the leaf-fringed sill
Leaned over and looked into his grey eyes,
    Where he stood perplexed and still.
But only a host of phantom listeners
    That dwelt in the lone house then
Stood listening in the quiet of the moonlight
    To that voice from the world of men:
Stood thronging the faint moonbeams on the dark stair,
    That goes down to the empty hall,
Hearkening[3] in an air stirred and shaken
    By the lonely Traveller's call.

> ### Reminder –
> ### Setting
>
> The setting is where and when a poem or story takes place. It is also the atmosphere of that place.

---

[1] tower   [2] struck/knocked   [3] listening

And he felt in his heart their strangeness,
    Their stillness answering his cry,
While his horse moved, cropping the dark turf,
    'Neath the starred and leafy sky;
For he suddenly smote on the door, even
    Louder, and lifted his head:
'Tell them I came, and no one answered,
    That I kept my word,' he said.
Never the least stir made the listeners,
    Though every word he spake
Fell echoing through the shadowiness of the still house
    From the one man left awake:
Ay, they heard his foot upon the stirrup,
    And the sound of iron on stone,
And how the silence surged softly backward,
    When the plunging hoofs were gone.

> ### Explanation – Alliteration
>
> When two or more words begin with the same consonant, the sound effect is very like rhyme, e.g. 'forest's ferny floor'. This is called alliteration.

Thinking about the poem

1 Describe the setting of this poem.

2 How would you feel about making a visit like this?

3 'The Listeners' is like a short drama. There is a whole cast of characters acting out a story. Who are the various characters in the poem?

4 What is going on in the poem?

5 How do you feel at the end of the poem?

Oral Language

1 There is a mixture of sound and silence in this poem. Find all the verbs that are used to describe sounds. What do you notice about these words?

2 Do you agree that 'The Listeners' is a good title for the poem? Explain your point of view.

3 How does the writer make the atmosphere so mysterious?

Groupwork

In groups of three or four, read the poem carefully and divide it into different parts to be read aloud in a choral style. For a choral reading, you need to break the poem into parts for individuals or groups to read aloud. Perform your own reading of the poem for the class.

Before you read ...

1 Look carefully at the photo. What are your thoughts and feelings as you look at it?
2 Talk to a partner in class about why you feel this way.

Stopping by Woods on a Snowy Evening

ROBERT FROST

Whose woods these are I think I know.
His house is in the village though;
He will not see me stopping here
To watch his woods fill up with snow.

My little horse must think it queer
To stop without a farmhouse near
Between the woods and frozen lake
The darkest evening of the year.

He gives his harness bells a shake
To ask if there is some mistake.
The only other sound's the sweep
Of easy wind and downy flake.

The woods are lovely, dark and deep.
But I have promises to keep,
And miles to go before I sleep,
And miles to go before I sleep.

> **Explanation –
> Sibilance**
>
> Sibilance is when 's' or 'sh'
> sounds are repeated to make
> a soft swishing sound effect,
> e.g. '... sound's the sweep ...'.

BE INSPIRED!

Thinking about the poem

1 What words can you find in the poem to prove that it is set in the country during winter?

2 Why does the poet interrupt his journey to stop in the woods?

Oral Language

1 Think about how the poem should sound. Work with a partner and experiment with different ways of speaking it out loud.

2 When you have finished, perform a reading for the class.

Writing Task

1 How does this person feel about stopping by the woods at this time of year? Choose from the following words and add your own:

> excited
> scared
> guilty
> glad

Write a short paragraph explaining how he feels. Give reasons for your opinion, using words or lines from the poem.

2 Complete this sentence: 'When I listen to the poem read aloud, I hear the sound of …' Mention key words and phrases from the poem in your answer.

3 What is happening at the end of this poem?

4 Do you agree that there is something very beautiful but also frightening in this poem? Explain your thoughts.

Before you read ...

1 What traditions do you have in your family as you prepare for Christmas?

2 Who decorates your home? When do you begin your preparations?

3 Do you have a favourite decoration?

The Christmas Life

WENDY COPE

If you don't have a real tree you don't bring the Christmas life into the house.
Josephine Mackinnon, aged 8

Bring in a tree, a young Norwegian spruce,
Bring hyacinths that rooted in the cold.
Bring winter jasmine as its buds unfold –
Bring the Christmas life into this house.

Bring red and green and gold, bring things that shine,
Bring candlesticks and music, food and wine.
Bring in your memories of Christmas past.
Bring in your tears for all that you have lost.

Bring in the shepherd boy, the ox and ass,
Bring in the stillness of an icy night,
Bring in the birth, of hope and love and light.
Bring the Christmas life into this house.

Author Biography
Check out the *Be Inspired!* website for Wendy Cope's author biography.

Explanation –
Stanza
A stanza is a group of lines in a poem. There are three stanzas in 'The Christmas Life' with four lines in each stanza.

BE INSPIRED!

Thinking about the poem

1 Write a list of all the nouns in the poem.

2 In your opinion, what are the 'things that shine' in people's homes at Christmas time?

3 Where might you find 'the shepherd boy, the ox and ass'?

Oral Language

1 Which do you prefer, a 'real' tree or an artificial Christmas tree? Give reasons for your preference.

2 Talk to another student and find out if he/she shares your point of view.

3 Have a class discussion about the benefits of both 'real' trees and artificial trees.

Writing Task

1 What, do you think, is meant by the line 'Bring in your tears for all that you have lost'?

2 There are many strong images in the poem. Choose the one you like the best and write a sentence saying why you picked it.

3 Write a paragraph beginning with the words 'It was a Christmas I will never forget …'

Research

Use the internet to find out as much as possible about one Christmas tradition. You might like to choose from the following:

> Christmas trees
> Christmas food
> a candle in the window
> wren boys
> midnight mass
> holly wreath
> carols
> Santa Claus
> Advent calendar
> Christmas cards

We all notice when one season ends and the next begins. It is one of the ways people have of measuring time. We can have mixed feelings about this as we leave one season behind and face into another.

 The Trees

PHILIP LARKIN

The trees are coming into leaf
Like something almost being said;
The recent buds relax and spread,
Their greenness is a kind of grief.

Is it that they are born again
And we grow old? No, they die too,
Their yearly trick of looking new
Is written down in rings of grain.

Yet still the unresting castles thresh
In fullgrown thickness every May.
Last year is dead, they seem to say,
Begin afresh, afresh, afresh.

> **Explanation –**
> **Onomatopoeia**
>
> Onomatopoeia is when the sound of a word echoes its meaning, e.g. 'thresh'.

BE INSPIRED!

Thinking about the poem

1 What time of year is it in the opening line?

2 How is the speaker feeling in the first stanza? How do you know?

Oral Language

1 There is an interesting simile in the second line. Explain it.

2 Say what you think Philip Larkin means when he writes about the trees' 'yearly trick'.

3 The word 'thresh' is used in the final stanza to help us imagine the sound the trees are making as they move in the breeze. Find another example of onomatopoeia.

4 Learn the poem off by heart. Notice all the rhyming words and the regular beat of the lines.

Writing Task

1 Explain how a tree could be like a castle.

2 Complete this sentence: 'When I read this poem I feel ...'

Choose from the following list or pick a 'feeling word' of your own.

> gloomy
> optimistic
> free
> worried

Say which parts of the poem made you feel that way.

3 Write out the moral, or lesson, of this poem in your own words.

Do you have a favourite place? Think about somewhere you really like to be. It could be indoors or outdoors, here in Ireland or in another country. Write a paragraph describing it. Use as many of your five senses as possible to help create a strong impression of this special place. When you have finished, read your answer out loud and listen to your classmates' descriptions of their favourite places.

Now read W.B. Yeats's poem about a place that was special for him.

The Lake Isle of Innisfree

WILLIAM BUTLER YEATS

I will arise and go now, and go to Innisfree,
And a small cabin build there, of clay and wattles made:
Nine bean-rows will I have there, a hive for the honey-bee,
And live alone in the bee-loud glade.

And I shall have some peace there, for peace comes dropping slow
Dropping from the veils of the morning to where the cricket sings;
There midnight's all a glimmer, and noon a purple glow,
And evening full of the linnet's wings.

I will arise and go now, for always night and day
I hear lake water lapping with low sounds by the shore;
While I stand on the roadway, or on the pavements grey,
I hear it in the deep heart's core.

> ### Explanation – Assonance
>
> Assonance is the repetition of similar vowel sounds close to one another in a line, e.g. 'b<u>ea</u>n-rows … honey b<u>ee</u> …'.

Thinking about the poem

1 What decision is being made in the opening line?

2 Close your eyes and listen to the poem being read aloud. Now complete the following sentence: 'When I hear this poem I see in my mind's eye …'

3 What words in the poem help to put these pictures in your mind?

4 What, precisely, does the speaker like about the island of Innisfree? Is it the sounds, the isolation, the thought of going back there, or something else?

Oral Language

1 How, do you think, is the person speaking in the poem feeling?

2 Find a place in the poem where the feelings change.

3 Look at the third line, where the words 'have ... hive ... honey' are very close together. The alliteration adds a musical quality to the line. Find another example of alliteration in this poem. Why, do you think, does W.B. Yeats use these sounds in his poem?

4 There are several other ways that the poet has of using the sounds of words to create an effect. Can you find them?

Writing Task

1 Imagine you are working for a travel agency. Write a short paragraph for a travel brochure describing your ideal holiday destination. In the text of your advertisement you might like to consider:

> weather
> food
> sights and sounds
> famous attractions
> landscape and wildlife
> facilities nearby

Or:

2 Write a poem about your favourite time of year.
Think about what you like about it.
Use your five senses to help build a picture of that season.

sights	sounds	smells	tastes	touch

Groupwork

Working with a partner, choose two of these poems:

> 'Stopping by Woods on a Snowy Evening'
> 'The Christmas Life'
> 'The Trees'
> 'The Lake Isle of Innisfree'

Compare the two poems using the diagram to help you.

Poem A How the poem is different — **Common features** — **Poem B** How the poem is different

Theme 2: Exploring

Before you read ...

1 Describe some of the things that can happen when you open a door.

2 What feelings or thoughts make us want to see behind a closed door?

The Door

MIROSLAV HOLUB

Go and open the door.
  Maybe outside there's
  a tree, or a wood,
  a garden,
  or a magic city.

Go and open the door.
  Maybe a dog's rummaging.
  Maybe you'll see a face,
or an eye,
or the picture
              of a picture.

Go and open the door.
  If there's a fog
  it will clear.

Go and open the door.
  Even if there's only
  the darkness ticking,
  even if there's only
  the hollow wind,
  even if
      nothing
          is there,
go and open the door.

At least
there'll be
a draught.

Explanation –
Form

The form of a poem is the shape the words make on the page. The form or figure that a poem makes is often a reflection of what the words are telling us.

BE INSPIRED!

Thinking about the poem

1 What do you notice about the pattern of the words in this poem?

2 Who, do you think, is the poet inviting to 'Go and open the door'?

3 The lines 'If there's a fog/it will clear' are very positive. Do you agree with this attitude of hope expressed by the poet? Explain your point of view.

4 What, do you think, is going on in the last stanza of the poem?

> *At least*
> *there'll be*
> *a draught.*

Can you find any humour here?

Check out the Against the Clock quiz on poetry terms on the *Be Inspired!* website.

Writing Task

1 The door mentioned in the poem could be a real door or it could be a symbol standing for something else. Can you suggest what the door might represent?

2 Write a paragraph describing an interesting door.

3 Complete this task in your portfolio, p. 54.

Write a very short story beginning with the words:

'Then I opened the door and …'

Think back to last August when you began secondary school. What do you remember about your first day? Talk to a partner about your memories of your first day in your new school.

The New Boy

JOHN WALSH

The door swung inward.
I stood and breathed
The new-school atmosphere.
The smell of polish and disinfectant,
And the flavour of my own fear.
I followed into the cloakroom; the walls
Rang to the shattering noise
Of the boys who barged and boys who banged;
Boys and still more boys!

A boot flew by me. Its angry owner
Pursued with force and yell;
Somewhere a man snapped orders; somewhere
There clanged a warning bell.
And there I hung with my new schoolmates;
They pushing and shoving me; I
Unknown, unwanted, pinned to the wall;
On the verge of ready-to-cry.

Then from the doorway a boy called out:
'Hey, you over there! You're new!
Don't just stand there propping the wall up!
I'll look after you!'
I turned; I timidly raised my eyes;
He stood and grinned meanwhile;
And my fear died, and my lips answered
Smile for his smile.

He showed me the basins, the rows of pegs;
He hung my cap at the end;
He led me away to my new classroom ...
And now that boy's my friend.

BE INSPIRED!

Thinking about the poem

1 The boy notices something as soon as he arrives in his new school. What is it?

2 What, do you think, does he mean when he says 'the flavour of my own fear'?

3 Describe the 'new-school atmosphere' that this poem captures.

4 The mood changes in the poem. Find the word, phrase or line where you think this change takes place.

> **Reminder –**
> ## Mood
> The feeling or atmosphere of a particular place and time in a poem is called the mood, e.g. a sad mood or a mysterious mood.

Oral Language

1 When the boy says he is 'on the verge of ready-to-cry' it is a key moment in the poem. How did it make you feel when you read that line?

2 What happens next?

3 What is going on at the end of the poem?

4 How did your feelings change from the start of the poem to the end?

Writing Task

1 There is a contrast between the two boys in the poem. Make a list of the words used to describe each boy.

New boy	Friend

2 Now write a short paragraph about how the boys are different.

Groupwork

Imagine it is your job to welcome a group of first-year students to your school on their first day. Think about what you would say to them. Work with a partner to write a short talk that you would both give to incoming first-year students. When you are happy with what you have written, practise speaking it to each other. Present your short talk to the class and compare it to the talks given by your other classmates.

Think of a time when you went exploring somewhere without permission.

> Where did you go?
> What did you do?
> Were you on your own or were you with a friend?
> How did it feel to be taking a risk?
> Did you get caught?

Write three paragraphs telling the story of your adventure.

Child on Top of a Greenhouse

THEODORE ROETHKE

The wind billowing out the seat of my britches,
my feet crackling splinters of glass and dried putty,
the half-grown chrysanthemums[1] staring up like accusers,
up through the streaked glass, flashing with sunlight,
a few white clouds all rushing eastward,
a line of elms plunging and tossing like horses,
and everyone, everyone pointing up and shouting!

---

[1] brightly coloured flowers

Explanation – Personification

Personification is a special kind of metaphor where something that is not human is written about as if it were human, e.g. 'chrysanthemums staring up like accusers'.

Thinking about the poem

1 Why is the title so important?

2 Find in the lines of this poem things that you might …

see	hear	touch

3 What do you notice about the weather? Does it matter?

Oral Language

1 Read the poem again and find all the verbs.

2 What is the effect of the sound of these verbs in the poem?

3 The child imagines the flowers accusing him like people. Find another comparison in the poem and explain it to the class.

4 Learn this short poem for homework.

Writing Task

Write the opening paragraph of a short story describing what happens next.

Or:

Write a short poem about adventure.

Climbing

AMY LOWELL

High up in the apple tree climbing I go,
With the sky above me, the earth below.
Each branch is the step of a wonderful stair
Which leads to the town I see shining up there.

Climbing, climbing, higher and higher,
The branches blow and I see a spire,
The gleam of a turret, the glint of a dome,
All sparkling and bright, like white sea foam.

On and on, from bough to bough,
The leaves are thick, but I push my way through;
Before, I have always had to stop,
But today I am sure I shall reach the top.

Today to the end of the marvelous* stair,
Where those glittering pinnacles flash in the air!
Climbing, climbing, higher I go,
With the sky close above me, the earth far below.

---

* US spelling

Explanation –
Rhyming couplet

A rhyming couplet is two lines of the same length
that rhyme and complete one thought, e.g.:

High up in the apple tree climbing I go,
With the sky above me, the earth below.

Thinking about the poem

1 Find a metaphor in the first stanza.

2 What is special about this day's climbing in the apple tree?

3 How is the child in the poem feeling?

> happy
> courageous
> free
> nervous

Oral Language

1 Check the meanings of these words in your dictionary.

> turret
> dome
> spire
> pinnacle

2 What do all these words have in common?

3 In the second stanza the word 'climbing' is used twice in the same line. Find two more examples of this type of repetition.

4 Repetition is a kind of rhyme. Can you think of any reason why the poet might use it in this poem?

Groupwork

Work in a group to give a choral reading of the poem.

Writing Task

Complete this task in your portfolio, p. 55.

Compare the poems 'Child on Top of a Greenhouse' and 'Climbing'. Look at ways in which the poems are like one another and look at ways in which they are different.

Wrapping up

> In groups of four, read back over the poems you have written during the school year.

> Ask your group to help you choose one of your own poems to include in a class collection.

> When your group has chosen four poems, read them for the whole class.

> Put together a booklet containing the poetry from your class.

> Discuss a good order or sequence for the poems.

> Think about a good title for your anthology.

> Draw a picture to use as a cover illustration for your poetry collection.

> Organise a reading of your anthology. Think about how each poem could be read aloud.

Poetry Reminder Chart

> **Alliteration** is when two or more words close together begin with the same consonant, e.g. 'the boys who barged and boys who banged' in the poem 'The New Boy'.

> **Assonance** is the repetition of similar vowel sounds close to one another in a line, e.g. 'bean-rows … honey-bee …' in 'The Lake Isle of Innisfree'.

> A **ballad** always tells a story, has a regular rhyme and a refrain that is repeated, e.g. 'What Has Happened to Lulu?'.

> **Character** is the term we give to a person in a poem or a story. Characters can be real people or fictional people invented by the writer, e.g. Dan Taggart in 'The Early Purges'.

> **Form** is the shape that the words of a poem make on the page, e.g. the pattern of lines in 'The Door'.

> A **haiku** is a type of short poem originating in Japan. It has three lines, seventeen syllables, and is usually about the natural world, e.g. 'Seaview Haiku'.

> An **image** is a group of words that paints a picture of something in your head, e.g. '… windsurfs/Skim across the bay' in 'Seaview Haiku'.

> A **limerick** is a five-line poem with the rhyme scheme AABBA. The humour is usually light and sometimes the rhyme itself is funny, e.g. 'pimple … simple … dimple'.

> Comparing something to something else is a **metaphor**, e.g. the trees in 'The Trees' are 'unresting castles'.

> The atmosphere of a particular place and time in a poem is called the **mood**. There is a mysterious mood in the poem 'The Listeners'.

> **Onomatopoeia** is when the sound of a word echoes its meaning, e.g. 'the unresting castles *thresh*' in 'The Trees'.

> **Personification** is a special type of **metaphor** whereby something that is not human is written about as if it were human, e.g. 'chrysanthemums staring up like accusers' in 'Child on Top of a Greenhouse'.

> **Rhyme** is two or more words that have a similar sound. It is common for words at the end of lines to rhyme. This is called **end rhyme**, e.g. 'meals ... feels' in 'The Vulture'.

> A **rhyming couplet** is two lines of the same length that rhyme and complete one thought, e.g. in 'Climbing':

> 'High up in the apple tree climbing I go,
> With the sky above me, the earth below.'

> The **setting** of a story or poem is where and when it happens. In the poem 'The New Boy', the setting is the cloakroom of a school.

> **Sibilance** is when 's', 'sh' or 'ch' sounds are repeated to make a soft, swishing sound effect, e.g. 'Begin, afresh, afresh, afresh' in 'The Trees'.

> A **simile** compares two things using the words 'like' or 'as', e.g. 'like a thunderbolt he falls' in 'The Eagle'.

> A **sonnet** is a poem made up of exactly 14 lines. Shakespeare's most famous sonnet begins with the words 'Shall I compare thee to a summer's day?'.

> A **stanza** is a group of lines in a poem. In 'The Eagle' there are two stanzas with three lines in each stanza.

> A **symbol** is something that 'stands for' or represents something else. In the poem 'The Door', doors are symbols of freedom, adventure and imagination.

> A **theme** is a key idea explored in a poem, play or story, e.g. the theme of growing up in 'The Early Purges'.

> **Tone** is the term given to the attitude or feeling in the lines of a poem, e.g. the happy tone in 'The Christmas Life' where people celebrate with 'music, food and wine'.

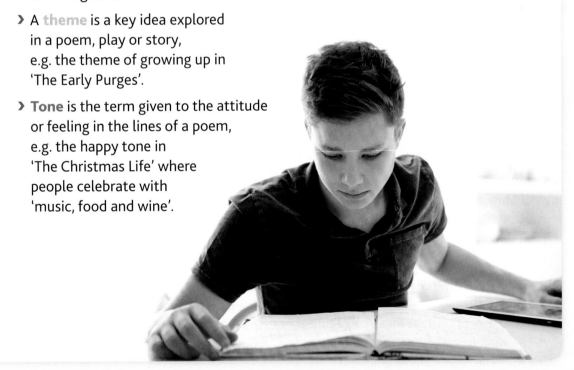

Young Writer's Toolkit

Writing Poetry

Here you will find tools to help you to write poetry.

1 Beginning to write   3 Using metaphors and similes

2 Making improvements   4 Shapes and forms

1 Beginning to write

Here are four things you can do to help you get started.

> Write quickly.
> Write down the pictures in your mind.
> Use all five senses in your writing.
> Try not to think too much!

There are a number of ways a poem can start.

> You could begin by writing random words on a page, nouns like:

    sky   flower   river   eye   cat   moon   fire   battle

Close your eyes and imagine a picture of one of these things. Now write a short phrase made up of several words describing the image in your mind. Repeat this for each of the words in your random list. Take five or six phrases and see what happens if you put them together.

    Remember, in a poem you do not have to explain or tell a story. Allow the phrases to hint at some feeling or atmosphere.

> You could take a familiar object or event and write about it as if it were a person speaking. Imagine that the object could say five things about itself without revealing its identity.

    I look ...   I sound ...   I smell ...   I feel ...   I taste ...

Finish with a question like 'What am I?' or 'Who am I?'

    Take each line and add any words that might help to make the images or pictures more interesting. Keep your pen on the page until you are happy with your poem.

> You could write an autobiographical poem. One way to begin this is by completing a series of phrases about yourself.

Line 1: Your first name only, or your nickname	**Line 6:** Who needs ... (three needs)
Line 2: Four traits or qualities that describe you (use adjectives only)	**Line 7:** Who fears ... (three fears)
	Line 8: Who gives ... (use three nouns)
Line 3: Brother/sister of ... (their names)	**Line 9:** Who would like to see ... (three wishes)
Line 4: Lover of ... (three ideas/people/ groups/activities ...)	**Line 10:** Who lives ... (brief description)
	Line 11: Your last name
Line 5: Who feels ... (three emotions)	

Remember, when you write a poem, ask yourself:

☐ Did I focus on making pictures with words?

☐ Did I write out the words quickly the first time?

☐ Did I try to use all five senses at some point?

☐ Did I make sure not to think too much about it?

Writing freely like this will help you to create strong images.

2 Making improvements

All poets edit their early writing to help improve their poems. You can edit your poems by reading back over the lines you have written and asking yourself the following:

☐ Are there words that sound or look wrong?

☐ Are there better words I could use to replace them?

☐ Do all the words on a line fit well together?

☐ Does each line end with a powerful word?

3 Using metaphors and similes

Metaphors and similes describe something by comparing it to something else. In Alfred, Lord Tennyson's poem 'The Eagle' he uses the metaphor of the eagle as a king or emperor, when he writes, 'the wrinkled sea beneath him crawls'. Metaphors and similes are very useful in poetry. The best comparisons are new ways of thinking about something by finding a suitable but unusual link between what you are describing and something else.

Try inventing comparisons by randomly describing some ordinary object as if it were something else:

> The moon is like … a dirty headlamp
> A question mark, mysterious … as a dark snake

Each of the above examples is a simile. Remove 'like' and 'as' and you have made a metaphor:

> The moon is a dirty headlamp
> A question mark, mysterious, a dark snake

An original metaphor can bring a poem to life by allowing us to see something familiar in a new way.

4 Shapes and forms

It's sometimes a case of editing what you have written and allowing the lines to follow their own shape. On the other hand, you can use some tried and trusted shapes or forms of poetry and make your writing fit them. *Riddles* and *haikus* are two popular forms.

Riddles

Some of the earliest poems were riddles (e.g. 'We are little airy Creatures', p. 38). Often something familiar is made to seem strange by speaking as if it were a person. Writing riddles is easy if you follow these guidelines:

Ri	Think of the answer – something ordinary. Make it speak in the first person – 'I'.
dd	Compare it to something unusual. Think of something it is and something it is not.
le	Say what it is used for. Describe its colour, feel, sound, smell, shape or number.

Haikus

A haiku is a short poem that comes originally from Japan. Writers from all countries have copied the style. John Foster's 'Seaview Haiku' (p. 38) is typical of the shape and style of the haiku.

Every haiku must follow three simple rules:

1 All haiku poems are three lines long.

2 Five syllables in the first line
Seven syllables in the second line
Five syllables in the third line

3 Haiku poems capture natural images.

When you are writing your haiku, count out the syllables by tapping out the beats on the top of your desk.

Try writing a haiku by starting with:

A season – winter, spring, summer, autumn

or:
A place – sea, mountain, woodland, fields

or:
A creature – fox, caterpillar, zebra, dolphin

Once you have selected the subject of your poem, make a picture and follow the rules.

Explanation – Syllable

A syllable is the smallest unit of sound in a word. Every syllable has at least one vowel (a, e, i, o, u) or y. For example, 'bat' has one syllable, 'battle' has two syllables and 'battlement' has three syllables.

Chapter Eight
PERSONAL WRITING B

In this chapter you will once again have the chance to learn from the writings of some very talented writers. The writing is personal and the topics range from children and parents to schooldays.

Communicating

> You will have the opportunity to work with others in pairs and small groups:
>> To listen actively
>> To explain your thoughts, feelings and opinions
>> To imagine, speculate and make judgements
> You will read these texts in order to:
>> Understand, enjoy and respond to them
>> Question and analyse them
>> Respond both orally and in writing in a variety of forms

Exploring and using language

> You will read these texts both for pleasure and to understand and appreciate all their aspects, including setting, atmosphere, language, imagery.
> You will understand and comment, orally and in writing, on how these texts are enhanced by their author's use of language and imagery.
> You will complete a quiz on the *Be Inspired!* website to check your knowledge of personal writing terms.

Understanding language

> You will also use sources such as a dictionary, websites and a thesaurus to help you with vocabulary.
> You will apply what you learn from these texts to improve your own writing.
> You will plan, draft and edit your own work and make helpful suggestions to others about their work.
> You will learn to choose appropriate language as you work alone and with others to write a diary/blog entry, a script, a short speech, use different tones, create a setting and atmosphere and design a Valentine card and a book cover.
> You will read an author biography on the *Be Inspired!* website and research topics online.

Wrapping Up

> To wrap up, you will be asked to read back over the details you gathered about yourself on p. 26 of your portfolio and to write your own autobiography.

www.edco.ie/beinspired

This piece is written by Gina Davidson about her teenage daughter and it was first published in the Guardian *newspaper.*

Treasure's Pocket Money

GINA DAVIDSON

Treasure was born to spend. She therefore needs huge amounts of pocket money. It is her life blood; she can scarcely move without it. She spends it, lends it, donates it, loses it. She buys snacks, tickets, make-up, bargain offers and presents. She is a fountain of pocket money and I am the source of her wealth – the magic porridge pot. Treasure says the correct words and up comes more pocket money. Because without it she is a prisoner in the house, an unpleasant option for both of us.

'I must have some,' she begs. 'I need it. I had to pay all the taxi fare because no one else had any money. They're all going to pay me back.'

'Good. Then you'll have some money.'

'But I haven't enough money to *get* to them.' Treasure is at her wits' end. 'You don't understand how much I spend on fares.' She is addressing an ignoramus. 'Fares are very expensive.' Her needs are always pressing. This month has been particularly pressing because it was Peter's birthday and Chloe's birthday *and* she had to buy Easter eggs.

I am keen to know how much pocket money her friends get. Treasure doesn't know. Her friends don't know either. They become confused when asked. They don't even remember if they have to earn it by doing the odd household task. This is a mysterious grey area.

Treasure is meant to do certain chores to earn her money. She doesn't refuse. She will do them, she promises, but she has other more urgent duties – dancing in her room, hugging the dog, phoning Rosie, going to sleep. In my weak way I have not always enforced these rules. Naturally people have criticised. 'You're making a rod for your own back,' bellows Grandma. She compares her indolent grandchild to the girls who used to live next door. They were paragons in Grandma's eyes. They peeled potatoes, made beds, washed up, never answered back. Having given up on me, Grandma tries Treasure.

'There's only one thing I want you to do,' she begs Treasure in a tragic way. 'Just help your mother. That's all I want you to do.'

This request always throws Treasure into a sullen fury. Grandma's wishes have never been realised. I continue to dole out pocket money regardless. But at least Treasure is a generous child. She spends the bulk of it on presents. I do rather well out of her pocket money. I even have a Teasmade.* I have chocs, flowers, tapes and my birthdays are sumptuous affairs. Nevertheless, I have cut the pocket money now and then when Treasure's behaviour has gone beyond the pale. But that ploy no longer works. Treasure has a new ally. The bank.

The wicked bank tempted Treasure with a cash card and tons of free gifts. It advertised on TV. All her saved up birthday and Christmas present money can now be frittered with ease. The bank is eager for Treasure to join our nation of debtors and be one of them. It does not wish to encourage thrift. I am no match for such an opponent. I dream that one day when all Treasure's savings are gone and I am bankrupt, necessity will force me to be strict about pocket money.

Treasure must have read my mind. 'I don't want you to give me all my pocket money,' says she out of the blue. 'I want to save it. I want you to put it in this piggy bank in your room so I can't get it.' She stuffs a fiver into the pig. 'Can I have some advance pocket money? I need three pounds. I must have it.'

'But you've got that five.'

'I can't spend that,' says Treasure, 'I'm saving it.'

---

* **Teasmade:** a machine for making tea

Explanation –
Tone

> Check out the Against the Clock quiz on personal writing terms on the *Be Inspired!* website.

The tone of a piece of writing lets the reader know the writer's attitude towards the subject of the writing. It is much the same as tone of voice in speech but, because we cannot hear the written word, it is a little harder to pick it up. In writing it is mainly conveyed through language – the kinds of words the writer chooses.

Thinking about the text

1 Why does Treasure need 'huge amounts of pocket money'? List all the things she does with her money.

2 What does the writer describe as 'a mysterious grey area'? Explain in your own words.

3 What kinds of things does Treasure do when she should be doing household chores?

4 How do we know that Treasure can also be generous?

5 Explain how the bank has become her new friend.

6 Watch the video 'Responsibilities' on the *Be Inspired!* website. Compare the attitudes of the parent in the ad with that of Treasure's mother when it comes to providing their children with money.

7 If your mother called you 'Treasure' what would that tell you about her feelings for you?

8 Find the meanings for any words you do not know in your printed or online dictionary and explain the following phrases from the piece in your own words:

> She is addressing an ignoramus.
> This request always throws Treasure into a sullen fury.
> Christmas present money can now be frittered with ease.

Oral Language

Highlight the words and phrases in the piece that best show: (a) the kind of mum Treasure has and (b) the kind of relationship there is between Treasure and her mother. Pair with another student to exchange opinions and to decide on areas of agreement. Then prepare two paragraphs, one about each of these areas, for an oral presentation to another group or the full class. Here are some words that might help:

kind	caring	considerate	cruel	affectionate
hard	generous	rigid	friendly	volatile	solid
healthy	positive	explosive	negative	excellent

Writing Task

Your friend has bought a new dress and she asks you for your opinion of it. Write a sentence, choosing your words carefully to convey your reaction. For example, 'That's lovely. It's like something my mother would wear!' might be described as insulting. Try to use language to convey each of the following:

> a sincere tone
> a jealous tone

> a sarcastic tone
> a humorous tone.

Groupwork

Work in groups of three or four for this exercise.

Tone can be more easily identified in speech than in writing (see Explanation above), and often it does not matter *what* you say but *how* you say it. Try this exercise in your group. Imagine that your mother says to you: 'You're such a wonderful little treasure.' Practise saying it using different tones. You can try to be affectionate, angry, sarcastic and so on.

Then read 'Treasure's Pocket Money' again with a view to figuring out the writer's attitude to her daughter. Pay particular attention to the kinds of words she uses. See if you can all agree what tone really captures the feelings in the piece. Here are some possibilities for you to consider – or you might prefer to think of your own.

> The tone is warm and affectionate.
> The tone is sincere and serious.

> The tone is humorous and playful.
> The tone is angry and reproachful.

Research

'Don't tell the teenagers: pocket money on the rise' (*Irish Times*, 23 February 2015)

Divide into groups of four to discuss the issue of pocket money and to devise some potential questions for a class survey. All the questions should be shared with the class and the best five chosen.

One group should take responsibility for distributing, collecting and collating the results of the survey for presentation to the class.

Before you read ...

Have you ever sat in a stuffy car for a long time? Have you ever queued for ages with nothing to do? Have you ever been embarrassed by an adult in your company calling attention to himself/herself in a negative way (like the father in this story)? Turn to your neighbour and tell each other one memory related to any of these experiences.

This is an extract from the memoir And When Did You Last See Your Father?
Here the author is remembering his father's impatience when waiting in queues.

Skipping the Queue

BLAKE MORRISON

A hot September Saturday in 1959, and we are stationary in Cheshire. Ahead of us, a queue of cars stretches out of sight around the corner. We haven't moved for ten minutes. Everyone has turned his engine off, and now my father does so too. In the sudden silence we can hear the distant whinge of what must be the first race of the afternoon, a ten-lap event for saloon cars. It is quarter past one. In an hour the drivers will be warming up for the main event, the Gold Cup – Graham Hill, Jack Brabham, Roy Salvadori, Stirling Moss and Joakim Bonnier. My father has always loved fast cars, and motor-racing has a strong British following just now, which is why we are stuck here in this country lane with hundreds of other cars.

My father does not like waiting in queues. He is used to patients waiting in queues to see him, but he is not used to waiting in queues himself. A queue, to him, means a man being denied the right to be where he wants to be at a time of his own choosing, which is at the front, now. Ten minutes have passed. What is happening up ahead? What fathead has caused this snarl-up? Why are no cars coming the other way? Has there been an accident? Why are there no police to sort it out?
Every two minutes or so my father gets out of the car, crosses to the opposite verge and tries to see if there is movement up ahead. There isn't. He gets back in and steams some more. The roof of our Alvis is down, the sun beating on to the leather upholstery, the chrome, the picnic basket. The hood is folded and pleated into the mysterious crevice between the boot and the narrow back seat where my sister and I are scrunched together as usual. The roof is nearly always down, whatever the weather: my father loves fresh air, and every car he has owned has been a convertible, so that he can have fresh air. But the air today is not fresh. There is a pall of high-rev exhaust, dust, petrol, boiling-over engines.

In the cars ahead and behind, people are laughing, eating sandwiches, drinking from beer bottles, enjoying the weather, settling into the familiar indignity of waiting-to-get-to-the-front. But my father is not like them. There are only two things on his mind: the invisible head of the queue and, not unrelated, the other half of the country lane, tantalizingly empty.

'Just relax, Arthur,' my mother says. 'You're in and out of the car like a blue-tailed fly.'

But being told to relax only incenses him. 'What can it be?' he demands. 'Maybe there's been an accident. Maybe they're waiting for an ambulance.' We all know where this last speculation is leading, even before he says it. 'Maybe they need a doctor.'

'No, Arthur,' says my mother, as he opens the door again and stands on the wheel-arch to crane ahead.

'It must be an accident,' he announces. 'I think I should drive up and see.'

'No, Arthur. It's just the numbers waiting to get in. And surely there must be doctors on the circuit.'

It is one-thirty and silent now. The saloon race has finished. It is still over an hour until the Gold Cup itself, but there's another race first, and the cars in the paddock to see, and besides ...

'Well, I'm not going to bloody well wait here any longer,' he says. 'We'll never get in. We might as well turn round and give up.' He sits there for another twenty seconds, then leans forward, opens the glove compartment and pulls out a stethoscope, which he hooks over the mirror on the windscreen. It hangs there like a skeleton, the membrane at the top, the metal and rubber leads dangling bow-legged, the two ivory earpieces clopping bonily against each other. He starts the engine, releases the handbrake, reverses two feet, then pulls out into the opposite side of the road.

'No,' says my mother again, half-heartedly. It could be that he is about to do a three-point turn and go back. No it couldn't ...

My father does not drive particularly quickly past the marooned cars ahead. No more than twenty miles an hour. Even so, it *feels* fast, and arrogant, and all the occupants turn and stare as they see us coming. Some appear to be angry. Some are shouting. 'Point to the stethoscope, pet,' he tells my mother, but she has slid down sideways in her passenger seat, out of sight, her bottom resting on the floor, from where she berates him.

'God Almighty, Arthur, why do you have to do this? Why can't you wait like everyone else? What if we meet something coming the other way?' Now my sister and I do the same, hide ourselves below the seat. Our father is on his own. He is not with us, this bullying, shaming, undemocratic cheat. Or rather, we are not with him.

My face pressed to the sweet-smelling upholstery, I imagine what is happening ahead. I can't tell how far we have gone, how many blind corners we have taken. If we meet something, on this narrow country lane, we will have to reverse past all the cars we have just overtaken. That's if we can stop in time. I wait for the squeal of brakes, the clash of metal.

After an eternity of – what? – two minutes, my mother sticks her head up and says, 'Now you've had it,' and my father replies, 'No, there's another gate beyond,' and my sister and I raise ourselves to look. We are up level with the cars at the head of the queue, which are waiting to turn left into the brown ticket-holders' entrance, the plebs' entrance. A steward steps out of the gateway towards us, but my father, pretending not to see him, doesn't stop. He drives ahead, on to a clear piece of road where, two hundred yards away, half a dozen cars from the opposite direction are waiting to turn into another gateway. Unlike those we have left behind, these cars appear to be moving. Magnanimous, my father waits until the last of them has turned in, then drives through the stone gateposts and over the bumpy grass to where an armbanded steward in a tweed jacket is waiting by the roped entrance.

'Good afternoon, sir. Red ticket holder?' The question does not come as a shock: we have all seen the signs, numerous and clamorous, saying RED TICKET HOLDERS' ENTRANCE. But my father is undeterred.

'These, you mean,' he says, and hands over his brown tickets.

'No, sir, I'm afraid these are brown tickets.'

'But there must be some mistake. I applied for red tickets. To be honest, I didn't even look.'

'I'm sorry, sir, but these are brown tickets, and brown's the next entrance, two hundred yards along, if you just swing around here, and …'

'I'm happy to pay the difference.'

'No, you see the rules say …'

'I know where the brown entrance is. I've just spent the last hour queuing for it by mistake. I drove up here because I thought I was red. I can't go back there now. The queue stretches for miles. And these children, you know, who'd been looking forward …'

By now half a dozen cars have gathered behind us. One of them parps. The steward is wavering.

'You say you applied for red.'

'Not only applied for, paid for. I'm a doctor, you see' – he points at the stethoscope – 'and I like being near the grand-stand.'

This double *non-sequitur* seems to clinch it.

'All right, sir, but next time, please check the tickets. Ahead and to your right.'

Thinking about the text

1 What are the Morrison family doing in Cheshire?

2 What caused the sudden silence in the car?

3 Why does the father not like queues?

4 What is the difference between the people in the writer's car and those in other cars around them?

5 'He is not with us, this bullying, shaming, undemocratic cheat.' Explain what you understand by this description of the writer's father.

6 If someone is described as 'magnanimous', it suggests that the person is being fair-minded, noble or generous, so it appears to be a word we would not apply easily to the dad. Why, therefore, do you think, the writer uses this particular word about him in this piece?

7 From what you've read here, would you like to have this man as your dad? Give reasons for your opinion.

Oral Language

1 Note down some ideas on how the writer creates atmosphere and gives us the setting for his story. Use these statements to record your thoughts:

> ❯ What I notice about the setting is …
> ❯ The kind of atmosphere created is …
> ❯ What I like about the information given is …

Share your notes with a partner. Together, have a conversation to consider what was good about the information. For example, was it clear what was happening and where the characters were? Was the atmosphere appropriate for the subject of the piece?

Or:

2 What kind of person would you say the writer's father was? What adjectives would you use to describe him? Here are some to help you make your choice, but you can also use your dictionary/thesaurus to add your own.

| patient | honest | truthful | deceitful |

| reliable | cunning | untrustworthy |

When you have made your decision, discuss with a partner and prepare a short report to help you both to move to another group and swap opinions.

Groupwork

Have you ever been amused or embarrassed by something one of your elders did – a parent, uncle, aunt, for example? Think about this for a few minutes before joining with a small group to hear each other's experiences. Then complete the writing task below.

Writing Task

Complete this task in your portfolio, p. 59. Choose the story from your group that you liked best and use it to plan and create your own new story. Write three paragraphs, concentrating on giving the setting in the first paragraph. Also try to create a suitable atmosphere throughout your story.

Research

Blake Morrison is a very well-known writer. Choose another famous writer, performer, musician or entertainer and prepare a short oral presentation for your class. If possible, use some visual element to help illustrate your presentation.

In 1996, Nuala Ó Faoláin published her memoir, Are You Somebody? *to great acclaim. In this extract, she writes about her mother.*

Mother

NUALA Ó FAOLÁIN

My mother didn't want anything to do with child-rearing or housework. But she had to do it. Because she fell in love with my father, and they married, she was condemned to spend her life as a mother and a home-maker. She was in the wrong job. Sometimes I meet women who remind me of her when I stay in Bed & Breakfasts around the country. They throw sugar on the fire to get it to light, and wipe surfaces with an old rag that smells, and they are forever sending children to the shops. They question me, half-censorious, half-wistful: 'And did you never want to get married yourself?' [...]

It seems that very early in the marriage my mother was overwhelmed. She foundered, and either he didn't see it, or he saw it but couldn't help. It must have happened quickly. A woman who worked for my parents when they came back from Donegal told me Gráinne and I were always identically dressed in pretty clothes. What I remember, from only three or four years later, is the teacher in Miss Ahern's school in Malahide calling me in to her office and fingering my dirty cardigan. 'Couldn't your mother find anything better to send you to school in?'

She was to have thirteen pregnancies altogether. Nine living children. She never had enough money. She did her best for years. She made crab-apple jam. She gave us jam sandwiches and a Milk of Magnesia bottle full of milk for our picnic. She bought us wellington boots for the winter. She fine-combed our hair, us kneeling before her, bent into the newspaper on her lap. Think of all the clothes she must have bought, washed, dried, sorted out, put on our backs.

Her life got harder. The Calor gas cylinder under the two rings she cooked on would run out, and she had no phone or transport. She washed clothes in the bath, with yellow soap and a washboard. We were no consolation. Once, when my father had gone down the country on a job, she broke the unwritten rules by daringly going into Dublin, and going to Kingsbridge station, and surprising him by being at the barrier, when he got off the train. He was with people. He leaned down to aim a kiss at her cheek before hurrying off with them. 'He didn't even take the cigarette out of his mouth,' she told me, not once, but over and over again, in years to come.

I imagine her making her lonely way back to us children. She was still in her twenties. She would have taken the bus out to the terminus, then walked out past the last street-lamp, then down the dark country road to the estate's gate-lodge, then ducked under a fence and followed the path we'd worn in the tussocky field across to the bungalow. … Nothing there but children. Another time – it was late at night, but I was awake in my bed because I was counting my Communion money for the twentieth time – I heard him come in and then I heard her shrieking: 'That's not my lipstick!'

Explanations –
Synonym

A synonym is a word that means the same as another word, for example **superb/excellent** or **huge/massive**.

Antonym

An antonym is a word that means the opposite of another word, for example **good/bad** or **arrive/depart**.

Language Alert

Appropriate words and phrases

If we think carefully about our choice of language when we are writing, it can make our stories much more exciting and interesting for our readers. Nuala Ó Faoláin has always been regarded as an expert in this respect.

Therefore, as you read, pay attention to the choices she makes. Underline or highlight any words or phrases that you particularly liked, or thought were out of the ordinary.

Thinking about the text

1 Explain why the writer says that her mother was in the 'wrong job'.

2 Underline all the signs you can find to show that the family had very little money. Which do you find the most touching or poignant? Explain.

3 What do you think of the comment made by the teacher to the young Nuala in the second paragraph? Explain how it makes you feel. Use one of these adjectives or find your own in your thesaurus.

angry	sad	unmoved	annoyed
indifferent	irritated	indignant	outraged

4 Describe in your own words the meeting between the parents in the train station. How would you describe the relationship between them? Explain your opinion.

5 Use your dictionary to look up the words 'censorious' and 'wistful'. Then say what these words tell you about the way the women questioned Nuala Ó Faoláin about whether or not she was married.

Oral Language

Choosing the right language is crucial when writing (see Language Alert above). Make a list of the words you underlined earlier and think about why you chose those ones in particular. Did you just like the sound of them? Did they surprise you in some way? Did they draw you in because they were different? Then turn to a partner and:

> Share your lists and the reasons for your choices.
> Take some of the words you have chosen and use a thesaurus to find the antonyms (see Explanations above) and discuss how substituting these new words would change the meaning of the sentences in which they appear.

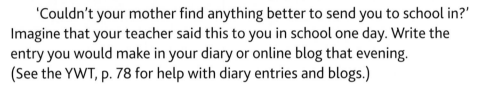

Writing Task

Complete this task in your portfolio, p. 61.

'Couldn't your mother find anything better to send you to school in?' Imagine that your teacher said this to you in school one day. Write the entry you would make in your diary or online blog that evening. (See the YWT, p. 78 for help with diary entries and blogs.)

Groupwork

In groups of three or four, take the final statement 'That's not my lipstick!' and imagine what might happen next. Write a script for a short scene (about three minutes), with each group taking turns to act out the scene for your classmates.

Each group should receive some feedback on both the script and the performance from the rest of the class as follows:

> One thing we like about your script/performance was …
> One thing we think would make it even better is …

Before you read ...

Think about your opinion of St Valentine's Day for a couple of minutes on your own.
Do you normally like or enjoy the day? Are your memories good or bad? Jot down
some thoughts for sharing with a partner.

This is an extract from the opening chapter of The Secret World of the
Irish Male, *in which the writer gives us his thoughts on St Valentine's Day
and relates a memory from his schooldays.*

St Valentine's Day

JOSEPH O'CONNOR

Author Biography
Check out the *Be Inspired!*
website for Joseph O'Connor's
author biography.

I have never actually met anyone called Valentine, and
I suspect there is a bloody good reason for this. Calling
one's child after one of the more obscure saints – Boniface,
say, or Begnet or Bede – I can actually understand. But
calling one's child Valentine would bring back wistful
memories to most people. What does
Valentine's Day really mean? I'm thinking of
the exuberant canter down to the letterbox
on the morning of February 14th, the blood
scuttling through the veins at top speed,
the tongue flapping with anticipation, the
nerves doing gymnastics, the exquisite
agony of it all, only to be followed by
disappointment, the bare doormat, the
poignantly cardless climb back up to the
scratcher, the placing of the head beneath
the duvet, the agonised screeching of
abusive epithets and the subsequent
moistening of the pillowcase with tears
so salty you could sprinkle them on chips.
Calling one's child Valentine would be
like calling him Disappointment. And
Disappointment O'Connor would not
be much of a name for a child, even
though, no doubt, it would eventually get
abbreviated to Dizzy O'Connor – and I've
met one or two of those in my time, God
only knows. Sappy O'Connor would be
another possibility, I suppose.

Anyway, in the whole dismal cornucopia of abject anniversaries, foul festive frolics and rancid rejoicings is there anything really worse than St Valentine's Day? Fresh from prising the shekels out of us for Christmas, the greetings card hucksters need a little extra to keep them in the style to which they are accustomed, and, let us face it, desire is the most marketable concept there is. The people who make greetings cards are bandits of the lowest order, if you ask me. They should be wearing tights over their faces.

When I was six I had a teacher named Miss Glennon. She was a very good teacher. She believed there was more to early education than the repetitive chanting of ideologically suspect nursery rhymes and the digital manipulation of plasticine, and so, when St Valentine's Day came around one year, she made every boy and girl in the class write a Valentine card, complete with a poem. For those less creatively gifted students, Miss Glennon explained that it was acceptable to start off with the time-honoured couplet 'roses are red, violets are blue'. We got ten minutes. The completed cards were then placed in two piles at the top of the class, one for boys and one for girls. We each had to pick one at random, and read it aloud to the assembled unwashed.

At the time I entertained an uneasy if quite fervent affection for Michele Killen, a tempestuous redhead who could play conkers like nobody's business, and whose pipe cleaner men were the talk of St Joseph of Cluny School. Michele did not like me much. On one occasion she called me 'a weird little fecker', I recall, but, hey, it was a kind of a Burton and Taylor thing. The card I picked out, however, came from a girl called Sheena whose hand I always had to hold whenever Miss Glennon took us on nature walks, which was a little too often for my liking. All I remember about Sheena is that she had a perpetually runny nose. The contents of her incontinent nostrils ebbed and flowed like the proud majestic Shannon, and the hand which she used to wipe said nostrils was also, invariably, the hand which she then used to hold my own as tightly as she could. My own hand, that is. Not my own nostrils. But anyway. Me and Sheena were frequently stuck together by something more than just love.

Reminder –
Alliteration

Alliteration is a device used in writing, particularly in poetry, in which the same consonant sound is repeated at the beginning of all or most of the words in a line, e.g. *Peter Piper picked a peck of pickled peppers*. It draws attention to the words used and it also establishes a connection between them. Can you find some examples as you read this text?

Flushed with romantic excitement, I stood up at the top of the class that morning long ago and began to read out the words Sheena had written. They were, and here I quote in full, 'Roses are red, Violets are blue, I think you're horroble [sic] and you are like poo.' I was shattered. Not only was the thought less than affectionate, but I mean, it didn't even bloody scan properly.

Every time I even think about it, I still blush to the colour of Ribena. Saint Valentine has an awful lot to answer for, in my book. In the unlikely event of my ever making it into paradise, be assured, I will certainly have a thing or two to say to him.

Thinking about the text

1 Whose card did the writer pick out of the pile and was he happy with his choice?

2 Why does he think that Miss Glennon is a good teacher?

3 What does the writer think of the people who make Valentine cards? How does he refer to them?

4 Why does he describe himself as 'shattered' having read the card?

5 'Calling one's child Valentine would be like calling him Disappointment.' Explain in your own words what the author means by this statement.

6 If the writer had picked Michele's card instead of Sheena's, do you think this might have changed his view of St Valentine's Day? Explain your answer.

7 What examples of alliteration (see Reminder above) can you find in this piece? Turn to your partner and exchange opinions about whether you think these add to the story.

Oral Language

In paragraph two, Joseph O'Connor makes the point that St Valentine's Day just provides an opportunity for 'greetings card hucksters' to make money by getting us all to buy cards. Talk to at least one other student to help you form your own views about St Valentine's Day and then write a short speech (about one minute) to give to a group or your full class.

Groupwork

Get into small groups of three or four for this task.

Imagine that it is a week before St Valentine's Day and that there is a school competition for the best Valentine card, which will be posted on the school website to celebrate the occasion. Your teacher has asked each group to design a card complete with an appropriate verse.

Research

Carry out some research into St Valentine's Day – origin, history, customs, practices – anything you find interesting. You will find quite an amount of data – websites, videos and so on. Prepare a colourful presentation for delivery to your group or class.

Wrapping up

Write your own memoir. Complete this task in your portfolio, p. 62.

In this chapter you have had the opportunity to read some pieces of writing from four well-known writers who are writing about a variety of topics concerning their own lives and memories. You have had the opportunity to learn from them and add considerably to your own writing skills, so you should be in a good position to write your own memoir.

Young Writer's Toolkit

Describing

Here you will find tools to help you to write descriptions.

1. Describing a favourite place
2. Creating an atmosphere
3. Describing a character
4. Describing your thoughts and feelings

1 Describing a favourite place

You have to write so that the reader can imagine the place clearly and also get a sense of what the place means to you. You are doing two basic things: you are making pictures in words; and you are saying how much the place means to you. Here's a quick guide.

> Pick out the most striking details and describe them, choosing your words carefully. You may end up concentrating on how a place looks, but also think of the other senses – the sounds, smells and texture of a place.
> Think of the place as a person and give it human qualities (warm, welcoming, cruel, unforgiving).
> Describe how being in the place makes you feel.
> Describe the kind of things you think about when you are there.

You can include all of the above in one paragraph. (If you're writing a poem, see 'The Lake Isle of Innisfree' by William Butler Yeats, p. 212.)

My Favourite Place

My favourite place is in the mountains not far from where I live. My dad first brought me there when I was little and I go there now as often as I can. It's a small clearing in the woods with a stream flowing through it. There are rocks in the stream and you can hear the water tumbling over the rocks before you see it. It's really peaceful there. All you can hear is the sound of water, the chirping of birds and the hum of insects. The trees shade you from the sun and filter the sunlight. I love the way the light falls on the ground, through the branches. The place is like an old friend to me and I always feel welcome there, and safe, too. Best of all, you can get rid of all the busy, silly thoughts in your head and be still.

> Use words that create pictures (nouns, adjectives, verbs) and that appeal to the senses.
> Use words that express emotions.
> Use comparisons to make your writing come alive.
> Pay attention to the sounds of words.
> Use repetition of sounds and words to create atmosphere. (Listing things one after the other is a simple but effective way of creating a sense of excitement or atmosphere about a place.)

Here's a checklist that will help you:

☐ Have I selected the most important features to describe?
☐ Have I described the place in terms of all the senses?
☐ Have I given the place some qualities?
☐ Have I set a mood?
☐ Have I used expressive words and phrases?
☐ Have I paid attention to sounds and the repetition of key words to shape my writing?
☐ Have I used good comparisons?
☐ Is my point of view clear?

2 Creating an atmosphere

It's the same as describing a place, but the emphasis is on how the place makes you feel. Pay attention to nouns, adjectives and verbs. Use comparisons to bring your writing to life.

The old house made my skin crawl. The biting wind whistled through the windows, or what was left of them. There was never enough daylight there. It was as if the house fed on light and devoured it all. And then there was the musty smell of things rotting and decaying. The old floorboards creaked and groaned when you walked across the floor.

3 Describing a character

When you are asked to describe characters in a story, you say what the characters are like and what you think of them. Think of this task: 'Describe the brothers in the story' (how you imagine the brothers in 'At the River-Gates', p. 27). Describe their appearance and the kind of people they are, as well as your response to them. This checklist will help you:

- ☐ Have I given a clear picture of each character's appearance and the differences and similarities between the characters?
- ☐ Have I described the personality of each of the characters and the differences or similarities between them?
- ☐ Have I drawn attention to the behaviour (the words and actions) of each of the characters?
- ☐ Have I mentioned what they say about each other and what others say about them?
- ☐ Have I focused on important details to support what I'm saying?
- ☐ Have I thought about the words and phrases I've chosen?
- ☐ Is my point of view clear?

4 Describing your thoughts and feelings

What you are being asked to do is to say what your thoughts and feelings are and to explain why you think and feel as you do. For your thoughts, you might find it helpful to use the following sentence starters:

- ❯ I think …
- ❯ This is why I think …

Describing your feelings can be a little trickier. You could, however, use these sentence starters to get you started:

- ❯ What excites/interests me about this is …
- ❯ What bothers me about this is …
- ❯ What I'd like to know more about is …
- ❯ What I think of this is …

It's a good idea to compile a list of adjectives for describing feelings; words like:

sad   angry   confused   energised   sympathetic   happy   ambivalent

When you're unsure of your feelings, you could ask yourself some of the following questions:

- ❯ If my feeling were a colour, what colour would it be?
- ❯ If my feeling were a sound, what kind of sound would it be?
- ❯ If my feeling were a taste, what kind of taste would it be?

Once you have named or identified your feeling, you have to remember to say why you felt as you did and this will send you back to the text for evidence.